FOR THE LOVE OF BASEBALL

"What this collection best represents is the full spectrum of the baseball experience, from romantic to nostalgic to eclectic. . . ."—*Boston Globe*

". . .[A]n all-star lineup. Ends with a piece by Roger Angell. Read it and you'll see why they waived the rules to give Angell the Spink Award even though he's not a member of the Baseball Writers' Association of America. . . . Frank Deford, Bart Giamatti, George Plimpton, Gay Talese, which makes it special, all that wit and wisdom between the same set of covers writing about a game they love."—Stan Hochman, *Philadelphia Daily News*

"This is one of the finest baseball anthologies of all time."—Jonathan Eig, author of *Luckiest Man: The Life and Death of Lou Gehrig*

"Exceptional—a lively, rewarding read."—Robert W. Creamer, author of *Babe: The Legend Comes to Life*

"These charming essays on baseball themes range from topics like first gloves—mine was a Rawlings Marty Marion model—to the tragic story of the Billy Southworths, father and son, to being relegated to right field or having troubles playing first base. These are tasty morsels."—Fay Vincent, former Commissioner of Major League Baseball

"Baseball is played only a couple of hundred nights a year. Here is a book that will help you fill up the rest of your time."—Seth Mnookin

Baseball's most lasting gift may be its power to stir our curiosity, memory and imagination into such a rich and loving tribute."—Robert Lipsyte, former *New York Times* columnist and author of *The Contender*

"For the Love of Baseball will remind you why you fell in love with the game. This is one of the finest baseball anthologies of all time."—Jonathan Eig

"An outstanding collection to be treasured by fans of baseball and personal essays."—*Booklist*

"Twenty wonderful writers—that's just enough for two full all-star teams—and two designated hitters."—Christine Brennan, *USA Today* sports columnist and author of *Best Seat in the House: A Father, a Daughter, a Journey Through Sports*

"This collection of 20 essays, most of them never before published, is not a New York book, per se, but it brims with lyrical reminiscences about the love affair between the city and the sport. . . . What ties these charming essays together? 'The collection,' Mr. Gutkind writes, represents 'the connective tissue' of the game, from the mitts to the stadiums that collectively constitute 'our common nostalgia for the way it was, and our fervent hope that the sport will endure the way we think it always should be.'"—Sam Roberts, the *New York Times*

FOR THE LOVE OF BASEBALL

A Celebration of the Game
That Connects Us All

EDITED BY

Lee Gutkind

AND

Andrew Blauner

FOREWORD BY

Yogi Berra

Skyhorse Publishing

Skyhorse Publishing books may be purchased in bulk at special discounts for sales promotion, corporate gifts, fund-raising, or educational purposes. Special editions can also be created to specifications. For details, contact the Special Sales Department, Skyhorse Publishing, 307 West 36th Street, 11th Floor, New York, NY 10018 or info@skyhorsepublishing.com.

Skyhorse® and Skyhorse Publishing® are registered trademarks of Skyhorse Publishing, Inc.®, a Delaware corporation.

Visit our website at www.skyhorsepublishing.com.

10 9 8 7 6 5 4 3 2 1

Library of Congress Cataloging-in-Publication Data is available on file.

Jacket design by Rich Rossiter
Jacket photogragh: iStock/Thinkstock

ISBN: 978–1–5107–0273–8
eISBN: 978-1-5107-0274-5

Printed in the United States of America

Contents

Foreword

Yogi Berra

Baseball to me is the greatest game. It's loved and played and watched all over the world. Whenever people ask what I would've done without baseball, I don't know. I played it because it wasn't work, but I worked at it because I loved to play. What I've truly learned is the game is more than a game. Sure it's a business, getting bigger all the time. But it still has an uncanny way of getting into people's hearts and minds—what other business can say that?

It's been over a half century since I last played a major league game, but I observe and follow and read about the game as much as ever. That doesn't mean I'll ever know all there is to know, and that's the beauty. Like I've always said, in baseball you don't know nothing. Or if you ask me a question I don't know, I'm not going to answer. But this much I know. Baseball remains a great game because people still worship and argue about it and they're going to games in record numbers. People still make movies about it. People dream up fantasy teams and go to fantasy camps. People keep analyzing and concocting statistics. And authors never stop writing about the game. Simply, baseball makes great baseball literature.

The title of an earlier edition of this collection was *Anatomy of Baseball*, but it was no medical book—if it was, I'm certain I wouldn't have read it. It's a baseball book, and a good one, and it's nice to be in a lineup that includes some pretty good writers. A good book makes you think about things you might not already think about. Or enjoy stories from writers you maybe don't know. Of course, I was never good with writers' names. A long time ago, somebody introduced me to Ernest Hemingway, mentioning that he was a great writer. So I asked, "Which paper?" That was when most of my reading consisted of the sports pages and comic books. But Hemingway was a big baseball fan. No surprise he used the game in his writing, especially in *The Old Man and the Sea*, referring to my old teammate Joe DiMaggio and the main character missing the daily box scores. Baseball has its own literature. It even has its own language. The game goes back to before the Civil War, but it never gets old. Neither does a good baseball book.

FOR THE LOVE OF BASEBALL

Introduction—Baseball: How Do I Love Thee?

Lee Gutkind

I want to say right off here that when our publisher suggested the title for this book, I was against it. The book had previously been published with a different title, one that my coeditor, Andrew Blauner, and I had very much liked, so it was initially annoying to have to change the title at all. It wasn't the subtitle that I was opposed to, by the way, *A Celebration of the Game That Connects Us*. It was the title itself. *For the Love of Baseball*. The whole idea of loving this game ticked me off—such a cliché. There are probably dozens of books that have love in the title or subtitle about baseball, so why join the common crowd? Our book is better than any other competing collection of nonfiction by a long shot—a great combination of original and previously published pieces, with George Plimpton, Roger Angell, Frank Deford, prestigious and accomplished veterans, and a bunch of rookies like Jake Young and Caitlin Horrocks, brand new fresh and vital voices reporting about baseball with a unique perspective.

So why use such an overused and unexciting phrase, with this gooey sentimental word—love? I mean, okay, I love my girlfriend, I love my mother, I love my son. But isn't loving a game where guys you've never met perform for nine or more innings with a bat and a ball, constrained by an encyclopedia of arcane rules and traditions kind of... over the top?

But then I started to think about my feelings toward baseball—and I began reevaluating. When I think back to my years growing up in Pittsburgh, I've got a lot of bad memories—my father was a tyrant. And we lived in a crummy blue-collar neighborhood where a fat Jewish kid like me was constantly demeaned and periodically pummeled by the Irish Catholics who believed that my people killed Christ. So I don't have many good times or comforting memories to look back on—except, I came to realize, for baseball. Even though they were cellar dwellers in the 1950s, I followed the Pittsburgh Pirates religiously, every inning of every game. Ralph Kiner, the slugging left fielder who one year clubbed 54 home runs, was my hero. Imagine! He was an All-Star player for six years in a row on a last place team. And he had a bevy of women he courted, including the very good-looking tennis star Nancy Chaffee, his first of four hot wives. He eventually left Pittsburgh for New York, became an announcer for the Mets, and he kind of faded from my regular awareness. But to me, he represented glamour, hope, and the ability to achieve despite your surroundings—and the relative flaws of your colleagues. My novel, *God's Helicopter*, featured Kiner as a make-believe character, and upon publication, I wrote him a fan letter telling him how much I respected and honored him, sent him two copies of the book, one to keep in his own library—I was assuming he had one—and one to autograph and return to me. I keep that autographed book in a prominent place in my living room today.

Kiner, like I said, was an All-Star, and I always picked him for my team when I played my favorite all-time board game, All-Star Baseball, invented by a player for the St. Louis Cardinals in the 1930s, Ethan Allen. Here's how baseball historian Jack Major describes the game which, in many respects is kind of a primitive model to the data-driven way in which we study and discuss the game today: "Allen…broke down hitting statistics into several categories and created pie chart representations of the performances of several major league players. He put those pie charts on paper discs about 3.5 inches in diameter. The discs were cut out in the middle to fit over a spinner, creating what you might call Baseball Roulette. Flick that spinner over a disc and the result would tell you what the player did in one at-bat. There were fourteen possibilities, from striking out to hitting a home run…If you played a season's worth of games, each player's statistics would approximate those he had generated on the field." Allen, a graduate of the

University of Cincinnati, created the game for kids between the ages of nine and twelve, but was startled and obviously pleased how many kids younger than twelve—all the way up to adults in their thirties and forties—played the game which became one of the top fifty board games ever created.

For me, All-Star Baseball was incredible comfort growing up. Summer mornings, I would wake up early and begin to plan my team for upcoming game of the day. The original All-Star game, when purchased, provided forty discs of players, but I actually made a number of my own by studying box scores and annual batting averages—mostly from the Pirates I loved. Those mornings, mostly in the summer, somewhere around 10 AM or 10:30 AM, I would take my discs and head down Beechwood Blvd. where we lived in a duplex above my grandparents, to Ronnie Rabinowitz's house—my best friend through grade school. Ronnie liked sleeping in, so I would wait on his porch until his mother awakened him and fed him breakfast, and then Ronnie would come out with his All-Star board and we would play—and play. Sometimes we played all day until Ronnie would have to go inside for dinner, and then I would go home and listen to the Pirate game at night—and play with my own board some more. Which is not to say that Ronnie and I didn't actually play the real game with ball and bat; we did so frequently in his backyard. And when Ronnie wasn't available, I walked further down Beechwood Blvd. to where my cousin Sonny Cofsky lived to play baseball-speedball with a Wiffle ball, until Sonny, also, had to go inside for dinner. Later, Sonny and I were on the same Pony League team together.

I didn't lose my connection to baseball as an adult. I went directly into the military after high school, and then when I returned to Pittsburgh I began taking classes at the University of Pittsburgh night school. Forbes Field, where the Pirates were then playing, was directly across the street from the Cathedral of Learning, Pitt's august forty-story classroom building, then, and maybe even now, the highest classroom building in the world. The Pirates traditionally opened the gates to anyone who wanted to watch the final 2.5 innings—at the seventh inning stretch—free. You could just walk right in and find an empty seat—anywhere! Classes ended at 9:15 PM, so when there was a night game, after classes, my friend Phil Willet and I would walk over to Forbes Field, literally across the street, buy an Iron City beer (or two) and watch the final innings of the game. The great Roberto (Clemente) was on that team, along with Willie Stargell and Maz (Bill Mazeroski) the super second baseman. Great memories—and during those years we were winning much more often than in those 1950 cellar dweller years.

I have to admit that I took a long sabbatical from baseball, beginning in the middle 1970s when I wrote my book about umpires. For one thing, I attended probably more than 200 games the year I researched the book and followed a crew of umpires from team to team and town to town, so I kind of OD-ed on baseball. And for another thing, the umpires were kind of flawed. What I mean is, I was traveling with some pretty nice fellows—Harry Wendelstedt, Nick Colosi and Doug Harvey, who became one of the few umpires inducted into the Hall of Fame. But that was the year the National League was trying to introduce the first black umpire into the game—Art Williams—and although Wendestedt, Colosi, and Harvey were, in many ways, well meaning, they weren't very considerate of his feelings. Nor were they sensitive to the pressures with which a black man was confronted in a totally white umpire world. The American League had introduced one black umpire the previous year. Williams had only two years experience umpiring in the minors—and it was a struggle to keep up with men who had gone through the ranks in a long and more traditional multi-year apprenticeship. Not to even mention the racial connotations and prejudices that frequently surfaced. Jackie Robinson was the change maker, but real change was decades away. I wrote about the difficulties and inequities with which Williams was confronted in *The Best Seat in Baseball, but You Have to Stand* in a way that infuriated the umpires and the National League. There were lawsuits and awful allegations. I was persona non grata in major league baseball for many years.

Time passes; people die or retire, feelings mellow. Few people in baseball remember or care about me, my allegations, and alas about the pioneering umpire Art Williams. And during that time, the game has matured. Racism hasn't been obliterated in America's national pastime, if we can still call it that, and certainly not in America itself. But we've charted progress, which is hopeful. And for me, gradually over the past few years, there's renewed hope and interest in baseball because, primarily, of the Pirates, no longer cellar dwellers. This is a very surprising never-say-die team with young and charismatic leaders like Andrew McCutchen, who was named National League Most Valuable Player, combined with recycled and reinvigorated veterans like the former Yankee All-Star catcher Russell Martin. Unfortunately, the Bucs did not make it to the World Series, but they extended the season for a few games and absolutely electrified the city of Pittsburgh—not to mention Andrew, although a New Yorker, a long-time Pirate fan—and me. I don't know if this feeling will carry over to next season, but I find myself once again engaged, if not obsessed.

Which brings me back to the title of this book and its meaning and symbolism for me. Do I "love" baseball? Is "love" the right word for my feelings for this game? I guess I can say that I love being once again so engaged, looking forward to the next game on TV next season, to seeing the guys I sometimes hang out with these days in the bar up the street, The Elbow Room, cheering the Bucs on, or texting my frustration or excitement to my friend P. J., who I know is watching the game and anticipating victory and fearing defeat and disappointment as am I.

And I can also say that the memories of being inspired by Ralph Kiner and his success with the hapless 1950s cellar-dweller Pirates, Wiffle ball with Sonny Cofsky, cold, invigorating Iron City drafts and the final innings at evening's end at Forbes Field with Phil Willet, and playing All-Star Baseball with Ronnie Rabinowitz on his front porch—make me feel good and connected in many ways to the world and the positives of my past, even though Ronnie and Sonny and Kiner and Phil, everyone else I shared baseball with in the past, are no longer in my life. So I guess, in the end, I am on board with my publisher regarding both parts of the title—*For the Love of Baseball*—and the subtitle, *A Celebration of the Game that Connects Us All*. It works for me.

The Green Fields of the Mind

A. Bartlett Giamatti

*In 2013, the Boston Red Sox won their third World Series in a decade
and established themselves as the dominant team of the new century.
Prior to 2004, the team and its fans endured one of the longest droughts
in professional sports—86 years without a championship. Their late-
season collapses were as predictable as autumn in New England. But
a byproduct of the team's haplessness was great writing about what it
means to be a broken-hearted fan. This piece by A. Bartlett Giamatti is
an extraordinarily fine example. [L.G.]*

It breaks your heart. It is designed to break your heart. The game begins
in the spring, when everything else begins again, and it blossoms in the
summer, filling the afternoons and evenings, and then as soon as the chill
rains come, it stops and leaves you to face the fall alone. You count on it,
rely on it to buffer the passage of time, to keep the memory of sunshine and
high skies alive, and then just when the days are all twilight, when you need
it most, it stops. Today, October 2, a Sunday of rain and broken branches
and leaf-clogged drains and slick streets, it stopped, and summer was gone.

Somehow, the summer seemed to slip by faster this time. Maybe it wasn't
this summer, but all the summers that, in this my 40th summer, slipped by
so fast. There comes a time when every summer will have something of
autumn about it. Whatever the reason, it seemed to me that I was investing
more and more in baseball, making the game do more of the work that keeps
time fat and slow and lazy. I was counting on the game's deep patterns, three

strikes, three outs, three times three innings, and its deepest impulse, to go out and back, to leave and to return home, to set the order of the day and to organize the daylight. I wrote a few things this last summer, this summer that did not last, nothing grand but some things, and yet that work was just camouflage. The real activity was done with the radio—not the all-seeing, all-falsifying television—and was the playing of the game in the only place it will last, the enclosed green field of the mind. There, in that warm, bright place, what the old poet called Mutability does not so quickly come.

But out here, on Sunday, October 2, where it rains all day, Dame Mutability never loses. She was in the crowd at Fenway yesterday, a grey day full of bluster and contradiction, when the Red Sox came up in the last of the ninth trailing Baltimore 8–5, while the Yankees, rain-delayed against Detroit, only needing to win one or have Boston lose one to win it all, sat in New York washing down cold cuts with beer and watching the Boston game. Boston had won two, the Yankees had lost two, and suddenly it seemed as if the whole season might go to the last day, or beyond, except here was Boston losing 8–5, while New York sat in its family room and put its feet up. Lynn, both ankles hurting now as they had in July, hits a single down the right-field line. The crowd stirs. It is on its feet. Hobson, third baseman, former Bear Bryant quarterback, strong, quiet, over 100 RBIs, goes for three breaking balls and is out. The goddess smiles and encourages her agent, a canny journeyman named Nelson Briles.

Now comes a pinch hitter, Bernie Carbo, onetime Rookie of the Year, erratic, quick, a shade too handsome, so laid-back he is always, in his soul, stretched out in the tall grass, one arm under his head, watching the clouds and laughing; now he looks over some low stuff unworthy of him and then, uncoiling, sends one out, straight on a rising line, over the center field wall, no cheap Fenway shot, but all of it, the physics as elegant as the arc the ball describes.

New England is on its feet, roaring. The summer will not pass. Roaring, they recall the evening, late and cold, in 1975, the sixth game of the World Series, perhaps the greatest baseball game played in the last fifty years, when Carbo, loose and easy, had uncoiled to tie the game that Fisk would win. It is 8–7, one out, and school will never start, rain will never come, sun will warm the back of your neck forever. Now Bailey, picked up from the National League recently, big arms, heavy gut, experienced, new to the league and the club; he fouls off two and then, checking, tentative, a big man off balance, he pops a soft liner to the first baseman. It is suddenly darker and later, and the announcer doing the game coast to coast, a New Yorker who works for a New York television station, sounds relieved. His little world, well-lit, hot-combed, split-second-timed, has no capacity to absorb this much gritty, grainy, contrary reality.

Cox swings a bat, stretches his long arms, bends his back, the rookie from Pawtucket who broke in two weeks earlier with a record six straight hits, the kid drafted ahead of Fred Lynn, rangy, smooth, cool. The count runs two and two, Briles is cagey, nothing too good, and Cox swings, the ball beginning toward the mound and then, in a jaunty, wayward dance, skipping past Briles, feinting to the right, skimming the last of the grass, finding the dirt, moving now like some small, purposeful marine creature negotiating the green deep, easily avoiding the jagged rock of second base, traveling steady and straight now out into the dark, silent recesses of center field.

The aisles are jammed, the place is on its feet, the wrappers, the programs, the Coke cups and peanut shells, the doctrines of an afternoon; the anxieties, the things that have to be done tomorrow, the regrets about yesterday, the accumulation of a summer: all forgotten, while hope, the anchor, bites and takes hold where a moment before it seemed we would be swept out with the tide. Rice is up. Rice whom Aaron had said was the only one he'd seen with the ability to break his records. Rice, the best clutch hitter on the club, with the best slugging percentage in the league. Rice, so quick and strong he once checked his swing halfway through and snapped the bat in two. Rice, the Hammer of God sent to scourge the Yankees; the sound was overwhelming, fathers pounded their sons on the back, cars pulled off the road, households froze, New England exulted in its blessedness and roared its thanks for all good things, for Rice and for a summer stretching halfway through October. Briles threw, Rice swung, and it was over. One pitch, a fly to center, and it stopped. Summer died in New England and like rain sliding off a roof, the crowd slipped out of Fenway, quickly, with only a steady murmur of concern for the drive ahead remaining of the roar. Mutability had turned the seasons and translated hope to memory once again. And, once again, she had used baseball, our best invention to stay change, to bring change on. That is why it breaks my heart, that game—not because in New York they could win because Boston lost; in that, there is a rough justice, and a reminder to the Yankees of how slight and fragile are the circumstances that exalt one group of human beings over another. It breaks my heart because it was meant to, because it was meant to foster in me again the illusion that there was something abiding, some pattern and some impulse that could come together to make a reality that would resist the corrosion; and because, after it had fostered again that most hungered-for illusion, the game was meant to stop, and betray precisely what it promised.

Of course, there are those who learn after the first few times. They grow out of sports. And there are others who were born with the wisdom to know that nothing lasts. These are the truly tough among us, the ones who can live without illusion, or without even the hope of illusion. I am not that grown-up or up-to-date. I am a simpler creature, tied to more primitive patterns and cycles. I need to think something lasts forever, and it might as well be that state of being that is a game; it might as well be that, in a green field, in the sun.

At the Park

Kevin Baker

---

*Baseball to me is an addiction, and as such, a distraction from
writing—but some distractions are badly needed. What I love about
baseball is that it doesn't have any greater meaning; it's just a beautiful
thing in its own right. I love its rituals, its carefully cultivated history.
I love the fact that it's a link to the American past, especially in its
peculiarities. Hence my love of old ballparks: they were eccentric
without trying to be so, which is appealing in our very purposeful,
homogenized time. Even the attempts to consciously re-create them,
worthy though they are, don't quite work. The past is quite dead, and
well beyond us, which gives it its luster.*

---

*Some boy too far from town to learn baseball, Whose only
play was what he found himself . . .*
—Robert Frost, "Birches"

It always was a city game, baseball. That's not how the old pastoralists
would have it, of course. They have so loaded the game down with country
imagery that it's hard to separate the mythology from the reality now—little
boys chasing fly balls into Iowa cornfields, The Natural peeling a bat off a
lightning-damned tree. When it came time to build a Hall of Fame the lords
of the game stuck it up in bucolic Cooperstown, seizing upon some old-tim-
er's letter about how the game was invented in Abner Doubleday's meadow.

Doubleday was the Forrest Gump of the nineteenth century, a Union
officer who was there at Fort Sumter, there at Gettysburg. But he wasn't even

around for the invention of baseball. The game required too many boys, as Frost's words imply. Only those who have forgotten the punishing isolation of American rural life would believe baseball came of age in the country. The old names give it away. It was called "town ball" because it was played on those days when everybody came into town for church or market. It was called "the New York game" because that's where baseball—real baseball—actually started, in vacant lots around what is now the West Side Manhattan neighborhood of Chelsea. It was played not by country boys but by clubs of middle-class merchants with a little leisure time on their hands; then increasingly by sharp-eyed immigrant professionals, Pat and Mick and Heinie.

The first major league parks, back in the nineteenth century, were little more than sandlots with rows of precarious wooden bleachers—one step up from those vacant, rock-strewn lots in Chelsea. Eventually they were ringed, frontier-style, with a stockade fence so the owners could monopolize what was going on inside—charge for admission and food sales; shake down or expel gamblers who dogged the game; expand the fan base to the growing middle class, to children, and even women. These changes were akin to Vegas going family—or to the incandescent cities of fire that rose along the sands of Coney Island during the same period, replacing the site of louche entertainments with the very first official amusement parks.

The crowds often broke the walls on the afternoons of big games. But like the cities in which they were contained, the parks were steadily improved by fire. Just as the city's wood shanties were replaced by ornate, block-long apartment buildings, by skyscrapers and bridges, and grand railroad stations and gorgeous, humming, electrical generators, the ballparks were replaced by concrete-and-steel structures that sprouted second tiers and outfield bleachers—everything getting bigger and better, all the time.

Just as the country seemed to stretch away forever before the first immigrants, so the ball field is theoretically infinite, the foul lines moving ever farther away from each other until they encompass all of existence. How to traverse this infinite landscape? Just as American industrialists, confronted with seemingly boundless plenty, invented time management, trying to convert all they saw before them into a rational system of production, so, too, have baseball's acolytes always tried to break the game down into more and more precise statistics, some narrative that will allow us to measure every movement on the field.

• • •

Air, space, and recreation were the crying needs of the American city by the mid-nineteenth century. They were considered vital to the continued health of both the individual and the polis. No city had a public park of any size. Those wishing relief from the city's racket and bustle resorted to the new rural cemeteries. These had begun to spring up with the consecration of Cambridge's Mount Auburn Cemetery in 1831, followed by Philadelphia's Laurel Hill (1836), and Brooklyn's vast Green-Wood Cemetery (1838). These were full-scale necropolises, laid out in the British landscaping style of improved nature, with deliberately winding roads and strategically placed trees, bushes, ponds, hillocks, and even boulders, designed to maximize dramatic views and uplifting vistas. The need for such spaces was quickly evidenced by their immense popularity. City dwellers poured out to the new cemeteries for Sunday afternoon picnics, whether a loved one was buried there or not. Green-Wood, by far the most splendid and the largest of the scenic graveyards at 478 acres, was drawing sixty thousand visitors a year soon after it opened for business.

"Rural cemeteries provided fresh air and greenery—and the illusion of a beautiful countryside," points out Frederick Law Olmsted biographer Witold Rybczynski.

Yet cemeteries were inherently limited by their utility, and there were still fears about the unhealthful "miasmas" that reputedly leaked up from the graves. Soon, Olmsted and his longtime partner Calvert Vaux had begun to lay out one magnificent public park after another in cities across the United States. These were deliberately intended as places of moral improvement as well as physical and cultural relief. Clean air and a place to stretch the legs were just the start. A dairy was actually built in New York's Central Park, intended to provide free, wholesome milk for the city's poor at a time when it was in short supply. Museums, concert halls, and other cultural institutions were to dot the park's perimeters. Beyond this, the poor were to benefit simply by exposure to their betters.

"There need to be places and times for re-unions [where] the rich and poor, the cultivated and the self-made, shall be attracted together and encouraged to assimilate," Olmsted wrote.

Baseball, on the other hand, wasn't thought to improve anybody. The game itself was all but banned from Central Park for decades. Yet it was in the new ballparks— the only other large open spaces in most American cities, coming into their own just as the first wave of public park building was coming to an end—that a true assimilation of American men of all classes would actually take place, and usually on a much closer and more intimate basis than ever occurred in other public parks.

The new ballparks were gloriously eccentric. For all of their corporate purpose, there was a specificity to them, an endearing individuality that would all but vanish from American business life. No other sport would ever boast such idiosyncratic playing fields. And in no other sport would the field become so critical to how the game itself was played, or such an enduring part of its lore.

Unlike the cemeteries and the English-style woods, or even the raucous amusement parks, the ballparks remained quintessentially urban structures. They were wedged into street lots, built around railroads and streetcar lines, factories and breweries and livery stables, rivers and highways, and the topography surrounding the parks gave rise to the quirks in their design. Brooklyn's Dodgers got their name because players and spectators alike had to dodge the trolleys to get to their old Washington Park field. Washington's Griffith Stadium featured a right angle in dead center field, a bulge where five homeowners had refused to sell. Cincinnati's Crosley Field shot some 377 feet out to right field, but was only 328 feet to left field, in which there was also a small hillock that sent Babe Ruth sprawling in the last year of his career. The Dodgers' later home at Ebbets Field featured a 20-foot-high chain-link fence in right field above a concave wall and a scoreboard with its immortal lower panel advertising borough president Abe Stark's clothing store at 1514 Pitkin Avenue: "Hit Sign, Win Suit."

Every stadium had its own peculiarities. The ones we know best are the thick ivy that clings to the lovely brick walls of Chicago's Wrigley Field and the great green wall looming over left in Boston's Fenway Park, but this is just because these are the only two major league parks to have survived from the era before World War I. So many of the others, now vanished, had their own gratuitous grace notes. As early as 1902, Cincinnati had built the short-lived Palace of the Fans, complete with grand Beaux Arts columns and pillars modeled after the White City at the 1893 Columbian Exposition in Chicago—the source of the City Beautiful movement in America. The new Polo Grounds was festooned with coats-of-arms along the top of the grandstand, representing all the National League clubs. The top of the original Yankee Stadium's upper deck dripped with white filigree bunting, and monuments to beloved former players and managers were actually installed on the playing field. Philadelphia's Shibe Park had a conical, domed tower, an escaped turret from some upper-middle class apartment house, over its main entrance. There was the Jury Box in Boston's Braves Field bleachers; the Coop, and the Crow's Nest, and the open-air promenade at Pittsburgh's Forbes Field. Ebbets Field had an eighty-foot Italian-marble floor in the image of a baseball in its rotunda, and a twenty-seven-foot-high domed ceiling, from which hung a chandelier with twelve baseball bat arms that held globes of lights shaped like baseballs.

The ticket windows at the old-time parks tended to look like boathouses Or beach pavilions, with fringed awnings and gentle arches. At Ebbets, they were gilded. The grandstands were always steep and close, dark and mysterious in their back rows after night baseball was instituted. Just beyond the walls of each park were comforting, orienting urban features of one sort or another: the Bronx County Courthouse, the flashing Citgo sign over Kenmore, the gloomy Cathedral of Learning towering over the left field wall in Pittsburgh, clouds of locomotive smoke billowing up from the Boston and Albany tracks behind left and center in Braves Field. There were usually, as well, huge, hand-operated scoreboards somewhere out in center field, visible to all. They showed the line scores of the same sixteen teams in the same eleven cities for fifty years, time moving on in the same stately progression, inning by inning.

The one feature all the old ballparks shared was outfields that were prodigious by today's standards. The old parks were routinely 420 feet to the farthest reaches of center field, and often 360–375 feet down the lines. It was 462 feet to center at Forbes Field, and 461 to left center in Yankee Stadium. The Yankees' previous home, Hilltop Park, stretched an endless 542 feet across the rough sod of Washington Heights. There were practical reasons for this. In the dead ball era, much of the scoring came from balls that found a seam and just kept on rolling. For an important game, the overflow crowd might be put out behind a rope in the outfield, and perhaps their cars or buggies too.

• • •

The most fantastic ballpark of all was the Polo Grounds, the home of the New York Giants, in upper Harlem. It was a strange place, and strange things happened there. The only man ever killed on a major league playing field, Ray Chapman, died at home plate, hit in the head by a pitch. A fan once died in the stands there too, between games of a doubleheader, struck by a stray bullet fired from a neighborhood rooftop. He went so quietly that no one realized he was dead at first; they thought he was only nodding off in the grandstand on a sunny summer afternoon.

No one ever played polo there; the name was carried over from the Giants' previous digs, James Bennett's old polo field down at 110th Street and Fifth Avenue. The new park the team built for itself in 1889 at 156th–157th Streets and Eighth Avenue was shaped like a gigantic horseshoe facing the Harlem River—the last major league ballpark that ever did or probably ever will disrupt the crowded streets of Manhattan Island. (In fact, as late as 1874, the whole site was under the Harlem River.)

Down the lines were the easiest home run shots in the big leagues, 279 feet to left and 257 to right. In some clairvoyant presentiment of

Frank Gehry's undulating architecture, the outfield walls stretched all the way out to a center field 483 feet from home plate. There, filling the gap in the horseshoe, were a multistory set of clubhouses and team offices, with a monument at the field level to Eddie Grant, a former Giants player killed in World War I; a large, square Longines clock crowning the top of the building; and a huge cigarette ad—"Always Buy Chesterfields"— in between. Two sets of stairs led to the field from the clubhouses, so that the players from both teams had to enter and exit the field matador-like, accepting the ovations and the jeers and barbs of the fans all around them.

It was the most glamorous park of the dead ball era, when the close, fast game was played mostly inside the infield, and always in the after-noon. John "Muggsy" McGraw, the irascible manager and part-owner of the Giants, would invite his show business celebrities up in the afternoon. They could park their beautiful new automobiles—as varied and idiosyn-cratic as the ballparks themselves—on the edge of the outfield and take in a whole nine innings before motoring back down to Broadway in time for the evening curtain. McGraw, "the Little Napoleon," did what he wanted: consorted with gamblers, owned part of a pool hall, punched umpires, and feuded with league presidents. It was a pitcher's game, and McGraw had the greatest one alive, his close friend and housemate, Christy Mathewson, the all-American boy grown up. A college man, Matty was as handsome and tall and well-spoken as McGraw was short and profane and dumpy; he had an easy grace about him and an out pitch known by the lovely old-fashioned name of "fadeaway."

Then everything changed, practically right before McGraw's eyes. The gamblers who hung out at McGraw's own favorite off-field stomping grounds, Manhattan's Ansonia Hotel—a confection no less unlikely in his-tory or appearance than the Polo Grounds, the building where Bette Midler would get her start in a gay bathhouse and Plato's Retreat would have its brief, notorious reign (but that's another story)— were busy plotting the fix that would throw the 1919 World Series. A hero was needed, and he would appear in the most unlikely dugout.

The Yankees were the Giants' tenants, their poor relations in the Polo Grounds, when they acquired Babe Ruth from the Red Sox. No deal ever irked Muggsy more. He hated Ruth, right from the beginning, with his seemingly heedless style of play and his ability to hog the spotlight. Most unforgivably, Ruth would transform the game, take it away forever from the control of the manager with his canny, small ball strategies.

Matty went off to fight World War I and returned a dying man, his lungs burned out in a training accident. Meanwhile, the Babe lofted one pop fly after another down the short foul lines of the Polo Grounds and launched moonshots all the way out to the distant bleachers. He had, somehow, transcended the old geometry of the game. It was all about power now. The infinite spaces of the old ball field had suddenly been spanned. The distant fans intimately connected with their hero as they scrambled for the balls he dropped in their midst, and roared their tribute during his leisurely, majestic strolls around the bases. The infinite spaces of the Polo Grounds—of baseball—had suddenly been negated.

McGraw hated it. So did all the old baseball purists. In every sport there are those—usually sportswriters—who remain irrevocably opposed to spectacular, flashy play. These individuals, who can be found on your sports page to this day, have yet to accept the home run in baseball, the forward pass in football, the long jump shot in basketball—even seventy, eighty, ninety years after these innovations came to pass. To purists, such plays make the game look too easy, almost cheap. They seem to negate the hard work and on-field canniness that defined the old Baltimore Oriole teams McGraw had cut his teeth on back in the nineteenth century.

• • •

Ruth was altogether too much, the consummate player of the 1920s. He himself had made the crossing from the old game to the new, the best southpaw in the now-dead dead ball game, before effortlessly converting himself into a slugger—the first true slugger anyone had ever seen. Before him, home runs were as likely to be inside-the-park jobs as they were to land in the stands. The leading power hitters rarely hit more than 12 or 15 in a season; the entire Yankees team hit all of 8 in 1913, their first year in John McGraw's park. But here was Ruth now, setting new records for home runs nearly every season—29, 54, 59...eventually 60 in 1927, or more than any other whole team in the American League hit that year. The suddenly rich, star-laden Yankees shook the dust of the Polo Grounds from their feet at McGraw's insistence, but the manager couldn't turn back time by banishing the team to the outer boroughs. The Yankees moved into their own stadium, "The House That Ruth Built," in the toney new Bronx and won pennant after pennant, setting new attendance records.

We know Ruth today mostly from a handful of salvaged photographs and film clips. He seems like a caricature now, a joke, with that big, puffy, tragicomic clown's face. A grainy figure with an enormous pot belly, flicking at the ball with his bat and then skittering around the bases on his spindly legs, smiling and nodding, smiling and tipping his cap. We have heard all the stories about his gargantuan appetites, about all the endless hot dogs, the oceans of booze, Ty Cobb seeing him in a whorehouse the night before a game with three—or was it four?—women, a tray of beer, and another one of pig knuckles...then watching him hit two home runs the next day, waddling around the bases complaining about how his stomach hurt.

That Babe surely existed, as did the Babe who seems to have actually put himself on the disabled list through overeating and the Babe who signed baseballs for sick boys in hospital beds and told them he was going to hit home runs for them. But there was another Babe too, an earlier Babe we don't like to dwell on so much because he reveals another side of the game. This was the young Babe, before he had grown the great gut, an athlete of phenomenal, almost frightening quickness and skill. To watch him in action, barreling around the bases, running through anything that gets in his way, is like watching a force of nature. In photographs his eyes flash under his dark brow, not yet safely encased in flesh. It is the look that suggests other appetites besides the culinary. It is the face of another street kid, with an eye out for his opportunities in the big city.

Contrary to Muggsy's assumptions, this Ruth was not inattentive to his game but had an innate, fundamental feel for the sport. This was the Babe who stole home seventeen times, who was an excellent bunter, hit to the opposite field, had a mean hook slide. The Babe who was an outstanding outfielder, who before games would sometimes give the fans a thrill by laying a towel down on home plate and seeing how many times he could hit it on the fly from deep right field. When he was in a slump at the plate, he might break out of it by pitching batting practice, or even catching a few pitches, trying to get his timing back.

Mobbed wherever he went, Ruth rarely lost his geniality, and then usually only when sorely provoked. He moved amiably through life, always smiling and winking, calling all the strangers who pursued him "kid." He took the vicious bench-jockeying of the era in stride and delighted in returning it.

The only taunt that ever got to him was when someone called him *nigger*. It infuriated him, which only made rumors persist. Could he have been? It is a repugnant question, of course, even if one might wish it were so—even if it would be the best possible joke on organized white baseball, which thought it had banned all African Americans from its midst. It is not worth the query, though; it is unknowable. Suffice it to say that Ruth was another mongrel American city boy like most of us—like all the rest of us, whether we want to admit it or not. The son of a Baltimore barkeep and his wife, he was handed over to a Catholic orphanage at a young age. The Jesuit fathers set him free in 1914—the same year Louis Armstrong was turned loose from the New Orleans boys' home he had been confined to for a youthful indiscretion. Two teenaged boys, released from two Southern homes, each about to transform his own piece of popular culture forever—such was the energy of America at the time.

The ban on black ballplayers—known black players—in the major leagues finally ended in 1947, with Jackie Robinson. Within four years, a final legend would be playing in the Polo Grounds. Willie Mays was in many ways the antithesis of Ruth. Shorter and more slender at five-eleven,

180 pounds, Mays was all elegance and fluidity, a player whose grace caused grown men to mourn his passing from New York for decades. If the Babe had been singular in conquering the two great poles of the game, pitching and hitting, it is doubtful there ever was as complete an all-around player as Willie Mays—a five-skill player, as the terminology has it. He could hit, hit for power, field, throw, run—how he could run. He ran out from under his hat, he was so fast. He was the first man in over 30 years to hit over 30 home runs and steal over 30 bases in the same season. He hit over 50 home runs on two separate occasions, once into the wind off San Francisco Bay.

He could do anything—gliding through life, it seemed, even more smoothly than Ruth had. Greeting all the adoring strangers with his own generic salute, "*Say hey!*" A good-natured if somewhat removed young man, up from Birmingham; up from nowhere, coached mainly by his father, a former Negro League star. Bursting on the scene a fully formed major-leaguer, it seemed. Bursting out with all that incalculable, bottled-up talent, that angry, channeled intensity those first, remarkable generations of no-longer banned black players brought to the big leagues—Robinson and Mays, and Newcombe and Frank Robinson and Aaron and Gibson and Clemente, to name just a few. Though Mays never seemed that angry. Enjoying himself, like Ruth. Even playing stickball out on the streets of Harlem with the neighborhood kids, waving a broomstick bat at the spaldeen, splattering it over the manhole covers.

September 29, 1954: the first game of the World Series at the Polo Grounds. The strange old park has less than ten years to live, and Mays, twenty-three, in his first full major-league season, is about to impress his image indelibly on the history of the game—and to ensure that a last glimpse of the old ballpark will be preserved in countless highlight reels. It's the eighth inning of a tie game, two on and nobody out for the visiting Cleveland Indians, and Vic Wertz, a muscular first baseman, is at the plate. Wertz will be red-hot throughout the Series, and he has already recorded three hits on the day, a triple and two singles. Now he rips another soaring fly, deep into the endless expanses of the Polo Grounds' right-centerfield.

Mays is after the ball. It keeps going, and he is right after it. Running and running, outrunning the ball, miraculously bisecting the endless expanses of the ball field, running all the way out over the vast, dark fields of the republic. Here is the weird center field clubhouse coming into view now, the monument to Eddie Grant, killed in the Great War, the war that took poor Matty's lungs. Here is a strange scene, frozen in still unfinished reaction: a few faces, peering out of the clubhouse windows, unable to see just where Mays is; a few of the fans, most of them men wearing hats and some in jackets too, even in the center field bleachers, just beginning to stand up, just aware something is going on that doesn't add up. They are all captured forever, in this first twitch of a great realization.

For Mays has already caught the ball. Running straight out, he has caught it over his left shoulder with barely a shrug. He is already turning back to the infield and about to throw, even as the crowd is still beginning to bestir itself. He windmills a quick throw back toward the plate, and the runners are kept from scoring. The Giants get out of the inning, win the game, sweep the World Series—the only one Mays will win in his whole long incomparable career. It was the greatest catch ever made in the World Series, perhaps the greatest catch ever. Bob Feller, the great Cleveland pitcher watching from the dugout that day, sniffed later that no one thought it was the greatest catch then. Feller, unaccountably sour for a man blessed with a hundred mile-an-hour fastball, claimed that everyone knew Mays used to deliberately wear his hats too small so they would fall off and make everything he did look faster, better, more incredible.

But the pictures of that frozen moment show that Mays's hat is just falling off then, obviously jarred off by how suddenly he has stopped and turned to make the throw. In fairness, it is easy to see how Feller or any other onlooker could be deceived. The over-the-shoulder catch is the hardest single play in baseball, but watching the film to this day, a casual observer will not see anything very dramatic, will notice little that stands out from the fantastic fluidity of Mays in motion. The greatness of the catch lies in how effortless Mays has made it look—lies in where he is, how far he has had to travel just to be there. He has bridged the same gap as Ruth did with his moonshots, but he has done it as a single running man catching up to the slugger's ball, closing the circle.

More than a decade later, they were still selling boys' models of Mays running down Wertz's ball—preserving at least some little, plastic representation of the old Polo Grounds. Mays would leave when Horace Stoneham, the Giants' drunk of an owner, was lured out to the West Coast, abandoning the stickball-playing kids on the streets of Harlem without a second glance. The Polo Grounds was torn down in 1964, replaced by an ill-considered housing project. Nearly all of the old ballparks met a similar fate over the next few decades—Ebbets Field and Shibe Park, Forbes Field and Crosley Field, Sportsman's Park and Comiskey Park, and Tiger Stadium—as the club owners squirmed and ran to get away from anyplace there might be black people; to where they could find something much more vital, which is to say, parking. The old parks would be replaced, at first, by new stadiums mostly out in the suburbs—round, interchangeable, all-purpose stadiums, many carpeted with artificial turf, that could be used just as easily for football games or rock concerts.

The Mets brought Mays back to play in what may have been the ugliest of them all, Shea Stadium, a park that already looked irredeemably shabby when it was brand-new. He was forty-two years old when he appeared in the 1973 World Series, and even though he managed to drive in the winning run in one game off a future Hall of Fame pitcher, he staggered sadly about the outfield, misplaying balls. Everyone gasped that Willie Mays had grown old, and in his embarrassment he retired after that fall.

He had lasted, in the end, nearly as long as the terrible new cookie-cutter ballparks would. Trying to capitalize on memories and luxury boxes, the owners found an excuse to tear down most of them after only a generation or so. In one town after another, baseball has returned to the inner cities, to new parks that were ostentatiously designed with quirky, eccentric features—a right field wall that is part of an old warehouse, a small knoll in deep center, even a swimming pool in the bleachers. They are improvements over the round, bleak stadiums of the 1960s—though somehow they never recaptured the beauty of the old parks, revealing themselves, ultimately, as what they were: an exercise in ready-made nostalgia. The past, once uncoupled, is not so easily regained.

My Glove: A Biography

Stefan Fatsis

*When I was asked to contribute to this anthology about the gorgeous
minutiae of baseball, I didn't have to think for even a second about a
topic. I'd wanted to write about my baseball glove for years. Not only
is it the single most personal object I own—the one thing I would be
devastated to lose—it is my last, best connection to the baseball that
defined my life as a kid. Not just playing the game incessantly, but
being a crazy fan of it, too. My glove is a reminder that the innocence
and thrill that made baseball so great and so important still exist
in this thirty-year-old hunk of leather.*

"I'll tell you what. It's sure broken in perfect."
 In my forty-three years on Earth, this ranks among the highest com-
pliments I have received. Right up there, definitely top five, maybe No. 1.
So tell me more, Bob Clevenhagen, you curmudgeonly craftsman extraor-
dinaire, you seen-it-all, stitched-'em-all Boswell of the baseball glove, you
National Archive of five-fingered-leather historical facts and figures, you
Ravel of Rawlings Sporting Goods.

"It's broken in as well as any I ever get," Bob says. On the other end of
the telephone line, I smile so hard that blood vessels threaten to pop in my
cheeks. After all, Bob has been making and repairing gloves for current and
future Hall of Famers for three decades. "The target for you is the base of
your index finger, not the web. That's the way the pro player would do it.
Not the retail market. Not a softball player."

Hell, no! Not the retail market! Not a softball player!

"This looks like a major-league gamer."

I move from happiness to rapture. In fact, I might just cry.

"That's high praise," I manage to say, filling dead air when what I really want to do is drop the phone and dance.

"Yes, it is," Bob replies, curt, gruff, no nonsense, Midwestern. He's just the third person in the 119-year history of Rawlings to hold the exalted title of Glove Designer, not a man given to bromides and bon mots, which of course makes his words all the sweeter. "Yours looks like—well, look in the Hall of Fame."

I may spontaneously combust.

"Those gloves probably look just like yours. Same color, same shape, same fadedout look," he says. "It's just a nice-looking glove."

· · ·

My glove isn't just broken in perfect, to quote Bob. I believe it is stunningly perfect, consummately perfect, why-would-anyone-use-anything-else? perfect. To play baseball well, you have to consider your glove an ideal; if not, it will let you down. A glove has to feel like an extension of your hand, something over which you have the motor control of a surgeon repairing a capillary. But my glove is more than just a piece of equipment that works for me. I really think it is empirically flawless.

Let's start with its shape: parabolic from the top of the thumb to the tip of the pinkie. This is the result of years of pushing those two fingers toward the middle; there's a slight break about three inches from the end of each digit. No ball is leaving my glove because it bent back one of the outermost fingers.

When I put the glove on, the first thing I inevitably do is press down the index finger. This transforms the parabola into a circle. Open your palm and spread your fingers wide. Now curl your fingertips forward. That's what my stationary glove looks like.

My glove is soft. It collapses of its own accord when set down. But, thanks to its aforementioned shape, it never falls completely flat, full thumb atop full pinkie. Instead, the tip of the thumb and the tip of the pinkie touch delicately, like God reaching out to Adam on the ceiling of the Sistine Chapel. I've never understood gloves that open to a V and shut like a book. The idea is to catch a round ball, not a triangular block. Roundness is essential. Softness is too. The trick is to create a glove pliable enough to respond to your slightest movement. To bend to a player's will, a glove needs to bend. Mine does.

The index finger of my left hand—I throw right-handed—lies on the exterior of the glove's back, the only digit not tucked inside. This technique provides bonus protection when catching hard-hit or fast-thrown balls. I believe it also helps me better control the glove's behavior. And it looks cool.

Each finger curves gently, like a suburban cul-de-sac. The adjustable loops surrounding the pinkie and thumb aren't tied too tightly, but their existence is palpable. The web isn't soft and deep, so that a ball might get lost, but rather follows the natural curvature from the top of the index finger to the top of the thumb. The heel of my glove aligns with the heel of my palm. The shearling beneath the wrist strap is matted but still recognizable. There are no garish personal adornments, just my first initial and last name written meticulously in black ink letters three-eighths of an inch tall just above the seam along the thumb. It looks as if I used a ruler to line the letters up.

Then there's the smell: leather, dirt, grass, saliva, sun, spring, childhood, summer, hope, skill, anticipation, achievement, fulfillment, memory, love, joy.

• • •

I bought my glove in the spring of 1977. I was about to turn fourteen, out of Little League and over my head in the ninety-feet-to-first-base Senior League in the inner suburb of Pelham, New York. A wall of leather graced the sporting goods store in a nearby town, soft porn in my baseball-centric world. I had to have a Rawlings—it would be my third or fourth Rawlings, one of them royal blue—because that's what major leaguers wore. And it had to be a good one because, while every other kid pined for his turn at bat, I happily chased grounders until dark. Five feet tall and under a hundred pounds, I was a typical prepubescent second baseman: all field, no hit. An adult-sized glove would make me feel bigger, and play bigger.

My choice, the XPG6, was expensive. I remember the price as ninety dollars, though old Rawlings catalogues tell me it was probably seventy dollars (or we were ripped off). I didn't know it then, but it was fourth-priciest glove in the Rawlings line. Thanks, Mom, for not blinking.

Not insignificantly, the XPG6 reminded me of the glove my eight-years older brother wore when he was in high school. Virtually all of my decisions at that age were influenced by my brother, who had taught me how to calculate my batting average when I was in the second grade. (At age nine, clearly my athletic prime, I hit .750, aided, no doubt, by some generous scoring.) He played shortstop and, like me, was a competent but unexceptional player. But his glove was just right: round and bendable. I didn't want his, just one like it.

So the XPG6 it was. It bore Rawlings's famous trademarks: HEART OF THE HIDE written inside a snorting steer stamped in the "DEEP WELL" POCKET. The TRIPLE ACTION web with a Spiral Top (in grade-school cursive). Along the thumb, Rawlings's familiar bright-red Circle R. Next to it, another classic, the EDGE-U-CATED HEEL. Below that, the patent number, 2,995,757. (And below that, my first initial and last name. And a single, mysterious black dot.) Along the glove's heel, XPG6 stamped just above the handsome Rawlings script, with a long, swooping tail on the R, itself resting atop the letters U.S.A. Only the U and the top of the S are discernible today.

Two other marks cemented my love. Explanation is unnecessary as to why, arcing along the pinkie, FOR THE Professional PLAYER was so seductive. The signature's allure was less obvious. My glove was endorsed by Willie Stargell, who (a) threw left-handed and (b) played 111 games at first base in 1976. Why his autograph—which looked fake, with penmanship-class loops and flourishes—was on what I assumed was a middle infielder's glove was incomprehensible, but I loved its cocktail-conversation quality. When you're fourteen, weird sometimes is good.

It's not a stretch to say that I've had a longer (and closer) relationship with my baseball glove than anyone or anything, apart, maybe, from my immediate family and a couple of childhood pals. I broke it in in the manner of the times: a couple of baseballs, string, the underside of my mattress, ceaseless play. It carried me through my last two years of organized ball, on a team sponsored by the local American Legion post.

A black-and-white team photo hangs framed on my office wall now. It's from the end of the 1977 season, and of the eighth grade. I sit smiling in the front row of wooden bleachers along the first base line at Glover Field with my friends Peter Derby (shortstop), John McNamara (left field), and Chuck Heaphy (right field, coach's son), and a younger kid whose name I can't remember. My wavy hair wings out from under the two-tone cap with the too-high crown. Black block felt letters spell LEGION across the chests of our double-knit uniforms. We wear what are essentially Detroit Tigers period road grays: black, orange, and white piping along the neck and sleeves of the buttonless jerseys, black stirrups with orange and white stripes stretched as high as possible to reveal as much of our white sanitary socks as possible. The Seventies rocked.

The XPG6 rests on my left knee. My index finger pokes out, pointing directly at the camera lens. The leather is dark and rich. I am young and small. The twelve-inch XPG6 is new and large—much too large for me, a glove worn, I have since learned, by big-league outfielders and third basemen. Joe Morgan used a ten-inch glove at second base at the time. But what did I know? (More relevant: what did the salesman know?) All that matters is that, in that photograph, the XPG6 and I look like we're starting life, which, of course, we are.

How did it do for me? Records of my glove's rookie year are lost to history. But my 1978 Legion season is preserved on a single piece of lined white loose-leaf paper, folded inside a schedule, stored with other keepsakes in the basement. It reveals that I played in 13 games—with 9 appearances at second base, 4 at shortstop, and a few innings at third base and in right field—and committed 5 errors, 2 of them in our 9–4 championship-game loss to Cornell Carpet. (The stat sheet also shows that I totaled just 4 hits in 23 at-bats, an average of, ouch, .175. But that I walked 16 times and had a robust on-base percentage of .404. Billy Beane would have given me a chance.)

I can still see and feel the ball rolling under the XPG6, and through my legs, during tryouts for the junior varsity the next spring, ending my competitive hardball career. But my glove's best years were yet to come. In college, on fast but honest artificial turf at the University of Pennsylvania's historic Franklin Field, my glove snared line drives, grabbed one-hoppers to the shortstop side, shielded me from screaming bullets, and started more 1-6-3 double plays than you'd expect. My team won back-to-back intramural softball championships, and my glove was one of the stars. Later, it performed well on the pitcher's mound again in New York City softball leagues. It shagged hundreds of baseball fungoes lofted heavenward on lazy afternoons by my best friend Jon.

As I aged—knee surgeries, work, a wife and daughter—my glove lay dormant most springs and summers, its color fading and leather peeling: wan, weathered, cracked. But it's always remained in sight, not stashed in a closet or buried in a box of moldering sports equipment. Single, on a couch in Brooklyn, the Yankees on TV—married, in Washington, in the attic, at a desk—I put on the XPG6 and whip a ball into its still-perfect pocket. My glove is a comfort.

• • •

My glove was manufactured in 1976 in Willow Springs, Missouri. It is made of tanned steer hide, specifically Code 5 Horween-X Catcher's Mitt Glove Leather from the Horween Leather Company in Chicago, founded in 1905. The exterior leather is 0.075 inch thick and cut from a durable two-foot stretch along the steer's backbone, the heart of the hide. The separate interior, a glove within the glove known as the lining, is 0.050 inch thick and hails from the softer belly. The web comes from the butt, the toughest part of the hide. Rawlings doesn't have a slogan for that.

I know all of this because Bob Clevenhagen tells me. To establish my glove's birth year, for instance, Bob has me look on the outside of the thumb, below the patent number. How many dots?

"One dot," I say.

"One dot. That's exactly right. Made in 1976. But it wouldn't have gone out in the marketplace until the first of 1977."

I'd noticed the one-sixteenth-inch dot years ago but had no idea what it meant. I thought it was an accidental factory mark. Bob explains that Rawlings used dots to establish the year of manufacture for warranty purposes. One dot meant a glove was made in a year ending in 1 or 6, two dots was a year ending in 2 or 7, and so on. That way, if someone returned a glove for repair or replacement, Rawlings would know whether it was still under warranty (and the owner would have no idea how the company could tell).

After working at shoe factories in Missouri and Massachusetts, Bob joined Rawlings as foreman of glove operations in Willow Springs in 1977. ("Leather was my life after I got out of the service," he says.) A workforce of two hundred made about 170,000 gloves there that year, including 15,000 or so XPG6s. As Rawlings and other glove makers began shifting production to Asia, the Willow Springs factory was closed in 1982. Today, Bob runs a four-person operation at Rawlings's main distribution center in Washington, Missouri, making gloves for a couple dozen major leaguers and for a custom catalogue.

The XPG6 and its progenitors were Rawlings's first fully functional modern gloves, created in response to Wilson's A2000, which revolutionized baseball when it appeared in 1957. The A2000 had a larger web, broader pocket, hinged heel, and flatter fingers, thumb, and heel than the standard puffy models of the time. In his artful book *Glove Affairs: The Romance, History, and Tradition of the Baseball Glove*, Noah Liberman explains that the A2000 dispelled a century-old belief: that the glove should look like the hand. "The evolution of the glove is, in large part," he writes, "the slow realization that a glove must reflect how a hand moves to catch a ball, not how it looks when you stare at it." (Liberman and I, it turns out, have something in common, glove-wise. "The XPG6? That was my glove!" he exclaims when I call. "That was my glove in high school!" Liberman swapped his with the shortstop of a women's pro baseball team for a jersey. She never sent him the shirt.)

Rawlings began making XPG prototypes—the initials stood for "experimental glove"—for big-league players in 1958. The first retail model, the XPG3, endorsed by pitcher Herb Score, appeared in the company's 1960 catalogue. The quarter-inch shorter but otherwise identical XPG6 debuted in 1962 and quickly became one of Rawlings's most popular gloves. The autograph inside helped: Mickey Mantle. According to glove historian Dennis Esken—who owns the glove Mantle used to make a one-handed catch in left center field that helped preserve Don Larsen's perfect game in the 1956 World Series—the model name bore a "6" because it originally was intended for Stan Musial, who wore that number. For Mantle, Rawlings designed an XPG7, but, Esken tells me, the famous No. 7 didn't like it. It had a newfangled Trap-Eze web with a vertical strip of leather connected to each side with laces; the Mick wanted a solid web. Since Musial was nearing the end of his career anyway, Rawlings put Mantle's name in the XPG6.

The original XPG6 was a "Personal Model," meaning the pattern of the glove, if not every detail of the glove itself, was the same as what the signer wore on the field. (Mantle wound up using an I-shaped web, as opposed to the two-piece Triple Action web in the retail version.) Mantle retired in 1968, but his name remained in the XPG6 until 1972. Bobby Tolan, a left-handed outfielder on Cincinnati's Big Red Machine, endorsed the XPG6 in 1973 and 1974. (Lefty signatures on righty gloves aren't unusual; glove makers don't sell enough lefties to segregate endorsers by throwing arm.) Then came Stargell. The future Hall of Famer had played in the outfield his entire career, but in 1975, the first year he signed the XPG6, he moved to first base. My glove was stitched in 1976, Stargell's name was shifted to a first baseman's glove (the FJ9) in 1977, and the XPG6 name was retired.

I tell Bob I think it's the ideal design.

"From a baseball standpoint, I agree with you," he says, quickly noting that he didn't design it. Credit for that goes to the late Rollie Latina, who in 1961 inherited the title of Glove Designer from his father, Harry, better known as Doc, as in the Glove Doctor, who joined Rawlings in 1922. The Latinas were the revered creators of most of the company's trademarked glove innovations and slogans. Bob became Glove Designer after Rollie retired in 1984. The shape of the pattern and the shape of the padding, Bob says, predisposed the XPG6 to excellence. "It's the perfect shape to play it anywhere you want to play it. Bill Madlock wore it at third base. Dwight Evans wore it for fourteen years in the outfield. That glove's been everywhere."

Tom Seaver, Hank Aaron, Mike Schmidt, Billy Williams, Doug DeCinces—I shared a glove with them too, I learn. "It was the first, most-streamlined model with that U-shaped heel and that nice pocket in it and a little less padding in it. It's more like what we use today," Bob says. "That same glove is still around. The truth is that it's the very same basic pattern. A-Rod's wearing it today," he says, referring to Yankees third baseman Alex Rodriguez. There are some differences, Bob notes. A-Rod's glove has a single-piece "Fastback" backside with a "Holdster" for the index finger. "The palm area. That's where it's the same as A-Rod, Dwight Evans, right back to Mickey Mantle."

Esken, the historian and collector, puts it to me this way. "Fifty freakin' years. That pattern glove has been synonymous with baseball for fifty years. It's still functional to this date. The A2000 from 1957 is not a functional glove today."

· · ·

Bob has made gloves for Presidents Carter, Ford, and both Bushes. He has made gloves for movies—Kevin Costner's *For Love of the Game*, *The Slugger's Wife*, written by Neil Simon, Billy Crystal's *61**. After the comedian paid $239,000 at a Sotheby's auction for a glove supposedly worn by Mantle circa 1960, he asked Bob to check it out. Bob could tell, based on the style of Mantle's signature, it was a 1965 model (an XPG3). "I could have saved him a lot of money in ten seconds," he says.

At sixty-two years old, Bob is one of Rawlings's longest-serving employ-
ees, and its de facto glove historian, fielding questions from reporters, fans,
even investigators. The FBI once called about a 1936 Joe DiMaggio rookie
gamer sold by a prominent auction house. It actually had been made two
decades later, after DiMaggio had retired. "Some of the experts who write
letters, they don't know shit," Bob tells me. "But it doesn't take a brain
surgeon to know a '36 glove from a '54 glove." One day when I call, Bob
is making a glove for a boy missing some fingers whose parents wrote
requesting help. (He made gloves for one-handed big-league pitcher Jim
Abbott.) "I get four or five of those a year," he says. "We don't advertise or
charge for it. I just do it for a nice letter from the kid. I've got a nice little
file of those."

Most big leaguers, Bob says, don't know much about their gloves.
"They don't even know what the hell they're getting. They get oil-tanned
leather. It's going to be darker from day one. Probably the last person who
knows how to make a glove is a pro ballplayer. . . . They've got a lot of bad
habits. They spit in 'em. That just rots the leather. Makes it feel sticky. It
just ruins the glove." (I don't confess that I regularly spit in the XPG6, but
only because those big leaguers did.) "They don't care today. It doesn't take
another year to break another one in."

Today's pros, Bob says, want supple leather right out of the box. They
don't want to have to work it in. Players like Dwight Evans who wear the
same glove for an entire career are as rare as perfect games. Modern players
burn through multiple gloves in a season; Bob pounds and shapes gloves
for Alex Rodriguez six at a time. Of course he does. It's good for business.

"Who wouldn't want A-Rod wearing their glove on TV?" Bob says.
"What's a lousy dozen gloves?" Compare that to the old days. "We wouldn't
even give Stan Musial an extra glove in the Fifties. If he wanted another one
he'd have to buy it."

Bob goes on. "These players are much different from your era." The
"your era" is simultaneously flattering (I lived in the old days? And there
was something good about them?) and horrifying (It wasn't that long ago,
was it?). "They don't care about durability."

They do care about the endorsement money—$100,000 or so a year for an A Rod or Derek Jeter—but they don't need it the way players did back in the day. Bob estimates Willie Stargell probably received "$5,000 and a set of golf clubs" to sign with Rawlings, plus royalties on sales above $5,000. "It mattered back then," Bob says. "I know Reggie Jackson made as much off us as he did playing ball. The Mantles of the world had to have a winter job to eat. I'm pretty sure A-Rod doesn't have to check in at Hardee's after the season's over."

• • •

On a bright afternoon two months into the 2006 season, my glove and I drive to Robert F. Kennedy Stadium—one year older than the XPG6—where the Washington Nationals are hosting the Houston Astros.

I collect my press pass and fast-walk to the home dugout. It stinks of sewage, thanks to some faulty piping manager Frank Robinson hopes the team's just-named owners will see fit to repair. As his players take batting practice, Robinson holds court with a clutch of reporters. He complains about how players won't accept instruction. He says they arrive in the big leagues sure they know everything. He outs slackers on his team by name. Of course, he does all of this off the record. Praise is on the record, though, because Frank Robinson loves and respects the game and loves and respects those who do, too.

When the beat guys finish their questions, I extract the XPG6 from my messenger bag. Everyone eyes me a bit warily—I'm not a regular, and I'm breaking the sportswriters' code of conduct by behaving weirdly in front of the people wearing uniforms. When he sees the glove, Robinson's expression falls somewhere between shame and disgust.

"You should be brought up on abuse charges," he says. "You ever oil that thing?"

Well, no, but I did have it restrung about ten years earlier, when the X-shaped lacing between the middle and index fingers broke.

"You don't even want to touch it," I say.

"No."

The manager asks who signed it, and I launch into an exegesis of the XPG6's family tree.

"Why would they change the Mickey Mantle model?" he asks. "Because he was retired," I say.

"So what?" Robinson says. "I'll tell you what. If they would have kept Mickey Mantle's name on that they would have sold more gloves than they would have with Bobby Tolan's name."

Ice broken, the other reporters join in. One asks Robinson, who won a Gold Glove in 1958, about his glove preferences. He tells us he used only a few in his twenty-one-season career. "Gloves are like shoes with me," he says. "I find a pair of shoes I like, I wear 'em. You just had a glove that felt good on your hand, you didn't quit playing with it."

Bill Mazeroski's glove was tattered, Robinson recalls. Willie Mays's glove was "beyond limit," he says. "It looked like those things they play jai alai with." Players couldn't be picky. "There were no specifications. They showed you models of gloves and you chose one that you liked." Robinson says he first signed with MacGregor, but didn't like the gloves, so he switched to Rawlings and wore a Spalding occasionlly.

Talk returns to my XPG6.

"That's the kind of glove you'd see guys playing with," he says. "Restrung, redone, whatever."

I take this as a compliment but seek a higher order of validation. "Do you like the shape at least?" I ask Robinson. "Say something nice about my glove. You're killing me."

"It's on your hand. It's not bad. How long have you had it?"

"Thirty years."

"It's not bad. It's not too bad. It's got a nice kind of shape for an infielder's glove."

But Frank Robinson thinks I need to move on.

"Get a softball glove," he says. "Retire that one."

"I can't retire it."

"Why not?"

"Because I love it."

"Sleep with it. But you don't have to abuse it. I love my wife but I leave her to come to work."

"I've had a longer relationship with my glove than I have with my wife."

"That's you. The way you're going with that glove, you're not going to know your wife much longer."

Across the infield, I wait for the Astros to finish batting practice. As the pitchers jog in from the outfield, where they've been shagging balls, I look for No. 36, Russ Springer.

Springer, Rawlings has informed me, is the only player in the major leagues using the XPG6, albeit under a different name, the Pro 6XBC. That model was also discontinued years ago, but the company makes him a couple every year. When Springer arrives at the dugout railing, I introduce myself. I tell him what we have in common, and he says he likes our glove because he played infield in high school and so prefers a smaller model (smaller for him, that is; he's six-feet-four). In his native Louisiana twang, Springer says the glove he's holding isn't his gamer, which is stashed in his locker. "It don't come out unless it's game time," he says.

Springer has used the same glove in games since 1993, his second year in the majors. "It's starting to show a lot of wear and tear," he says. "Sun-bleached on the outside. It's starting to get a couple of tears on it. The only thing I've ever had done is have the top laces replaced, all through the fingers. Just to show you how old it is, and yours is too, they don't make 'em with metal rivets anymore. And mine's still got the metal rivets. You'll see mine. It's a lot like that."

He gives my glove a once-over, examining the pocket.

"Mine actually looks worse in here than yours does."

"Can we go compare?" I ask.

"Yeah."

"Let's go."

We walk into the visitors' clubhouse and over to Springer's locker. A few days earlier, the right-handed reliever had been suspended for four games for throwing at Barry Bonds, possibly because Bonds had 713 home runs at the time and Springer didn't want to give up No. 714, possibly to let Bonds know how he felt about alleged steroids-using sluggers. (After throwing one pitch behind Bonds's back and three more inside, Springer plunked Bonds on the right shoulder and was ejected from the game. As he exited the field, Springer received a standing ovation from the home crowd.) I tell Springer our glove originally was worn by Mickey Mantle, which elicits no response. Not a historian, I guess. He pulls his gamer from the locker.

His Pro 6XBC has the crosshatched (and trademarked) Basket Web.

Instead of "DEEP WELL" POCKET, Springer's glove is stamped with GOLD GLOVE. His also doesn't have an EDGE-U-CATED HEEL. His red rectangular Rawlings label on the wrist strap says "Made in U.S.A."; mine says "Est. 1887." Springer's glove is broken in a bit flatter than mine. Otherwise, they are identical: same shape, same stitch patterns, same lace holes, same curves, same feel.

"So when you look at something like this"—I hold up the XPG6—"you don't think: old piece of leather?"

"Heck no," he says. "That's personality."

Springer says he's a creature of habit. He wears the same spikes all season. His black batting practice T-shirt (featuring his once and future teammate Roger Clemens) has a giant hole around the underarm. "I just don't like new stuff," he says.

When it comes to our glove, I tell him, I'm the same way. "I was a kid when I got it," I say. "I played softball with it for twenty years, so it's a little bit fatter and wider. But you could play with this? You wouldn't have a problem putting this on?"

"No, that's got personality," he says. "It's better than a new one."

• • •

"You need a little TLC on it," Craig Biggio says.

We're sitting on metal folding chairs on the other side of the Astros' locker room. The second baseman holds my glove gently, his thick fingers resting just beneath the wrist strap, but not inserted into the slots. "Never put your hand totally into someone else's glove," he says. Indeed, I always avoided lending my glove. The borrower inevitably would, to my horror, stick his index finger inside it. A few months earlier, I'd shown my glove to Cal Ripken Jr., who, as if testing me, inserted his hand and then admonished that I "should have been more territorial with it." Ripken said the only person he had ever allowed to use his gamer was Ronald Reagan, when the president threw out a first pitch in 1984. (Of the XPG6, the future Hall of Fame shortstop/third baseman said, and I proudly quote, "You break yours in similar to me.")

Bob Clevenhagen had recommended talking to Biggio, who won four consecutive Gold Gloves in the 1990s and, more important, appreciates the art of the glove. "It's what you make your money with," Biggio says. "A lawyer goes to work with a nice suit on every day. We've got to put a glove on our hands. If you don't know how to use it, you're not going to have a job very long. It is personal. And everybody's different."

Biggio uses one glove per season. He's a throwback, preferring firmer leather that requires attention and work on the part of the owner. But he says he's not an extremist. Steve Buechele, a third baseman for Texas, Pittsburgh, and the Cubs, used one glove his entire career, Biggio tells me, as did journeyman shortstop Jay Bell. Oakland shortstop Walt Weiss's glove was so ravaged it had a nickname: "The Creature." Biggio says the great Cardinals shortstop Ozzie Smith took the opposite approach. He could remove a new glove from its box and play with it the same day. "But he had some of the best hands ever," Biggio says.

Biggio does more work on his gloves than Smith did, but not much more. Bob sends the nineteen-year veteran a few gloves before spring training. Biggio picks a future gamer and plays catch with it. He puts a little pine tar in the pocket for "tackiness," which he says helps in cold weather when the ball is slicker. By the start of the regular season, the glove is ready. By the end, the fingers have stretched just enough to force its retirement. Biggio gives the old ones to his two sons. "They can't wait to get this one," he says, showing me his Pro CB (his initials), which is similar to the XPG6 but smaller. "It seems like a good one right now."

Like a diamond cutter appraising a stone, Biggio studies my glove. I ask what he sees.

"It's got a story to it," Biggio says. "Classic, old, beat-up. This is a classic glove of somebody who would use it every day, who wouldn't change it at all. It's got a lot of character."

"Thank you," I say. Craig Biggio understands.

"For me, the pocket's a little deep," he continues, "so it's more like a third baseman's glove. But actually, it's not all that bad. If [the ball] goes in it, I know it's not coming out. I'd have the whole thing restrung." His glove has extra laces connecting the sides of the fingers to minimize separation between them. "The leather's a little dry." He points to the pocket and fingers. "That can be padded. They can patch it up."

Biggio tells me to send my glove to Bob.

"He'll fix it up for you."

· · ·

Bob tells me what he'd do to restore my glove. "It needs new insides and new leather trim all the way around on the inside. And new laces, of course."

The trim curves around the wrist and fingers, holding together the pieces of my glove. Bob says he'll replace the interior lining—the glove within the glove, against which my palm and fingers, back and front, have rested since I was fourteen—with the same durable Horween leather as in the original, not the softer stuff pros and amateurs expect today. ("It took a man to break it in," he says of the glove of yore.) The challenge will be making the new lining fit snugly inside the old exterior; since leather stretches with use, the original pattern for the innards of the XPG6, which Bob has, probably won't match the current size of my glove.

In short, Bob says he will rebuild my glove from the inside, "everything underneath that you can't see." On the undersides of the three middle fingers, he'll install fresh wool-blend padding (minus the asbestos fibers it contained thirty years ago). Beneath the wrist strap, a synthetic wool will take over for the old shearling. The two frayed red Rawlings labels—the rectangular script Rawlings and the Circle R—will be replaced with modern likenesses. "I don't have any more of these antique ones," he says. Antique! The exterior will remain unchanged; if he replaced that, Bob says, he'd just be making a new glove.

Letting the XPG6 out of my possession had been traumatic. I first packed it at the post office, but decided I didn't trust the government, unpacked it, and shipped it FedEx. I called Bob to make sure it arrived. I had wanted Bob's expert opinion, assuming that perhaps he would offer to string some new lacing or perform some trick to revive the worn leather. I hadn't considered a total makeover. But now, listening to him explain the restoration process like an archaeologist entrusted with preserving the Parthenon, I grow excited at the prospect of new life. I tell myself I finally would be treating the XPG6 right. I finally would be making amends for years of what Frank Robinson called abuse. Spontaneously, unhesitatingly, I give Bob the go-ahead.

"I don't think you'll be upset with the way it looks," he says.

• • •

A few weeks later, a brown box arrives. I pull out the XPG6 and say, aloud: Oh. No!

It's my glove, but it isn't. It stays open of its own accord, rather than flopping shut on release, the tip of the thumb kissing the tip of the pinkie. The finger slot no longer lies permanently in the off position, pancaked to the lining. I slide my hand in. The XPG6 is snug and stiff. I can't even close it enough to obscure Stargell's too-neat signature.

The insides are burnt sienna, rich with the aroma of new leather. The laces and trim Bob had promised are bright and prominent, mod orange racing stripes on a battered Chevrolet. The replacement Rawlings patches shimmer like freshly washed fire engines drying in the summer sun. The spongy synthetic wool rubs prominently against the back of my hand; I can't even recall feeling the old stuff, tamped as it was. New internal padding forms a thick ridge along the index, middle, and ring fingers, functionally useful but interrupting the pocket's old, uniform concavity. There's even a bump in the new leather exactly where the top of my thumb rests. An imperfection! Bob, how could you?

I feel disappointment and then panic: I'll never again hold my glove, the one that accompanied me through adolescence and into adulthood, a life partner whose advancing years were undetectable because we had aged together, an anti–Dorian Gray. I didn't want a trophy wife. But now I have one.

For a second time, I feel like I'm going to cry because of my baseball glove. The XPG6 was comforting because it was so familiar. It had earned its cracks and bruises on the field, over time. Holding the remodeled version, I close my eyes and picture my glove, trying to imprint permanently its sensory qualities on my brain. How I could make the upper half flap by snapping my wrist back and forth. How I could wield it like a lobster's claw to snatch a ball off the ground. Its gloriously battered and decomposing personality, in Russ Springer's apt anthropomorphization. Even if my preschool daughter becomes a softball superstar, there's no chance I'll play enough to return the XPG6 to its old form—not enough throws to catch, not enough grounders to field, not enough time. I feel I've committed a horrible betrayal. I set down the imposter and vow not to pick it up until I'm emotionally willing to give it a chance.

• • •

The pain begins to lift a month later. What made the XPG6 special was its artistry, I realize, its shape, form, and feel. The essence of those remains unchanged. In fact, the shape and form are truer, the parabola stronger and more confident. Propped upright, resting on its wrist strap, the XPG6 reminds me of the Gold Glove trophy itself. Its new contrast, I realize, is beautiful: I. M. Pei's glass pyramid at the Louvre.

More than I have in years, I bang the pocket with my right fist, flattening the new padding. I grab the pinkie and ring finger in my right hand and open and close the glove to resuscitate its natural hinge. With my left thumb, I push and flatten the bump under my thumb (caused, I guess correctly, by the difference in size between the XPG6's lining pattern and my stretched-out glove) to which I'm sure Bob was referring in the note that accompanied the glove home: "I wish it was a little better! But!! Good Luck, Bob."

Inside the box, Bob deposited the battered core of the XPG6. It looks like something that's been worn since Honus Wagner was playing short-stop. The leather is as weather-beaten as a cowboy's chaps. Waxy remnants of the grease that affixed the lining to the glove's exterior form a dark, mottled circle on the palm. Where the fleshy part of my heel rested and sweated, there's a hole the size of a half dollar and the shape of Wisconsin, and a tear next to that. The padding beneath the three middle fingers is shredded. At the point where the nail of my ring finger touched the leather, there's another hole—the result of untold thousands of repetitions of finger sliding into glove, right fist pounding left hand, balls batted and thrown striking that precise spot.

Then, finally, there's the index finger slot, pressed as flat as a stone made for skipping across a lake. I peek underneath. The leather is smooth, dark, unblemished, my glove in 1977. Still with me today, still perfect.

I'm going to use my new glove as much as possible. What's left of my glove—My Glove—I'm having framed.

Giants Favor New Slim Look For Men in Gray Flannel Suits

Gay Talese

Baseball players, wearers of the gray flannel suit long before it became the uniform of Madison Avenue, generally try to look fashionable in their baseball suits, all of which are tailor-made, unshrinkable and free.

Although the style of the baseball suit has not changed much in the last two decades, there is a trend toward slimmer lines and away from baggy pants. Oversized or chemise-like, shirts also are not considered chic nowadays in the big league's *beau monde*.

Ray Kolas, a seasoned baseball uniform fitter, who currently is measuring players for their 1958 trousseaus, says it is now customary for players to look at themselves in the locker room mirror before going on to the field.

"They want to make sure they look right," Kolas said with conviction.

What concerns them most about their attire?

"Oh, I guess it's the angle of their hats," Kolas said. "Players like to wear their hats at a precise angle. Dusty Rhodes of the Giants, for example, wants his hat to set at precisely the same angle of that felt fedora worn by Adolphe Menjou in the movies".

Baseball hats, belts and socks, together with shirt and pants, cost $55 wholesale. Every season each player gets two gray flannel suits for "away" games and two white flannel suits for "home" games. The club pays for the suits and hats, but players buy their own shoes and gloves. After one season, the suits are too weary for major league play and they are sent down to the minors.

The minor league teams that inherit one-year-old suits from their parent clubs all find that the suits rarely fit. This is one disadvantage in playing minor league ball. Suits, for instance, that were tailored to the pint-sized measurements of Phil Rizzuto, formerly with the Yankees, or to the towering specifications of the ex-Brookyln first-baseman Howie Schultz, are now said to be floating around down in the Class D territory. It is suspected that these uniforms have been cut up by this time, however, and would make first-class windshield wipers for a Class D team bus.

The San Francisco Giants already have ripped off the "New York" lettering that appeared on last season's road uniform. In its place the Giants have the thirteen-space "San Francisco". But it is difficult to see all the letters on the shirt because no Giant is big enough to bulge out the shirt lettering. There are no plans to re-obtain big Ernie Lombardi as far as can be determined.

Kolas, who works for Wilson Sporting Goods, twirls his tape measure around 600 players each season. He keeps a measurement chart report on each player that would do credit to Brooks Brothers. For instance, on his chart of the Detroit pitcher, Jim Bunning, Kolas noted: "Taper shirt—has small hips (no seat)."

Kolas does not know anything about batting averages or who's on first, of course, but he is strictly the man to see "if one must know about Ted Williams' inseam, Virgil Trucks' girth or the size of the smallest head in the major leagues."

According to Kolas' official record book, Williams holds the record for inseam, 34 inches; Trucks, the Kansas City pitcher, has a waist of 40 inches; and the smallest head in the majors belongs to Billy Pierce of the White Sox, who is size 6½.

(from the *New York Times*, February 24, 1958)

My Brilliant Career

Susan Perabo

*Why is there so much written about baseball? Why do writers—
even fiction writers, like me—feel compelled to weigh in on the
subject? As with love, the topic is inexhaustible because it feels
like personal property to everyone who holds the sport dear. As
with love, there is always something new— something original,
something crucial—to add to the conversation.*

This past summer I went to see my St. Louis Cardinals play the
Washington Nationals at RFK Stadium. Turns out, when a batter
approaches the plate at RFK, not only do his stats appear on the Jumbotron
but also his date of birth. Now, I'd come to terms some time ago with the
fact that I'm considerably older than a lot of major league players. Albert
Pujols has only a few years on the kids in my creative writing classes. Kerry
Wood, A-Rod, Renteria—I might have babysat them. But it was a most
unpleasant surprise when Jim Edmonds came to bat and I was informed in
five-foot-high letters of his date of birth: 6/27/70. I literally blinked to clear
my vision—those lighted numbers get blurry sometimes in the glare of a
night game. I had always thought of Edmonds as the old man of the team,
the seasoned vet, the big brother (*my* big brother), the guy who could put
things into perspective and buy you a frozen Coke afterwards. Could it
possibly be that I was *older* than Edmonds? And yet the numbers, when I
looked again, were the same. My big brother had, in an instant, become my
little brother. And in the next instant the sobering truth came clear: it was
nearly time for me to retire.

Retiring from a pretend baseball career is more difficult than a nonpretend baseball player might imagine. My career, though entirely imagined, has been long and rewarding. Am I a superstar? Far from it. Even in my fantasy life some tenuous grip on reality must be maintained. My lifetime average is .268; my fielding percentage is regularly among those of the top five second basemen in the league; I once won a Gold Glove; one season my on-base percentage was so high I was moved to second in the order; I played in one All-Star Game (purely for the sake of novelty...I know when I'm the ballplayer and when I'm *the girl*) and I hit a double down the right field line that scored the go-ahead run for the National League; I got tossed from a game for arguing a called strike; I'm too slow to steal, but I'm the worst kind of pest on the base paths; I once tumbled into the stands to catch a foul ball; I'm always the first to the ballpark.

A friend who knows of my pretend career recently asked me if I thought a woman would ever play major league baseball. You might think I would have mulled over this question considerably in the course of my career, but you'd be wrong. Once it became clear I would not be the first woman stepping onto the diamond at Busch or Wrigley or Fenway, I went about the business of baseball fandom and my pretend career and have not worried much about the state of women in the game. But perhaps, with my pretend retirement on the pretend horizon, this is the perfect time to consider the question.

One thing's for certain: my *personal* glass ceiling had nothing to do with gender and everything to do with talent. When I played college baseball, I was the backup second baseman for a team so new—it had turned from a club sport to a varsity team just the season before—there were no tryouts; I made the team by showing up at the organizational meeting. Barring divine intervention (not that I didn't consider this a real possibility for a good while), it was clear my actual baseball career would and should begin and end with my beloved Webster University Gorlocks. But of course there have been other women since who have played at the collegiate level, in programs far more established than my own. The best known is Julie Croteau. Sometimes referred to as the first woman to play NCAA baseball

(I'm mostly over this), she started at first base for St. Mary's College, went on to become the first woman to coach college baseball, and eventually played for the Colorado Silver Bullets, a professional women's baseball team that played against professional men's teams for five years in the 1990s. Croteau is now affiliated with the American Women's Baseball Federation, an organization that promotes women's amateur baseball. Was Julie Croteau good enough to play in the majors? She was not. How about Ila Borders, who pitched for three years in the Northern League in the late '90s? She neither, nor the often overlooked Toni Stone, who played in the Negro Leagues in the early '50s. But were these women the cream of the crop?

The answer is no. With all respect to these women, they were not the best of the best. The best of the best, I firmly believe, are lost before they are found. They are discouraged by well-meaning parents, steered in other directions. Billie Jean King once dreamed of playing big league baseball but was encouraged by her parents (thank goodness, we must think now) to pursue tennis instead. Most girls who love baseball are, of course, steered to softball, and the fact is, at the earliest level—the elementary school level—the two sports are fairly interchangeable. The softball used for young girls is smaller than a regulation softball, just slightly bigger than a baseball; it can be driven, thrown, and fielded almost exactly like a baseball. The size of the field, the distance between bases, the speed of the pitches (often thrown by coaches)— all these are very similar, at first. But when the size of the ball changes (usually when girls are around twelve), the whole game begins to change; softball gradually becomes a game of small-ball, of bunts and infield hits, of manufacturing runs with a huge ball on a tiny field. What had once been nearly interchangeable with baseball becomes, by high school, an entirely different sport, and a young woman hoping to shift from softball to baseball might as well be trying to shift from soccer to football. Besides, a star player on her high school softball team may have her eyes fixed on a scholarship to play college softball, and why would she give that up to play a sport in which she has no future? And what adolescent athlete wants to have to wage a battle against the status quo? Being a teenage girl is difficult enough; who wants to be the girl who's *different*? The girl who may even have to sue her high school to be allowed to play with the guys? (Julie Croteau tried this, without success.) Gina Satriano, another former Silver Bullet, told *The Sporting News*: "We had to fight to play Pony League, we had to fight to play Colt League. When I got to high school, Mom asked me if I wanted to fight to play there, too, and I said, 'I'm tired of fighting. I just want to play.' So I played softball. I just didn't enjoy the game as much." Lest it seem I'm demonizing a wonderful sport, I must point out that softball— which became widely popular in large part due to Title IX—has given countless girls and women opportunities they would never have had otherwise. But it's also been a convenient way to keep young girls out of baseball.

So we come to the sticky question: even if the best women did play baseball, would they be able to compete with the best men? The answer's even stickier: no way. The physical differences between men and women are too vast. Asked about the possibility of women playing major league baseball, Babe Ruth said, "They will never make good. Why? Because they are too delicate. It would kill them to play ball every day." As was often the case, the lovable old pig missed the point entirely. The problem is one not of endurance, but of physical strength (primarily upper body strength) and speed. In no sport is the best woman better or faster than the best man. And the numbers are drastically against us. Say one in ten thousand men have the natural ability that—with the best coaching and the right attitude— could take them to the majors. The numbers for women? Maybe one in one hundred thousand. Couple those staggering odds with the early social pressures to play a "girl's game" rather than a boy's, and it's pretty clear why the gender barrier has not yet been broken.

But, as we all say when we buy the Powerball ticket despite the enormous odds: well, *somebody's* got to win, right? Indeed, even if the odds of a woman playing in the bigs are one in a million, it's logical to assume that the one can't be too far off. And the more girls play baseball, the more the odds are with us. The American Women's Baseball Federation, with Julie Croteau and other former Silver Bullets on board, is seeking to bring women into the game earlier, offering baseball camps for girls only and holding regional, national, and international baseball tournaments for young women. It will take opportunities like this, and a powerful parental influence, to create the first woman major leaguer. There's no doubt in my mind that had Richard Williams decided to groom his daughters into baseball players rather than tennis players, at least one of them—probably Serena—would have had the ability to play in the majors.

So here's my fearless prediction: look for her in 2024, a control pitcher with great lower-body strength, a middle reliever with brilliant placement and dagger eyes. Or possibly a second baseman with quick hands and feet, a player with the skills I've honed in my pretend career: a contact hitter and excellent fielder with fierce determination. Mark it in pen on your calendar: she's coming soon(ish) to a dugout near you.

But for now, for today, there's only me: Susan Perabo, DOB: 1/6/69. Aaron and Mays played past forty, but I am no Aaron or Mays. I am not even an Edmonds. Some infield greats lose a step or two in their mid-thirties but still manage to make amazing plays. But I don't have a step or two to lose. And my pretend average this year is five points lower than last, a trend I fear is irreversible, no matter how much time I spend in the gym or the cages during the off-season. Perhaps the dignified thing to do would be to retire. There's nothing worse than watching a ballplayer play one season too long, nothing worse than wondering "Doesn't she know it's over?"

But here's where the *pretend* part of my pretend career comes in handy. This winter, against all odds, my hours in the gym will pay off. And in the cages I'll find, inexplicably, that I'm seeing the ball a little better. Yes, my retirement still looms, but it now seems I have at least one more season left in these legs and hands and eyes. There's a bounce in my step, a fire in my belly, and my fingers grip invisible balls even as I sleep. I feel fresh. I feel young. I feel like...a girl.

Field of Dreams

George Plimpton

*There probably aren't many writers who would volunteer to pitch in
the majors. In fact, there's probably only one: George Plimpton, who,
while sitting in the stands at a game in 1960, started to wonder what
the view was like from the mound. His curiosity led him, as it did with
football and boxing, to talk his way into the sport, and before the start
of the 1960 All-Star Game, Plimpton faced the National League lineup.
In this essay, written more than forty years later, Plimpton reflects on
being put out to pasture, demoted over the years from the pitching
mound to first base to rightfield. [L. G.]*

I can't remember whether it was last summer, or the one before that, or
maybe even three years ago, when, in a pickup baseball game after lunch,
I was the last one picked. The captain, a teenager, referred to me as "Mister."
He asked me if I would play rightfield. Sure, I said. I thought longingly of
the half-finished glass of white wine back on the porch.

The others ran to their positions. The first baseman, a twelve-year-old,
stretched out his length like a big leaguer to receive the warm-up tosses
zipped across the infield.

There were two of us who walked to our positions—the young pitcher
(a third my age), because that is in the nature of pitchers, and myself. Even
in pickup softball games, pitchers move with a kind of smug, imperial

elegance to the pitching mound. As for me, I walked out to rightfield because there was no need to hurry. I don't run much—perhaps a burst of speed to get to a subway door before it closes. I was without a glove that afternoon, unless I had been able to borrow one from the rightfielder on the other team, which was unlikely. That year, if I recall correctly, she was a young Romanian ballerina who'd never played baseball.

Rightfield is where nothing happens. In softball games, just about everyone, except the ultrasuave, bats righthanded and they tend to pull the ball, which means that the left side of the infield and outfield gets almost all the play. When on rare occasions lefthanded batters step up—I say they are ultrasuave because they are a minority and cause consternation—everyone shifts around to compensate. The centerfielder encroaches upon the quiet refuge of rightfield. When a fly ball drifts out, he moves in front of the right fielder. "Mine," he calls out, not with any degree of urgency but in a muted, condescending way as if it were better that he helped out in this situation, very much like a Boy Scout guiding an elderly lady across a street.

So rightfield is where the inept and those who are getting on in years are sent. They nurse the injury of being the last picked. They trudge out there by the oak tree and turn around.

It has always been my contention that great thoughts have been generated in the lonely wastes of rightfield. I have no doubt that Albert Einstein was playing rightfield when he came up with the theory of relativity. So was George Gershwin when he suddenly hummed to himself the upward scale that provides the opening notes of *Rhapsody in Blue*. Wasn't Woodrow Wilson playing rightfield when he came up with the concept of the League of Nations? Was not Edwin Hubble staring up into the heavens hoping a baseball would never materialize when the first inklings of the Big Bang theory came to mind? William Randolph Hearst dreamed up his newspaper empire playing rightfield in a softball game more than a century ago. Hugh Hefner was in rightfield when... well, you get the drift.

For me, it wasn't always like this. In high school, during college, at the Sunday games for years after graduation, in the grass field beyond the A&P, I affected a studied, nonchalant walk as I ventured to the pitcher's mound.

Then one year I was asked if I would play first base. "First?"

"Well, Tim is a pretty good pitcher."

"Tim? Who's Tim?"

"The young kid over there warming up."

"Oh."

And then that summer afternoon last year, or was it a year or so before, a glass of white wine left on the luncheon table, I found myself in rightfield.

There are many rightfields in our lives; the ones you find on athletic fields may just be the most obvious. The equivalent in touch football is the position of center. He is invariably the last person picked in the lineup.

What the centers hear in the huddle, usually from quarterbacks scrabbling the play in the grass, is this: "OK, Jack, you go long to the right, down toward the bushes; Penny, you go long on the other side and cut right behind Steve; Warren, you go down the middle, then cut for the sideline. Who's the center?"

"I am."

"OK, you center it on three, take five steps down and if everyone's covered I'll throw it to you."

So the center does this—the five steps, the turn, arms up plaintively. Nothing. On offense, it was possible to spend the entire afternoon taking those five steps, turning, and watching the ball arch far overhead on its way downfield.

In soccer, the equivalent of rightfield is being picked to play goal— the least active of the positions, and thus suitable for a boy (or girl), or someone's grandfather. The unlucky person stands in line, shifting worriedly from one foot to the other, hoping not to be the last picked. Upon that indignity, "Hey, Joe"—or "Jill" or "Mister",—you're the goalie, OK?" the chosen person then trudges to where the two piles of coats mark the goalposts.

If one has been picked for the better team, a whole chilly autumn afternoon can be spent standing between two piles of coats waiting for something to happen, some movement from the other end.

Shep Messing, a professional goaltender who played for the New York Cosmos, told me once that he whiled away such moments of inactivity by talking to the goalposts. He felt he had to talk to someone, not very serious stuff. He'd say things like "Be there when I need you."

I remember from my brief playing days as a goaltender with the Boston Bruins (as a participatory journalist) that when my team was attacking the other net, the expanse of ice in front of me was so vast, I could hardly make out what was going on at the opposite end. I wrote about it thus: "With the puck at the other end, it was not unlike standing at the edge of a mill pond, some vague activity at the opposite end almost too far to be discernible— could they be bass fishing out there?—but then suddenly the distant, aimless, waterbug scurrying became an oncoming surge of movement as everything—the players, sticks, the puck—starts coming on a direct line, almost as if a tsunami, that awesome tidal wave of the South Pacific, had suddenly materialized at the far end of the mill pond and was beginning to sweep down toward one . . . a great encroaching wave full of things being borne along full-tilt—hockey sticks, helmets, faces with no teeth in them, those black, barrel-like hockey pants, the skates, and somewhere in there, that awful puck."

Alas, that is the sort of thing that can happen to disturb one's reveries in rightfield—the thwack of the distant bat, the faces of the infielders sud denly turning as the bills of their caps tilt first upwards, then directly toward right-field where the ball is beginning the downward curve of gravity's rain-bow. If the rightfielder thought to look, it would be the first time while standing out there he had seen the infielders' faces, now staring at him with horror; instead he is staring up transfixed, arms stiff as poles, reaching for the sky as if praying to an almighty being.

I had a friend who, while playing rightfield in a pickup game, was frightened by a ball hit his way and tumbled backward into a thicket. While extracting himself from the bushes, he was bitten by a bee, probably a yellow jacket. He turned out to be violently allergic and was hurried to a local hospital where he fell in love at first sight with the receptionist. This chance meeting quickly resulted in a marriage, which turned out to be a disaster.

I never mentioned it when we had lunch on occasion years later, but I've often thought that if he had caught that long-ago fly ball he might have escaped a rather unfortunate five years of his life.

Peter, Paul & Mary had a song about playing rightfield, echoing all this:

> Playing right field it's easy, you know,
> You can be awkward
> And you can be slow
> That's why I'm here in right field
> Just watching the dandelions grow.

Oddly, at the conclusion of the song, with the rightfielder daydreaming as usual ("I don't know the inning/I've forgotten the score"), a ball is hit his way that he actually catches! Startled by everyone suddenly yelling at him ("And I don't know what for"), he looks up and the baseball falls into his glove for an out! Poetic license indeed! Hyperbole! No rightfielder worthy of the tradition would catch a ball.

I once played briefly with a softball team many of whose players refused to catch the ball at all. It was not because of age. They were "The Penguins"— a team put together from members of the New York Philharmonic orchestra. Almost all of them depended upon their fingers for their livelihood. So if a ball was hit to a violin player in rightfield, he (or she) would turn and run alongside the ball until it stopped before picking it up and throwing it toward the infield. I don't recall that we ever won a game.

Of course, rightfielders go to bat—the enormous moment, perhaps three or four times an afternoon, when the focus is on you, so unlike the peace of the grass out by the oak tree. You hear the cries of encouragement, and then it's over, a soft liner to the shortstop, the heads turned as you walk back to the others ("Nice bat, Pops!").

So, what's on my mind as I set out for rightfield and the oak tree beyond? Sometimes I remember the sphinx's famous riddle that befuddled so many who were devoured by the winged lion when they couldn't solve it. What had four legs in the morning, two at midday, and three in the evening? The answer (which Oedipus solved and in doing so, saved the city of Thebes): man, who crawls as a baby, walks upright in the prime of life, and supports himself with a cane when he's old. The three stations in softball, if one extends the metaphor, would start with pitching, then first base, and end with rightfield. Too melancholy a thought. Better to consider Alexander Pope—"to be swift is less than to be wise."

And besides, one can consider the great rightfielders who have occu- pied the same area—Roger Maris, Hank Aaron, Reggie Jackson, Al Kaline, Frank Robinson, Enos Slaughter, King Kong Keller, Mel Ott. The latter played rightfield for the New York Giants in the Polo Grounds, very often standing in what became known as Ott's Spot because the stands behind him ("The Porch") were so close that there wasn't much to do except turn and watch the home run balls sail overhead. And, of course, the great Babe Ruth played rightfield.

I turn to face the infield. The game has begun. A pop fly goes up. Was it caught by the shortstop? The third baseman? Who knows. It is time for reverie, and the mind begins to soar....

(from *Cigar Aficionado*, March/April 2000)

Who's on First?

Diana Friedman

I am standing at first base watching my six-year old daughter Naomi swing. And miss. And swing. And miss. With each strike (and there will be eight—this is rookie league), it seems the bat rounds home plate all the way into my stomach. When she finally does connect, a small dribble to a boy fielding for the adult pitcher, I begin to bellow: "Run it out! Don't stop! Run it out!" As team manager and first base coach, this is my official job. But when the boy's foot, ball snug in his glove, touches first base a split second before hers, I am certain my face reveals that I have slipped from manager to mother. The umpire, a parent from the other team, comes out from behind home plate and nods gently. I pat Naomi on the back. "Way to hustle, you almost got it," I tell her, and brace for the flood of tears. But she just nods and trots back to her teammates on the bench, disappointed, but hardly heartbroken. Nothing like me.

If there is such a thing as a six-year-old girl wannabe, I claim that title shamelessly. What I wouldn't give to be in kindergarten today, huddling with friends and teammates in matching T-shirts and hats as we slap high fives to the coach and celebrate pins and trophies at end-of-season ice cream parties.

Nineteen-sixty-eight hardly qualifies as the dark ages, but in those last few years before Title IX legislation prohibited gender discrimination in federally funded educational programs, before Little League bowed to law-suits and public pressure finally allowed girls to play, my organized team sports were limited to weekend pick-up softball and touch football games with my brothers and father in Central Park. My mother had hoped for a girl she could parade in lace and tights; I was otherwise preoccupied pulling dirty T-shirts and jeans out of the hamper and wrestling my brothers on the basement carpet. My father was just as happy to have an extra second baseman or wide receiver. Once she saw I had no plans to trade my sneakers for stockings, my mother became my biggest advocate. Particularly when I tried in first grade to join the all-boy Friday after-school softball game.

"You're a girl, you can't play," my classmates told me as I stood clutching my Ken Harrelson glove. But I could, I knew. And so did those boys who played with me every day in gym class. My mother, believing a simple resolution at hand, approached the other mothers, many of whom were her close friends.

"It's not a good idea, she could get hurt," protested one.

"This is a special thing for boys," said another. "The girls are so advanced with their small motor skills. Let the boys have their own activities, something they can feel good about."

So opening day, a muggy Friday afternoon, I stood, my fingers curled around the backstop fence, as I watched my two closest friends, Dennis and Rusty, for whom I had fielded endless grounders, choose up sides. Without me.

I know that the options Naomi and her friends have are partially the legacy of girl athletes of my generation, even though we led the fight without a clue that's what we were doing. We just wanted to play.

In high school, finally: varsity volleyball, basketball, softball. My freshman year, the standard girls' skirts and bloomers were tossed and as each season unfolded, we broke the seal on the boxes for our new uniforms— stretchy shorts, three quarter length baseball pants that covered our knees, short sleeve jerseys with black numbers, white for home games, orange for away. We traveled on the bus with the boys' teams for many of our games. From a distance, the difference between the genders was scarcely discernible.

But there were more boys' teams; their gym and locker room were bigger, cleaner, more accommodating to the larger fan base that attended their games. In our gym, basketball was not a contact sport—elbows remained politely tucked in, even under the boards.

My brothers also played varsity sports, openly fantasizing: if only they were a little taller, a little better with the hook shot, more precise with the fast ball, that call from senior management might still be coming in from the Knicks or the Mets.

One afternoon nearing the end of my softball season, I was met by my younger brother as I came home from school.

"Look at this," he said excitedly, handing me the sports section of the *New York Times*. I dropped my pack, anticipating an article or photo signaling a new women's basketball league. Instead, I stared at a short blurb indicating that females were increasing their ranks as ball girls for professional baseball teams.

Not until many years later, when I was a graduate student in upstate New York, did I begin to understand how I had buried all this sorrow. Late one afternoon as the sun was dropping behind the hillside, I noticed a soccer field across the street from my bus stop. From where I stood, I could just make out the red and white blur of the players racing up and down the field. I had never played, soccer not being introduced to girls until I was finishing high school. But waiting for the bus I found myself compelled to cross the street. And from closer up, I saw the majesty of the game for the first time: flawless passes placed with Zen-like accuracy, powerful sliding and diving, an almost collective ego which seemed to power both teams forward to the goal. And then I noticed something else: all the players had pony-tails. I was late for dinner that night and most Tuesday and Fridays thereafter, often sneaking out from my lab to catch the games. Every time one of the players tackled an opponent or dove for the ball and emerged splattered with mud, I would twinge—not for them, but for how much I wanted to be on that field, playing a game in which I had never touched the ball, barely knew the rules.

I could not possibly have known that some of these women would later share a field with the women of the powerhouse U.S. women's soccer team of the late 1990s, the same team that would bring the world the indelible image of Brandi Chastain circling her shirt wildly over her head, that same team that would ratchet up the legitimacy of women's sports 20 notches in 20 seconds. But at 28, as I watched these women not even a decade younger than me—these women with quads bulging shamelessly from under their shorts, these women who showed no fear about crashing into one another, these women who threw themselves into the game like their lives depended on it—I felt the door to my buried psyche blow open. It was immaterial, I realized, whether my brothers or I, my teammates or I, had ever been good enough to be professional athletes. What had mattered was who had had permission to dream.

Naomi, my first child, was born a few years later into this brave new world of women's sports, a reality I never could have imagined even in those moments when my mother would sit me on her lap, whispering "soon, soon," in response to my asking once again when girls would be allowed into Little League. Yet, while Naomi was drawing her first breaths, more than two million girls were enrolled in soccer leagues, women's softball was now an Olympic sport, and basketball, sweaty, pushy, elbows-out, in-your-face basketball, was the most popular women's sport in high school and college.

The day we came home from the hospital I clutched Naomi's tiny curled body against my chest, letting my mind wander gleefully. Her first pair of shoes were going to be cleats. She would be just like me in a picture my parents have of me at age two where I am lugging a bat across my shoulder, except Naomi wouldn't be in a pink dress, she'd be in her team uniform.

Of course the plans we conjure up for our children and the blueprints they unfold for themselves seldom travel parallel tracks. Naomi was physical—neither my husband nor I can recall her sitting still for more than a minute between the ages of one and four. She was also competitive, constantly arguing with her best friend who was first, fastest, best.

Yet. If I threw her a ball, she looked the other way. If I handed her a bat she'd whack the couch. As Naomi approached the age of team eligibility, my excitement seemed to rise in direct proportion to her lack of enthusiasm.

The more I suggested, the more she resisted, until I backed off. I consoled myself: if there were a candidate ripe to mutate into a stage mom forcing her child to accomplish all that had been missed, I was staring at her in the mirror. My pushing her into team sports would only result in disaster: Take one stubborn daughter, an over-interested and frustrated mother, throw them in a pot and watch it explode.

Eventually, urged on by my husband who is from Spain, a promise of junk food snacks at half time, and peer pressure from her gaggle of five-year-old friends, all of whom played in our city's Pee Wee league, Naomi did sign up for soccer. From time to time, when she wasn't squatting in the field contemplating blades of grass, she chased the ball. But soccer mornings had been punctuated with shouts of, "I hate soccer. I'm not going." It was, to say the least, far from an auspicious beginning.

My mother, a freelance writer, tried to sell an article, "My Daughter, Jackie Robinson," about my fighting to play in that Friday afternoon game. The story climbed its way up past all the senior female editors at a woman's magazine, until it landed on the desk of the editor-in-chief, a man, who read it, liked it, and then dismissed it: "Who would want to read about girls and sports?"

But on the field, my mother had not stopped even when her friends challenged her: "Are you doing this for Diana, or for you?"

The more they resisted, the angrier my mother got, smoking out the women huddled in the school lobby, pointedly asking them if they would be saying the same things if I were black. And still, they refused to yield. "What if she's not serious? What if other girls wanted to play? Why are you making such a fuss?"

When I called one of those mothers recently, she denied her involvement. "I had a girl too," she said. "It wasn't me. It was the mothers of the boys."

Another mother of three sons, who is still a good family friend, was more forthcoming. "It seems so impossible to understand now," she told me, "but back then the idea of a girl on boys ball team? It simply wasn't in our lexicon."

She paused then, almost as if to apologize, before adding: "Your mother—she was the conscience of that group."

The spring Naomi turned six she arrived home from kindergarten one warm March day and threw a form on my lap. "Sign me up," she announced.

"This is baseball," I said. I wasn't sure she understood what she was signing up for.

"I know," she responded, throwing me that look that six-year-olds reserve for their idiotic parents. "I want to do it. Lowell's playing." Lowell was a friend of hers from school with whom every interaction turned into a major competition.

For a fleeting moment I thought perhaps we should discuss it; she'd never even thrown a baseball. But that thought was quickly erased as I realized she might change her mind, so I grabbed a pen and filled out the form.

And then, a few weeks after she'd registered, another surprise: a message on my voice mail informing me that I should be at the managers' meeting Sunday night for the team drafts.

"There must be a mistake," I said to the rookie league commissioner when I called back. "I signed up to bring snack." As required, I had agreed to help the team since Naomi was only six.

"No," he replied. "There's no mistake. And we're short managers, so I can't accept no for an answer." Apparently I had checked the wrong box.

"Wait a minute," I started. "You don't understand."

But he cut me off. "Really. I can't take no. It's not that hard. Do you play?"

"I used to," I said.

"All right, then. You know the rules. The other parents will help you out."

"That's not the problem," I began, but he was already dictating directions to his house.

During soccer games the coaches' children were easily recognizable—they stood in the middle of the field melting down, unable to stand their fathers paying so much attention to other children. "Where's my water! Daddy, I need you NOW!" I could think of little more that would make Naomi hate the game than to have me unavailable, as well as barking instructions to her.

"You mean you'll be in charge, like every game? In charge of all of us?" Naomi asked after I hung up the phone.

I nodded, expecting a fit. But she ran and got her glove.

"Let's go practice. Now!"

In a bit of a stupor, I followed her to the backyard where we set up bases using an old Frisbee for home plate. She ran to the disc and jumped on top looking at me eagerly. I moved behind her, silently edged her feet back, lifted the bat of her shoulder, and wrapped my arms around her to frame a batting stance.

I threw the first pitch and my mouth opened all on its own. "Keep your eye on the ball, don't look at me." When she connected on the third try, sending the ball behind the magnolia tree, my anxiety ratcheted down a notch. Maybe, I thought, maybe we can do this.

When the season began I told my mother about how gut-wrenching it was to watch Naomi bat. My mother laughed. "Now you know how I felt."

"How do you mean?"

"Don't you remember what finally happened? In first grade?"

The other mothers, tired of being hounded by mine, reached a compromise. They would allow me to play if the boys would agree. My classmates, convinced by my friend Dennis, decided after brief debate that I was not in fact technically a girl, but a tomboy, and therefore eligible. The next Friday afternoon I headed to the field with the boys for team selection. After everyone was picked and headed off to start the game, I stood by the pitcher's mound, waiting.

"Hey, what about her?

"Who?"

"Diana."

"You take her."

"No, you take her. We have too many."

I stood there until finally someone motioned that I should play left field. Far, far, left field. Eyed through my lens, I viewed this as nothing more than normal first grade behavior. Surveyed through the infinitely more complex prism of motherhood, I imagine now how my own mother must have felt, her heart inured by defense, yet each setback a chisel, chipping away a little piece.

I didn't come up to bat until the last inning. With two outs and the bases loaded, my team trailed by one. The first pitch came and I swung and missed. On the next pitch I swung and missed again. My mother sat alone at the end of the bleachers chewing her nails.

Baseball is not for the faint of heart, I say to her as we recount this story.

No, she replies, especially if you're a mother.

The night before Naomi's first practice, I called a friend who had coached sports for years.

"What do I do? What kind of persona should I take on? Fierce? Friendly?" I was referring to how comfortable some of the soccer fathers seemed in their skin as they raced around with the children. Inside, I was worrying about how I was going to lead Naomi and her peers through something I'd ached for so badly myself.

"Just be yourself and shower them with praise," responded my friend warmly. "Accentuate the positive."

Which, I immediately discovered, required some creative thinking. Naomi and her teammates arrived at the first practice clueless when or where to throw the ball.

"Let's run the bases," I said, watching them charge confidently off to first, turn the corner, and head straight across the pitcher's mound to third. It didn't take long for the other parents to agree that if we could teach them how an out was made, get them running the base path correctly, and help them have fun, we'd consider ourselves successful.

By the time the season started, the children were so excited that positive reinforcement spilled out effortlessly. With high hopes we dubbed the team "Green Magic." Every time someone made it to first base we had a rousing cheer. Each run scored warranted high fives from the whole team.

I stayed close to the kids, running the bases with them before every game, positioning each batter at the plate, showing them over and over how to dig their toes in, until by the middle of the season the kids began to absorb the mechanics of the game in that osmotic fashion they use to slurp up information. There was Riley, a lanky boy who often couldn't remember where to throw the ball, fielding a grounder near the pitcher's mound and galloping home to tag the runner. Zeke, the only lefty on the team, finally remembering on his own which side of the plate to stand on. And Naomi, in the last game of the season, lowering her glove for a ground ball and upon finding it there, throwing it to the first baseman, who caught it and got the runner out. I stood with my mouth open, and after clapping vociferously, turned away from the players and the parents and pulled my hat down over my eyes to hide my tears.

At the end of season Naomi asked me how long I would coach.

"Maybe until you're 18," I joked. And then more seriously: "I had a great time. What about you?"

She was quiet, but I knew from the way she had followed my every instruction without a peep or protest, the way she charged out of bed Saturday mornings to get dressed in her uniform, the way she had loaded the balls and bats into the car without being asked.

And truthfully, I wasn't joking either. I'd been arm twisted into the job, but after watching her learn the mechanics of the game and dissect the rules of baseball, it was clear that my stage mom demons were not nearly as fierce as I'd imagined. One season of watching her enjoy herself on the field and I knew I honestly didn't care whether she played team sports her whole life or not, whether she became a professional athlete. I just wanted her to have what most parents want—the opportunity to play and believe that that anything is possible, such as the afternoon she came home from a game and said, "Mom, I hope someday I can be the Mia Hamm of baseball."

And, for me, there was this: each time I turned a kid's shoulders at the plate, each time I reminded them to bend their knees, each time I lifted their rear elbow to level their swing, I found my own sadness surfacing, hovering for just a moment, but then quietly dissipating, like the dust in the base path swirling up and away into the outfield.

Naomi likes my first grade baseball story and I like telling it to her, although every time I say, "They used to think girls couldn't do that," I worry what she hears. What if I say it so many times she starts to believe girls really can't do things?

But now that she understands baseball she wants to hear the story again.

"So what happened after you had two strikes?"

"I fouled off."

"And then what?"

"I fouled off."

"Again?"

"Again. That's baseball."

If this is a bedtime story she's usually half way to sleep by now. But she strains to hear the end.

"How many foul balls?"

"Six."

"And then were you out?" She is laboring her way through the rules. Her league had an eight-strike rule.

"Nope. I hit it."

"A big hit?"

"Nope. A dribble to the short stop."

"And he caught it?"

"Nope. It went right between his legs."

She is quiet, calculating the runs, the outs, the bases.

"So your team won?"

"Yep." I kiss her goodnight and turn out the light. "We won."

The Southworths

Michael Shapiro

I found out about Billy Southworth and his son by accident. I was doing research on baseball in wartime and wondered whether there was anyone in the big leagues whose connection to events in Europe and the Pacific extended beyond the papers and the radio. In 1942, the game and those playing it seemed removed from the seismic events of the day, as if baseball were a world apart—which is, of course, its beauty. Then I discovered the story of Billy Southworth and his son. Billy also had a daughter, Carol, and it was she who shared with me her brother's diary, which is the basis for this story. This is a baseball story, I suppose, but really, it is the story of a father and a son and the bond between them. It breaks my heart.

There are a lot of stories about baseball during World War II, and the more they are told the more they almost succeed in making those years sound like a foolish time, when a man with one arm played outfield for the St. Louis Browns and a fifteen-year-old pitched for the Reds. They played because most of the major leaguers had enlisted or been drafted, even the reluctant ones like Joe DiMaggio, who was said to be upset about the drop in pay. Only the old or very young or, in a baseball context, the infirm, remained, which perhaps explains why it was only in wartime that the Browns, who fielded a team of older players known to drink like fish, ever made it to the World Series.

These stories might suggest that the war touched the game deeply, but that really wasn't the case. A few weeks after Pearl Harbor, the owners and the commissioner, Kenesaw Mountain Landis, met to consider canceling play for the duration. President Roosevelt, however, suggested the games continue so that an anxious nation might have something besides the war to think and talk about. Considering that in its early stages the war did not go well for the Allies and there was ample reason to believe they might even lose, this was a wise idea.

The war did intrude upon the game. There were scrap iron drives at the ballparks and signs reminding people to buy war bonds. Attendance was down, even though servicemen were admitted free of charge. The major leaguers, by and large, stuck around through the end of the 1942 season but were almost all gone by the spring of 1944. By then the teams had stopped traveling south for spring training in order to keep railroad cars free for the troops. Some major leaguers saw combat. Several were injured and were never the same again. Two little-known big leaguers died in battle. Many more spent the war playing exhibition games overseas.

Still, whatever the players were thinking and feeling about the war seldom made its way into clubhouse conversation. A rare exception was the case of Larry French, who pitched for the Brooklyn Dodgers and in the spring of 1942 reacted to the report that the Japanese had invaded his native California by telling Cliff Dapper, the backup catcher, that he was going home to fight. Dapper would have gone with him, had the story turned out to be true.

More common was the sentiment conveyed in a story I heard from Marty Marion, the tall and skinny St. Louis Cardinal shortstop. I asked Marion how often his teammates talked about the war, considering they were all of draft age and might even have had friends or relatives in the service. Marion, by then an elderly man, recalled the first summer of the war well: The Cardinals were chasing the Brooklyn Dodgers—they'd begun August ten games out of first place and then went on a tear of historic proportions. "The war?" Marion said. "What war? We were in a pennant race." Yet there was at least one man in that clubhouse thinking about the war, even if he was not disposed to speaking about it. To speak about the war would have meant revealing something of his feelings, which was just not done. Billy Southworth, the Cardinals' manager, had a son, Billy Jr., who was a captain in the Army Air Corps and who in the summer of 1942 was preparing to ship out.

The story of this father and son is the sort too seldom told when people talk about baseball in wartime. That is a shame, because more than most, their story captures the true and complex nature of life on the home front: people going about the business of their lives but pausing every hour to listen to the news; young men deemed unfit for service feeling too ashamed to come out of the house; mothers sitting and weeping on the always-made beds of their sons in uniform. Stories of the American home front tend to suggest that life consisted of little more than watering victory gardens, collecting scrap, suffering the occasional air raid drill, and reading about ration cheats in the paper. They too often leave out the terror. This was not the terror of an attack; that was over by 1943. Rather, it was the terror of the Western Union man bringing the worst news imaginable, the terror that came from walking past a neighbor's house and seeing a gold star affixed in the window and wondering when your turn would come. There were two kinds of people on the home front: those who had men in the service and those who did not. They might have been friends before the war, but for the duration they really didn't have much to talk about.

Billy Southworth had a son in the service. He also had a team in a pennant race. This left him to straddle the world of the war and a world where the war did not seem to exist. He spent the war doing what everyone with a son, husband, or brother in uniform did: he waited.

• • •

Billy Southworth Jr. was a ballplayer. But unlike his father he did not make it to the major leagues. Instead, he had the distinction of being the first professional ballplayer to enlist. That he did so eleven months before Pearl Harbor made his act of bravery greater still. Billy Jr. had been a well-regarded minor league prospect when, after spending the 1940 season with Toronto in the International League, he decided to sign up. His father had hoped Billy Jr. might follow him to the big leagues and tried to get him to change his mind. The story of their conversation was often told in the early days of the war, when America was finding itself hard-pressed for heroes.

Billy Jr., the story went, came to his father to break the news.

His father asked him to reconsider.

The son replied that there were things more important than baseball. The following morning the father came to his son and said, "This is a beautiful day to enlist."

Maybe the conversation took place just this way and maybe the sportswriters who told it were trying to get other young men to be like Billy Southworth Jr., which was not necessarily a bad idea. Billy Jr. was tall, wore a mustache, and looked like Clark Gable. He carried himself with the bearing of a young man who knew that other young men envied him because of the way young women looked at him. He was a heartbreaker. Some of the men with whom he served found him a little too full of himself, but then, once they got to know him, became his friends.

There were women who wanted to marry Billy Jr. Though he did give the matter serious thought, he did not feel inclined, as others did, to rush to marry before he shipped out so that he could leave knowing someone was waiting for him. He was not the sort of young man given to fretting and dark thoughts about the perilous future that awaited him. He seemed the least burdened of men and took to leadership as if it was a naturally occurring gift. He possessed a swagger and confidence that left his father, for one, a little bit in awe. He, for his part, thought his father was "a grand fellow."

They were as close as a father and son could be. His mother had left them when Billy Jr. was still young. His father, who had played thirteen major league seasons, was by then managing in the minors. They spent the winters together and, when school let out, Billy Jr. would join his father on the back-roads circuit. He was the batboy.

The elder Southworth had had his struggles. He had been a solid, if unspectacular, outfielder whose career was built not upon size or muscle but on grit. He was also something of an innocent to city life— in New York and later St. Louis—and his attempts to keep up with his harder-drinking teammates ended badly. He managed the Cardinals briefly in 1929 but was fired when he tried too hard to emulate the harsh and exacting ways of his mentor, the great Giants manager John McGraw. Southworth slipped out of the game, found work as a salesman, remarried, and then had his career resurrected by Branch Rickey, the teetotaling general manager of the Cardinals, who sent him back to the minors to manage after Southworth swore off the bottle. He made it back to the big club in 1941, a changed man. Gone was the out-of-character brutishness; he was still demanding, but in a far less abrasive way. He seldom raised his voice. The Cardinals that year barely lost out to the Dodgers for the National League pennant, and Southworth's comeback was all but complete.

In the meantime, his son had grown into a ballplayer of considerable promise. In 1939 he had been voted most valuable player in the Canadian-American League after batting .342 for the Rome Colonels, a minor league team in upstate New York. He played the outfield, ran well, and possessed a strong throwing arm. In 1940, he batted .280 for Toronto, a step below the majors. But by the early winter of 1941, he was at Parks Air College in East St. Louis, Illinois, learning to fly planes that barely held together. His father had driven him there from their farm in Sunbury, Ohio, on New Year's Day. He had woken his son early that morning and helped him pack before they set off together on the long drive. They arrived at Parks at ten o'clock that night. "A quick handshake and I was off," Billy Jr. later wrote.

That memory appeared in a July entry in the diary Billy Jr. had decided to keep. The diary would be for his father, and was dedicated to him too. This way, in addition to the letters home, his father would have a record of the time they spent apart.

The diary of Billy Southworth Jr. is remarkable not so much for its content but in the way it captures the particular way men—especially baseball men, who have seldom been given to introspection—talk to and about each other. On page after page, spread over weeks and months and years, Billy Jr. logged the events of his days, beginning in the summer of

1942: flying barely airworthy B-17s over the Arizona desert, news of yet another training crash, tales of friends taking the marriage plunge, complaints about superior officers who in his view were anything but. But there is something more: baseball scores. All the while, Billy Jr. chronicled his father's pennant race: "Cards won 3–1 from Pirates, 71/2 games back. My day off, worked all day yet did not fly." It is as if he were saying, I was thinking of Dad, all that time. He would write, "Must write to dad."

It was as if he were speaking to his father through his diary, but in the oblique way in which men of a certain sort convey their feelings. There was, for instance, a story of a two-day pass to visit his father in Chicago, where the Cardinals were playing the Cubs: "It sure was great to see him again. We talked til three or four in the A.M."

The Cardinals kept winning, and in his diary, Billy Jr. grew ever more excited. "One more game in two to play will clinch the pennant... got a wonderful letter from dad today."

By October, Billy Jr. who'd become something of a celebrity, was invited to fly over Sportsman's Park for the opening game of the 1942 World Series, which the Yankees were favored to win. But after dropping the first game, the Cardinals swept the next four and with them, the championship. "October 5—will be a memorable day in the history of Southworth," Billy Jr. wrote. "Dad proved that he was the best manager in baseball today. Wired him immediately after the game, congratulations."

They saw each other one more time before Billy Jr. left for England. His unit had been transferred to Bangor, Maine. His father visited for five days and Billy Jr. introduced him around. The elder Southworth signed autographs and wrote his name on his son's plane, The Bad Check (so dubbed because bad checks always come back). He also gave him the cap he had worn that season. Billy Jr. had it rigged with extra wiring so he could wear it into combat. "He's the grandest guy that I know," he wrote. "Sure tired of this sitting around—I want to go to combat."

He would not have long to wait. Whatever thoughts and fears Billy Southworth had in all the many months his son flew combat missions over

France and Germany he seemed to have kept to himself. But he followed the news of every mission. As a manager, Southworth was a stickler for lists; he kept running tabs on opponents as well as his players. As a father, he kept a running account of bombing runs, and with each letter from his son, crossed off all the missions that ended with his safe return.

His Cardinals won the National League pennant again in 1943 but lost the World Series to the Yankees. They won again in 1944, and this time defeated the Browns in the one and only all–St. Louis World Series. His son, meanwhile, kept his own account of the team's fortunes.

He was by now stationed in Molesworth, England, and the life he describes seems a numbing routine of rain, mud, and fog interspersed with early morning takeoffs for bombing runs with frighteningly high casualty rates. Men died all around him, and in his telling of what took place in the skies over Europe, it seemed important that his father know his son's resolve and nerve never flagged. Within three months of arriving in England, half his unit was gone: "We still lack nose guns. The enemy is stronger and keener than ever and we don't miss a trip. Our effectiveness has been great. Our accuracy good. Courage and intestinal fortitude, as much as Napoleon or Washington might ask for." The waist gunner on his plane goes AWOL. The navigator is hospitalized. There is a raid on a submarine base in St. Nazaire. He gets irritated describing commanders who are slow to pick up on his ideas. He goes to parties on leave in London. Missions are scrubbed at the last minute. Billy Jr. kept a list of each of his missions, the position in which he flew, whether it was a win, and how significant the losses. He also wrote, "Little worried—Dad was sick at last writing and letter is overdue."

From time to time his picture appeared in the newspapers—gathered with his crew, joking with Bob Hope. He flew twenty-six missions and won the Distinguished Flying Cross and the Air Medal with three oak-leaf clusters. And then he came home.

"I never realized until he returned what tremendous pressure I was under," his father told Arthur Daley of the New York Times. "But now he's back home, safe at last."

Billy Southworth Jr. was not going to become a major league baseball player. The airlines wanted him as a pilot. The movies wanted him too. The producer Hunt Stromberg gave him a screen test and then signed him to a contract. His father seemed quite excited about this. But the war was not yet over, and so Billy Jr. remained in uniform. The army sent him on tours to sell war bonds. Crowds of people came to see him. Enlisted men who accompanied him were grateful for his willingness to sneak them into officers' clubs. His future seemed one of endless possibilities. His father was regarded as one of the best managers in the game. And they were back together, at last. This is where the story should end.

But this is a wartime story, and such stories, even in a baseball context, too often end sadly. In February of 1945, Billy Southworth Jr. who had managed to survive the hellishness of flak and German fighter planes over Europe, was killed on a routine training mission as he was about to land a B-29 at Mitchel Field, in New York. His father rushed to New York and kept a vigil for weeks, waiting for his son's body to be recovered. It was not found until August.

Billy Southworth returned to Ohio and then to the Cardinals, but he was never the same man again. Several years later he made a winner of the Boston Braves, but he had begun drinking again, and in time the Braves let him go. Years later he quit for good and ended his career as a scout. He died in 1969. He never saw the diary his son had written for him.

As it happened Billy Jr.'s friend and navigator, Jon Schueler, had borrowed the diary. Schueler had dreams of becoming a writer and had asked Billy Jr. if he might borrow the book to draw ideas and inspiration from it. Schueler, a sensitive man, had had a difficult time in the war and saw in Billy Jr.'s ease and bravery qualities he believed he himself lacked.

Schueler was also disposed to self-absorption, and so it never occurred to him to part with a diary whose front page bore a dedication to a man whose name was, after all, often in the news. Years later, Schueler did write about the war, and briefly about Billy Jr. but mostly about his own life of struggle in a book called *The Sound of Sleat*. He also became an artist of some acclaim. His paintings, many of the sky, suggest a man searching for something in the clouds that had eluded him in wartime. Perhaps he was searching too, in the words that Billy Jr. had intended for another man, a baseball man, who would have surely understood his meaning.

The Bat

Philip F. Deaver

Long before I knew how strangely literary the game is, I wrote and dreamed about baseball, because for me it's all tied up with memories and early initiations. A friend of mine who lived down the street when I was growing up was the son of a man who actually caught Warren Spahn, apparently during a lull in the action, at the Battle of the Bulge in World War II. As the story went, the mess sergeant provided this guy, who was a catcher back in the world, a slab of ham to put in his glove to take out a little of the bite while Spahnie aired out his heater to the delight of his war-weary pals. That catcher was the county surveyor in this story about the priest and the bat and the fly balls, the guy who allowed us to play baseball on the big green lawn of the Douglas County Court House in Tuscola, Illinois. I'd long wanted to write this piece as nonfiction, but it seemed so odd that our parish priest, the guy who hit me the pop-ups, was named Casey, really, and so there was this odd entanglement with the poem "Casey at the Bat." I call the priest Kelleher in my fiction, but I had to go with the truth here.

For perhaps ten years now the golden summer evenings I remember from growing up have been gone. Did they slip by and I didn't notice? And is it innocence or the light I'm missing? In my hometown in Illinois, the grass isn't as green as it was. When the rain comes, it comes in deluge and flood, or, for a long time, it doesn't come at all. In the 1950s, the winters were cold from well before Thanksgiving to well beyond April Fools' Day. Now the weather's a crapshoot.

The year I turned eleven, we ballplayers plunged into the summer as if it would be our last. We were bigger than the year before. Could greatness be far behind? We gathered in the mornings and played until about ten with an ash-gray rubber-coated baseball, heavier than regulation, that gave off a smacking sound when you hit it. By ten the dew would have burned off and from then on we used a regular ball. There was a park on the north side of town where we played, and on the south side, where I lived, there were a couple of insufficient lots we managed to play in sometimes if nothing was shaking out at the park. Frequently, we used the southwest corner of the block occupied by the Douglas County Court House, a huge expanse of green. Home plate was under a giant silver maple, and third was a sugar maple lightning-damaged into a strange shape and much smaller than the silver. We'd use the batting team's ball gloves as first and second bases. Right field was closed because of the courthouse itself and two stalwart limestone boulders chiseled to make a stand to display a Civil War cannon, the cannon long since gone, so we didn't encourage the participation of left-handed hitters (there weren't many anyway), and left-center was very deep, if you got the ball high in the air early enough so it didn't tangle in the rangy green limbs of third base. The courthouse venue was far from perfect, but the grass was cool and always mowed, and in afternoon sun, the shade was worth the trouble of the trees.

The courthouse was two blocks from my home. The summer we were mostly eleven but turning twelve was the only summer we played there.

You have to picture this. There wasn't really a diamond; we made it all up. There was no backstop, and the batting team supplied both the pitcher and the catcher. If the ball went between the catcher's legs, it skipped a few times and went across Van Allen Street right into the front yard of the Forty Martyrs Catholic Church and rectory.

In those golden evenings that year, Father James Casey, our pastor, would walk at a peculiarly fast pace up and down the sidewalks around his house, saying his office. He'd been injured a few months before in a one-person car wreck returning to town from the Kaskaskia Golf Course, and the walking had been prescribed as a way of rehabbing his hurt leg. Father Casey, first-generation Irishman, was a helluva golfer. It amazes me to calculate that at the time I'm talking about he was younger than I am now as I sit here writing about him. He was in his midfifties, and was an institution in our town, having been in Tuscola for twenty-five years. Among the Protestant townsfolk, he was known as tough, perhaps a little cranky and mysterious. In fact, my Catholic classmates saw him that way too. He barked at us in catechism classes, in a brogue so thick we couldn't understand him. He was a great friend of my dad, though, and frequently came to our house for Sunday dinner, so I did "get" this fellow a bit better than my friends did. Anyway, to a man, the kids I played ball with were afraid of him, and if the ball went across the street when Father Casey was out in his yard, I was the one who had to go after it.

One evening, I'm sure it was a Wednesday, I trotted over to the court-house after dinner to meet my friends—you only needed about six to have a good game—and sat under the silver maple waiting for them to show up. Andy would soon round the corner on Houghton (that was center field on the courthouse diamond), Gary would come down from the north side via Court Street, and Alan would come on Central up from where his folks had an apartment on the highway. Bill would show up probably, and maybe bring a brother, hopefully not the littlest one. I waited. It was never perfect. We never got the time of the rendezvous quite right and unexpected circumstances would always arise. (Bill's folks might load up the family and go out to the drive-in if there was a good Western showing; Gary's dad might make him work.)

I waited for them. I was used to it—in fact we all were. They waited for me plenty too, in those days. We were eleven and flexible. Sometimes nothing happened, and whoever was waiting would finally walk home kicking a rock. That evening, though, Casey was fast-walking and reading his breviary, and I sat under the tree so that I wasn't completely visible to him, so he wouldn't call me over to talk. I hated to stand around and talk to adults. "How's your dad?" "How's your mom?" "When you gonna learn your Latin responses so you can serve mass?" "How's school?"

I knew he knew I was sitting under the maple, but if I was on the other side of the tree, that seemed to let us both off the hook. He wouldn't have to talk nice to me just because he was pals with my dad and knew me and came to dinner sometimes. And I wouldn't have to talk to him a whole lot so next time he'd recognize my voice in the confessional, which was precisely the sort of thing an eleven-year-old boy worried about if the family was friends with the priest and the boy was me.

So, on this evening apparently none of my friends were coming, and after a while, when his walk got him directly across the street from me, he called over. His voice came around the tree.

"Danny. You over there?"

Because my father and I had the same name, my nickname was Danny in those days, after the Kipling poem "They're Hanging Danny Deever in the Morning." Things like that can affect your destiny.

"Want me to hit you some?" he called to me.

Right, I was thinking. Hundred-year-old Irish priest—a golfer—with a broken leg—is gonna hit me some. Plus, my Protestant pals start filtering in from the neighborhood and see the priest duffing around with our ball bat, they'd just go back home. "That's it," they'd be thinking. "No baseball tonight!"

"Sure," I said.

He looked both ways on Van Allen, limped across the street. He gimped up to me, and I got up off the ground where I'd been sitting.

"How's your dad?" he asked.

"Fine."

"Fine what?"

"Fine, Father."

"Lemme see that thing," he said, and I got him my bat, which was leaning against the tree. It was a twenty-nine-inch Larry Doby Louisville Slugger. I always brought it to our games. Bill had a thirty-inch Hank Aaron we all used, and Andy had a thirty-two-inch Jackie Robinson we'd broken sometime in the past year but still used after it was repaired, using a well-placed nail to hold it together plus two miles of electrical tape around the handle and over the nail, which effectively removed the nail from our consciousness. (After it broke, this repaired bat logged most of our tape-measure home runs, and we had a theory that the nail and the tape were responsible. It didn't occur to us we were growing.) Anyway, Father Casey handled my Larry Doby like it was a foreign object.

"Where's the ball?" he said, and I took it out of my glove over by the tree. He handled it a minute. It was the rubber-coated one. We often used it at the courthouse because the leather ones got torn up on the sidewalk and the street. All it took to tear the thread was for the ball to skip once on the concrete—one little tear in the thread and a leather baseball was on borrowed time.

Father Casey, wearing black pants and a white shirt with rolled-up sleeves and a Roman collar, scanned the big west lawn of the courthouse. That's how it would have looked to him—a big lawn. He couldn't see the baseball diamond so clearly imagined by us kids. He said, "Okay, I'll go over there by the steps and then hit 'em this way so we miss the trees."

"Yes, Father," I said.

As he lumbered away, he said, over his shoulder, "How's your mom?"

"Good."

"Good what?"

"Good, Father."

I watched him as he slowly strolled through the courthouse lawn's green grass until he was right up to the building itself, right under the window of the county surveyor (Bill's dad). I watched him go, on his sore leg, sort of slumped like the ancient guy he was. This would never work. Golf and baseball aren't the same. If you didn't know that already, you could tell by the way he handled bat and ball as he walked. I looked around for the approach of my friends from their dinners. Nobody was coming. Okay.

I guessed trying to hit a baseball to some kid was the sort of thing that would make Father feel better. Step across the street and hit some balls, try out the mending leg in something besides walking around the house two hundred times. He put his black breviary on one of the courthouse steps and pushed up his already rolled sleeves. He looked down the long lawn my way like he was scoping out a tee shot, took a couple of practice swings, very golfish. This would never work. Then he took the ball and laid it out in front of himself on the evening air and quickly brought his hand back to the bat handle so both hands were on it . . .

. . . and smacked the mightiest fly ball almost straight up that I had ever seen hit by priest, man, or real baseball player, straight up damned near out of sight . . .

. . . and yelled to me as it went up, "HaHA! Catch that one, Danny boy!"

Well, it turns out golf is not baseball but when it comes to hitting, the two sports do have some things in common. We who grew up hitting a baseball (and, since, have played a little golf) have learned to dream of hitting one that would fly like a shot off the tee, launched effortlessly, rocketing away in a white streak breathtaking in the beauty of its flight against the background of trees and green grass, taking to the air in an upward swoop that would make the best-hit line drive into the gap seem lumbering by comparison. It turns out Father Casey could whack some mighty fly balls.

There were many evenings after that when I chased pop-ups at the courthouse. Casey, grumbly old parish priest, seemed to love coming over and hitting, and I loved trying to track those giants down. It was fun despite the obstacles: the trees, the cannon rocks, the crisscross of sidewalks and telephone wires. I imagined sometime getting him to hit flies to me at the Pony League field in the park, but this wasn't that kind of thing. We were stuck in the circumstances of sandlot baseball contrived within available space convenient to Father Casey if he wanted to wander across the street on a summer afternoon. It was a situation confined to a certain situation. One night toward the end of summer as I watched him launch me pop-ups, I finally noticed something I hadn't before. The ball wasn't being pitched to him; rather, he was tossing it up and hitting it by himself. Now I noticed he was tucking a shoulder and shortening the stroke. Many times he was fouling the ball off, though they were mighty fouls to be sure, and sometimes you could tell even when he hit it on the sweet spot he didn't get it all. And I thought to myself:

If only. He had. A better bat.

In those days, an eleven-year-old could spot a good bat. Even the sand-lot kids could eye the ash or hickory and see promise in the grain of the wood, tell what felt right in the distribution of the weight between the handle and the barrel. They could take a couple of practice swings and know if it was good in the hands. It was intuition and experience, not science; it was also partly faith. If the bat felt right, so did the batter when he stepped to the plate.

The Saturday morning after my birthday—twelve!—I had a little birthday cash. I biked uptown seven blocks to the Western Auto, where I found Father Casey a thin-handled hickory beauty: a thirty-four-inch Mickey Mantle Louisville Slugger, beautiful, the wood a dark tan, browned in fire with a varnish. Powerized, it said on the bat above the label in parentheses shaped like lightning. The grain was very interesting. The lines that ran the length of the bat were distinct and spaced, and the wood was harder and sweeter than the thin-grained cheapos we had in Little League.

It was four years before Mantle and Maris, using this new bat style, made a run at Babe Ruth's single-season home-run record. The older bat style was thick and heavy; old-timers often said people should remember Babe Ruth set that famous record basically hitting a sock with a fence post. The Mickey Mantle model was thin-handled, the barrel too, thinner than you'd expect. The knob on the end of it was pronounced so it didn't slip out of the hitter's hand. Think about a golf club, the metal shaft light, with plenty of whip. And of course the golf ball was packed with rubber bands instead of yarn. Yarn! Anyway, I imagined this was the kind of bat Father Casey needed if he was going to take his talent for hitting fly balls to the next level. Light, the sweet spot farther away from him for whip action and so he wouldn't have to tuck in his shoulders as he turned but rather could extend his arms, the handle so he could grip it tight and transfer arm speed and shoulder ballast directly into pop.

"Where'd this come from?" he asked me that first evening.

"Try it," I said.

He started meandering up the lawn toward the courthouse to his usual spot. "It looks brand-new. Did I break the other one?"

"Nah, it's at home."

"Uh-huh." He was standing up there by the steps taking practice swings. "I might knock somebody's window out with this thing."

"Yes, Father," I said.

I wanted all the fly ball this man could whack into the sky.

That evening some of my Protestant friends showed up and watched him hit—the mysterious local Catholic priest hitting pop flies at the courthouse. Only in America. And what a thrill it was, the crack of that new bat, how the ball sailed above the full length of the courthouse lawn, high over the silver maple and the little dwarf maple we called third base, passed over Central Street like a Russian satellite a couple of years later, flew over Charlie Price's garden in the next block and a yard beyond that, so high it was nearly out of sight in the pink dusky sky of a rural Illinois evening, summer 1957. I ran back for it, across Central and down the alley. I ran for it as far as I could go, right up against Judge Gray's handsome wrought iron fence. Lined up in windows behind Father Casey, the county surveyor and his staff looked on. Across the street to the south on the curb in front of the Catholic church, friends saw it happen and would testify.

"Yikes," my friend Andy said without really knowing he said it, sitting by the silver maple looking up. The ball, as it returned to earth, seemed to fall straight down out of the pink and blue, straight into Judge Gray's wife's flower garden, and didn't even bounce in the loam.

"Yikes indeed, lad!" Father Casey called. "Ha HAA!" he laughed. I'd never seen him happy like that. "Now that's a ball bat!" he said so we coul-hear him and he laughed again. I can hear him this moment. Will you cry with me right now for the loss of that innocent, beautiful time?

My Outfield

J. D. Scrimgeour

Winner of the *Creative Nonfiction* Baseball Essay Contest

This essay originated from my experiences playing the outfield. From Little League through high school, my outfields rarely involved fences. Somewhere far behind me would be a cornfield, or a softball diamond, or just grass. Where did the game end and the world—or imagination—begin?

The outfield stretches from the flat, dried brown grass of Fairview Park in Normal, Illinois, to the thick green behind the high school tennis courts in New Milford, Connecticut, to Furlong Field in Salem, Massachusetts, booby-trapped with gooseshit, hemmed in on three sides by an auto junk-yard, a playground, and a street, but on its fourth side—is that fair terri-tory?—sloping down into the mouth of the North River as it drifts into the Atlantic.

Its boundaries are inexact, and infinite—a state of mind.

It's a dumping ground for the weak-armed, the unskilled, the lefthanded; its grasses are littered with failures. Even Whitman, the supreme outfielder (unshaven, musing, great range), would be perplexed by grass so full of misjudgments.

The outfield is tainted with mercury and lead paint; it's an old Indian burial ground. Ambiguous weeds make love to lost strands of grass in the shadow of an imaginary scoreboard. The brown patches where the outfielders usually stand weep like bullet holes. A hollow, anonymous voice slurs facts that pile in soggy heaps down the leftfield line. Where the grass turns to yellow stalks of prairie, an ant skitters into the husk of a baseball, empty leather hide that has birthed whatever was inside it.

There are no fathers and sons in the outfield. There is, somehow, not enough room. Beyond the foul lines, there have been sightings of gnarled gods with curious, knobby protrusions and unpronounceable names—the sentimental call them angels.

The low line drive skims the infield and bounds toward you, a little to your right. Nobody on, one out. You need simply to stop the ball. The throw, which needn't be rushed, will go to the shortstop, who is lining himself up with second base. The ball is still moving fast, but it's on the ground. Plant one knee in the grass, the other bent, leg opening out. The glove touches the ground, your throwing hand beside it, fingers splayed. Watch the ball into the glove, closing your hand over it, getting hold of it as you push yourself up, angling your body in line with second. The arm drops and rises behind you, your glove points to your target, then falls as you shift your weight and release. Whooshhhhhh—snap! into the shortstop's mitt. The shortstop turns and jogs the few steps to the infield dirt, watching the runner retreat to first, then flips the ball to the pitcher. Single.

Mostly, the outfielder runs to back up, to collect a poor throw or a surprising bounce, to limit others' mistakes, to assure everyone that things are not that bad. Hustle behind third base. Be ready for the pickoff to second, the overthrow from third to first. Mostly—and ideally—these efforts are unrewarded. The play is made, the outfielder jogs back to his post, glove unused, breath easing to normal, perhaps hollering "Good play" or "Way to do it" as he folds into position, knees bent, hand on one knee and glove on the other. Settled, he spits, as if saying, *That's done*.

If things go perfectly, the pitcher never lets the ball leave the infield. Logically, the outfielder's ideal game is one in which he does nothing. There he is, scuffing the grass with his cleat, spitting sunflower seeds, offering some bland encouragement that the pitcher may not even hear. There he is, lying down and staring up at the empty, endless sky, the greatest outfield, uncoverable. He plucks a blade of grass and pins it between his teeth. A plane leaves a contrail that connects one cloud to another. It is just cool enough that when a breeze passes, goose bumps appear on his arms.

The outfield, even center field, is not for strivers, those cursed with ambition or pride. Lear ends up in the outfield, raging in a storm (why didn't they call the game?), but he never imagined he would be out there, rain spilling from his cap's brim.

The outfield is democratic. Anyone can play it, and, let's admit, any number can play it. Twelve players on your T-ball team? Have six outfielders.

This country, drifting toward empire, more proud than democratic, has little interest in the outfield. In the major leagues, the fences keep getting closer and closer. The possibilities, the players, must be hemmed in.

Watch an infielder groom his position, bending every now and then to pick up a small rock and toss it beyond the baseline, out of play. Such fastidiousness! Obsessive-compulsive, clean-shaven or finely mustachioed, they are too tidy. *Are my pants too loose? My socks the right height? Is my cap precisely centered and angled off the forehead?*

What can an outfielder do? The task is Sisyphean. One can't tidy the universe. Pick up a rock or dirt clod and move it . . . where? And what about the other rocks, pebbles, twigs? The logs and memories and boulders? A ball could go anywhere. One must resign oneself to fate—the ball will collide with what it chooses. The world will go where it goes. You are not central to its outcome. The bombs will fall, and you can do little to stop them. Back up! Always back up! Or, if the situation calls for it, run like hell, holding your glove ahead of you like an offering, or a prayer.

In a time of war, the outfield may be your only chance.

Don't believe them when they tell you all fields have fences now. Don't even believe them when you see the fences yourself, when you collide into them running back, back, back for that endless fly ball. There is always more air than chain-link, and some nocturnal animal will have dug a rut underneath. There must be a way out.

· · ·

An inside pitch, and eight-year-old Javier drops the bat and jumps back, out of the box, pulling his chest in, his arms rising on either side like wings. He turns to his bench wide-eyed. "That ball almost hit me!" he exclaims, not with anger, or fear, but with simple astonishment that the world has the potential for such cruelty. The coach simply nods.

Oh Javier, there is room for you in the outfield. You don't need to wear cleats. You don't need to wear sneakers—go barefoot. You can forget your hat in your mother's boyfriend's car. You can forget to pee between innings, and then, in the privacy of right field, drop your gray baseball pants down to your thighs in full view of those parents in the stands, of your own team-mates on the bench, of your coach. Your only audience is yourself. You had to go bad, and now you're going, the stream making an impressive arc, leaping into the air like a well-struck ball. A few drops glisten on the grass, rivulets putter and fade into the earth, a map of some unknown country appears and quickly recedes.

· · ·

Turn to the right fielder, the young guy who is supposed to be good, the one who aches for your position, and yell "Kevin!" When he turns, open and close your mouth as if you are talking, but, rather than say words, just let out occasional syllables—"Ah-Bo-Ace-Ta-Ta-Jedda." Smile as if you've said something clever. Watch him smile, nod, and offer a weak laugh. What plea-sure to be goofy! He thinks you're annoying, or nuts. He's certain you're not as good as he is (he belongs in the infield). Lift your cap off your head, rub your long hair off your brow with your arm, then get ready for the pitch.

In the outfield, I smoked pot. I cracked stupid jokes about sex I only half understood. I rode in cars, their tires cutting the turf, making ridges in the moonlight. I stood in line, waiting for my turn, for the coach to hit me ten fly balls in a row until my arm burned from all those throws back in, until my lungs burned from all that running. In the outfield, I composed the great song of the spheres I will never sing aloud, that I have half forgotten now, as I enter middle age.

In the outfield, worms eased between the nubs of my cleats, trying to write their damp hieroglyphics on my soles.

Yes, we were naked in the outfield, and I can hardly remember her now, but it was good.

In the silences of center field, I etched haikus on the back of my glove:

I was of three minds,
like an outfield, in which there
are three outfielders.

From a distance, the outfielder stands, small and thin, a young boy's erect penis, so insignificant on the huge body of the field. Something passing over him that is vague, unknown, presexual, keeps him from dropping limp on the grass. The breeze? The clouds? Whitman's trembling hand? The pitch?

The outfielder's pleasure is simple, unencumbered by guilt or desire: See ball. Chase ball. Get ball. Throw ball. Oh, joy!

The outfielder does not wear a protective cup. He does not speak of fences.

• • •

You have taken turns on the pitcher's mound and spent a little glamour time at shortstop, but you have always been an outfielder. When you were nine, playing in a league of nine- and ten-year-olds, you were the worst hitter on a first-place team. You spent that season excited and terrified, standing on the fringes of the outfield. Kids rarely hit the ball farther than the edge of the infield dirt. One game, the main slugger on the other team, a kid named Todd Whitehouse, hit a monstrous fly ball out toward you. You watched it. You stepped toward it. You caught it. And you were baptized an outfielder, teammates slapping your back and hollering. Since then, you've believed you can catch any ball you can reach, and many you can't.

And to throw! Not like infielders, the wrist snap and quick release. Outfielders throw with their lungs, their soul, their groin. The body flings itself open, as if to hug the world, one arm somewhere behind the back, the other hanging in front, and then the swift arc of the body and arm, nearly a somersault, and the ball zings off.

A secret: true outfielders—not those who toil in the major leagues—abhor hitting. To be the spectacle—how distressingly public. And it's so violent, brutal. Batting is something the outfielder accepts, penance for the joy of hunting fly balls, a kind of tax.

It is hardly worth running hard if you don't get to dive, stretching parallel to the ground and falling into it at the end. The batter begins to swing, and before he even hits the ball, you're taking a step left or right, depending on the pitch location and the speed of the swing. The ball moves up and out, and you are moving too, your body calculating geometry on the run—the best angle, the quickest route, exactly where the little fucker is going. You're running so hard you forget you're running, and you lose all the awkward hitches that make you slower than you should be. Whisk, whisk, across the grass, whisk, whisk. And the ball comes down, and your body calculates again—is a dive necessary? If so, how? What angle? Off which leg? Now! The arm stretches.... Snap! Thud! It's in the glove. You're on the ground. You hop up and hurl the ball back to the infield, back from whence it came, and feel your chest rise and fall, rise and fall. When you lie down tonight, your side will be tender, and you will be unable to sleep, your chest still rising and falling, your mind chasing that ball down in the great dark field of night.

An Ode to Baseball Caps

Frank Deford

*Each week since 1980 (with a few breaks—I am not the Cal
Ripken of radio commentators) I've aired a sports commentary
on National Public Radio. Unlike most sports journalists, who are
communicating with a distinct audience of fans, I know that my NPR
listeners form a broad spectrum. Many of them have only a minimal
interest in sports. As a consequence, I often try to find subjects that
may be idiosyncratic and hardly hard-core sports. My little essay
(if I may dignify my remarks so) here on baseball caps is one of my
favorites of that genre.*

An ode to baseball caps: Oh, baseball cap—

I know. I know. Why in the world am I talking about baseball caps at all, let alone in December, when it isn't baseball
season? But, you see, that's exactly the point. Baseball caps
are now bigger than baseball. Around the world, they now
may well even be the most familiar American artifact, passing Coca-Cola and blue jeans and bad movies. Think about
it. How many baseball caps actually end up on the heads of
baseball players? Well, I'd wager that fewer people in baseball
caps play baseball than people in tennis shoes play tennis or
people in polo shirts play polo. Not only that, but baseball
caps have risen to preeminence at a time when headgear in

· 89 ·

general has been in decline: the fedora has gone the way of spats. The beret remains the favorite choice of a few noggins, but as sure as English has replaced French as the language of diplomacy, so has the baseball cap swamped the beret sur la tête—the final indignity to Gallic pride.

Baseball caps have become so ubiquitous largely because women have taken to them, too. Name another hat that is so unisex. This is largely because of the most brilliant clothing invention since the zipper, namely, the hole in the rear of the baseball cap so that ladies might let their glorious long locks stream through the gap in the cap, absolutely Dr. Seussian. Actually, I'll bet you never thought of this. We shouldn't be surprised that women now wear baseball caps, because as millinery experts have divined, the baseball cap is closest in shape and utility to the old-fashioned Victorian sunbonnet. Visualize that now, right? And it also helps the hegemony of baseball caps that they have the adjuster with the little holes in the back. This way, one size fits all. I have a pinhead. I had an old friend with a noggin the size of a watermelon, so big that we called him the head of the school. The two of us can buy the exact same baseball cap; they fit men's heads, women's heads, big heads, little heads. The baseball cap may be the most universal article of clothing ever designed.

One of the ironic things about baseball caps is that so many people in other sports wear them. Tennis players and golfers wear baseball caps when they're playing tennis and golf. Football quarterbacks put them on as soon as they take off their helmet—so, too, automobile racers. I don't understand, though, why so many people wear baseball caps backwards. This doesn't keep the sun out of your eyes, and the gap in the cap looks foolish on your forehead. Of course, a few young knuckleheads even wear baseball caps sort of sideways. Whatever. What you don't see much of anymore is folks who wear their baseball caps way back up on the head. These are the types who tend to scratch their heads. That seems to have mostly gone out, too. Oh, but it'll probably come back in style.

(originally aired December 14, 2005,
on NPR's "Morning Edition")

My First Day with the Yankees

Matthew McGough

I grew up a huge fan of the New York Yankees. When I was very small, I'd go to games maybe once a year with my father and watch Reggie Jackson. When I was a little bit older, we'd watch Dave Winfield. And then when I came into my teens, Don Mattingly, who was my absolute favorite player.

I went to high school in New York, and it was a big moment when I started going to Yankee games by myself. It was at one of these games, sitting in the bleachers in the fall of 1991, that I noticed for the first time this kid in right field wearing a Yankee uniform playing catch with the right fielder.

I'd been to Yankee Stadium so many times, but I had never noticed the batboy before.

And this kid could not play catch for his life. He was throwing the ball over Jesse Barfield's head, or he was one-hopping him. And I was like, *I'm not a great athlete, but I can play catch at least as well as this kid can. I don't understand why he has that job, and I'm sitting in the bleachers.*

So I went home that night, and I tore a page out of the program that listed all the different Yankee executives. I wrote a handwritten letter to everyone from Steinbrenner on down to Stump Merrill, who was the manager at that point, and basically said, "My name is Matt, and I'm 16 years old, and I'm a huge fan of the Yankees. I don't know if you can apply for this batboy position, but if you can, I really would like an application. And I'm so excited to hear from you that if I don't hear from you soon, I'm going to follow up with a phone call."

I sent these off. After two weeks I hadn't heard anything, so I picked up the phone and called the Yankees switchboard number.

The secretary answered the phone, "Hello. New York Yankees."

I said, "Hi, this is Matt McGough. I sent a letter in a couple weeks ago about applying for a batboy position. Nobody got back to me."

So she's like, "Okay, well, I'll take your name and number down, and I'll have somebody get back to you."

Another week goes by, and I don't hear anything. So I pick up the phone again and I call and the same woman answers the phone, "Hello. New York Yankees."

I say, "Hi. This is Matt. I've sent some letters in about the batboy position, and I called last week and somebody was supposed to call me back."

I thought it was kind of rude that they hadn't.

And she laughed, and asked me, "How old are you?"

I said, "Sixteen." And she laughed some more. I didn't really understand what she was laughing at, but she took down my name and number.

She said, "I'll make sure that somebody gets back to you."

A few days later, sure enough, a letter arrived in the mail on official Yankee letterhead. It invited me to come up to the stadium for an interview with Nick Priore, who was the clubhouse manager.

So I put my jacket and tie on. I didn't even tell any of my friends about this, because it was way, way too weird to explain. I took the 4 train up to the stadium. This was October, and the Yankees weren't playing in the World Series back in '91, so it was very quiet. I walked into the Yankee lobby and there was a security guard there.

I introduced myself, and I said, "I'm here for the batboy interview."

He picks up the telephone, and he's like, "Nick, some kid's here to see you," and he says to me, "Have a seat."

So I sit down in the pinstripe lobby, and I'm passing about ten minutes waiting for this guy, Nick, to come up for the first job interview of my life.

I'm trying to think of the questions that he might ask me. I'm ready to tell him what my favorite subject is in school, why I think the Yankees need a big bat behind Mattingly to win the pennant next year, and what Mickey Mantle's batting average was in 1956.

I'm passing the time, when these double doors burst open, and this guy walks in—obviously Nick, but he doesn't introduce himself. He could be anywhere from forty to eighty years of age. He has this greased-back hair and a stogie between the two teeth left in his mouth and a chaw of tobacco. He's wearing a wife-beater T-shirt, blue Yankees shorts, and white athletic socks pulled up to his knees. He has these black sneakers that are obviously shoe polished.

He looks at me and says, "Are your parents gonna mind you taking the train home late at night?"

So I say, "I take the train to school every day. I think it'll be fine."

And he says, "Well, come back Opening Day."

I go home. I think I have the job. I'm not really sure. Six months later, Opening Day in 1992, I put on my jacket and tie, and I show up at the stadium at 9 AM. I go back downstairs, through these tunnels, and come to this big steel door—the Yankee Clubhouse.

I walk inside, and it's complete pandemonium.

All these ballplayers that I'd only seen before on TV or across rows and rows of stadium seats are here in the flesh, right in front of me. I had a poster of Don Mattingly above my bed for my whole life, and he's standing on the right. Jimmy Key, the ace of the pitching staff, is over there.

Opening Day at Yankee Stadium is not just a sports event. It's a news event, and it's the beginning of spring in New York City. Mayor Dinkins was in the clubhouse with his entourage, and like, it's Mayor Dinkins and Don Mattingly, you know? I'm walking around, and I'm kinda lost, and I figure I better go find Nick.

So I walk up to Nick, and I say, "Nick, I'm Matt. We met a couple months ago. This is my first day of work. What do you want me to do?"

And he says, "Stay the f--- outta my way."

I kind of shrink back and throw my backpack over on the side, and I'm wandering around in a daze, when I feel a tap on my shoulder. I turn around, and it's Don Mattingly.

He sticks his hand out, and he says, "How's it going? I'm Don Mattingly. Are you gonna be working with us this year?"

I'd never really thought about the experience in those terms. He could've said so many other things that wouldn't have been as cool.

He could've said, "Who are you? Are you the new batboy? Are you gonna be working for us this year?"

But he said, "I'm Don Mattingly. Are you gonna be working with us this year?"

So I said, "I know who you are, Mr. Mattingly. I'm Matt. I'm the new batboy."

He says, "Great to meet you, Matt. I have a very big job to ask of you. I've just unpacked all my bats from spring training, and I don't know if it was the altitude of the flight up from Florida or the humidity down there or what, but the game starts in about two hours, and I need you to find me a bat stretcher."

I say, "Okay."

I go and find Nick, but Nick is busy. Probably half a dozen ballplayers are bothering him for batting gloves or AA batteries or this or that.

I walk up to him, and I'm like, "Nick, I need a bat stretcher for Don Mattingly."

Nick lets loose with a stream of expletives that fell on—I swear—completely virgin ears. I'd never heard that type of language in the movies before or anywhere, let alone directed at me.

So I rock back on my heels and go and find Nick's assistant, Rob.

And I say, "I need a bat stretcher for Don Mattingly, and Nick told me to go f--- myself, and I don't know what to do."

So Rob goes, "Chill out. I saw Danny Tartabull using one in his locker." Danny Tartabull is the new power-hitting right fielder.

I go to Tartabull's locker, and he's getting dressed in his uniform. I stand off on the side, and he says, "How's it going?"

And I'm like, "Fine. I'm Matt. I'm the new batboy. I need a bat stretcher for Don Mattingly, and I heard you were just using one."

Tartabull says, "Well, I was using one, but I left it in the manager's office. You should probably go check in there."

I say, "Thanks," and I go into the manager's office. I walk in, and Buck Showalter, the manager, is having a press conference with probably eight or ten reporters. I stand off on the side, and the conversation comes to a standstill basically because there's a sixteen-year-old kid there in his Easter blazer and jacket, standing in the manager's office at Yankee Stadium two hours before first pitch on Opening Day, looking very lost and anxious.

Showalter turns to me, and he's like, "Can I help you?"

And I say, "I'm Matt. I'm the new batboy. I really sorry to interrupt, but I need a bat stretcher for Don Mattingly, and Danny Tartabull says that he left it in here."

So Showalter looks down beneath his desk. Then he's like, "Well do you need a right-handed one or a left-handed one?"

This is the first question I'd heard all day that I could answer with complete confidence, because you couldn't have grown up in New York at that time without knowing that Mattingly was the best left-handed hitter in baseball.

I say, "I need a left-handed bat stretcher."

Showalter says, "Well, I think we maybe have a right-handed one around here, but probably not a left-handed one. You should try down at the Red Sox clubhouse. See if they have one."

So I said, "Okay, thanks. I'm sorry to interrupt." By this point, I'm sprinting down the hallways in the tunnels beneath the stands. I run into the Red Sox clubhouse and find their equipment manager and give him the whole story [talking very quickly]: "I'm Matt. I'm the new batboy for the Yankees, and Danny Tartabull left his right-handed bat stretcher in Buck Showalter's office, but I need a left-handed one, and the game's about to start."

He's like, "Calm down. We don't have one, but we need one. Here's twenty bucks. Go up to the sporting goods store on 161st Street and River Avenue and buy two—a left-handed one for Mattingly and a right-handed one for us—and then bring me back the change." He gives me the $20. I put it in my pocket. I run upstairs.

By now, it's an hour before first pitch on Opening Day. Fifty thousand fans are coming down from the subway in the opposite direction that I'm walking. I'm the only person in the world who knows that if I don't come through on this mission, Mattingly's gonna go up there against Roger Clemens and the Red Sox on Opening Day at Yankee Stadium with a toothpick in his hand, basically.

So I'm fighting against the crowd and feeling so much weight on my shoulders. I'm making my way through and I'm about to cross the threshold of Stan's Sporting Goods, when it dawns on me... I've played a lot of baseball in my life, and I've been a big fan for a while, and I don't even know what a bat stretcher looks like.

At that moment it dawns on me for the first time: *Is this a joke? Could this possibly be a joke?*

But I had so much fear, because if I go back, and I tell Don Mattingly, "I'm too smart to fall for your BS bat stretcher story," and I'm wrong, I'm gonna be back in the bleachers before my first game and lose my dream job.

So I take three laps around Yankee Stadium, convincing myself, *It's gotta be a joke. It's gotta be. It's gotta be a joke.* Then I walk back in. I go down the stairs. I walk into the clubhouse. Mattingly winks at me from across the clubhouse, a couple of the other ballplayers laugh.

Mattingly went three for four that day. Yankees win. It was my first day in pinstripes.

I didn't learn until later on that I was the first kid in anyone's memory to have gotten the job without having a connection, without somebody knowing somebody or their dad knowing somebody. And you know, as naïvely intense as I was in chasing that bat stretcher, I was perhaps as intensely naïve to think I could get a job working with the Yankees.

But the lesson to me is that with a great deal of persistence and a little bit of common sense, even if the thing you're chasing may not exist, you can sometimes will it into being.

Pesäpallo: Playing at the Edge of the World

Caitlin Horrocks

*For a long time, I avoided writing about sports. American baseball,
especially, has always had so many talented writers to do it justice—
people who play the game better, know the game better, love the game
better than I ever could. On the field, I'm likely to drop the ball. In the
stands, I'm easily distracted by soft pretzels. I don't have a head for
statistics, either—I've lost many games of Trivial Pursuit trying to earn
that Sports & Leisure wedge. So pesäpallo provided several firsts for
me: it was the first species of baseball I encountered that I was actually
good at, and the first I felt I could say something about that people
hadn't already read. This essay also marks the first time I tried to look
at any part of my own life through the lens of sports. Why did my
father spend so many hours playing catch with his clumsy daughter?
What did it mean to be one of the only Americans in a small Finnish
town? And am I ashamed of taking joy in being the twentysomething
pesäpallo MVP of the fourth grade? No, I am not.*

We're leading by one, but with two outs, when I come up to bat. The
staff-student baseball game is a yearly tradition at Päämajakoulu,
and part of the tradition is that the game isn't played for any set number of
innings. Whoever is winning when the bell rings for the next lesson is that
year's champion, so the game's normal rhythms are speeded up and slowed
down, tense, the leading team moseying through the batting order and the
trailing team fielding with a frenzy. Our opponents are a handpicked lineup
of sixth graders, mostly the boys who are hitting puberty faster than their

peers. Finnish sixth graders are the age of American seventh graders, and a few of the boys are already much taller than I am, which admittedly is not saying much.

I am buried somewhere in the middle of the batting order, but there's only one runner on base, the school handicrafts teacher, when I come up to bat. I don't remember now which student is pitching, but I believe it was Jukkis, the monosyllabic nemesis of my Conversational English classes. Tall and broad and sullen, with spiked, naturally platinum hair, he's barely talked to me all year. This wouldn't be such a problem except that being talked to is nearly my only function here at Päämajakoulu. Jukkis, I imagine, after nine months of being asked about his favorite animal, his favorite sport, his favorite flavor of ice cream, finds me as infuriating as I find him. We eye each other balefully, the bright yellow ball seeming to glow in his hand.

Because this is a game of pesapallo, Finnish baseball, Jukkis is standing beside me, across home plate and just out of range of my swing. To pitch he will throw the ball in the air, at least three feet above my head, and I will try to hit it on its way down. If it falls and hits the asphalt of the school-yard, that's a ball. Two balls and the batter walks. If it falls and hits the base, that's a strike. Three strikes are an out. I have no intention of missing the pitch, but bats and gloves and balls of all kinds have traditionally not paid me much heed. As a clumsy, pudgy kid, a girl who really did throw like a girl, I long ago convinced myself not to care. On this May morning in Mikkeli, Finland, 60 miles west of the Russian border, 140 miles northeast of Helsinki, 325 miles south of the Arctic Circle, eyeing a thirteen-year-old student across the plate, I care desperately. I bend my knees, raise the bat, my stance the same as in the American game, and wait for Jukkis to fling the ball upwards. I concentrate on its speed, its height, and at the same time keep repeating to myself: *Remember to run towards third! Run towards third!*

The pitching style is not the only thing that separates American baseball from the upstart Finnish version: the base running pattern is also radically different, with first base roughly where third should be. Second is over by first, and third is across the outfield, somewhere in leftfield close to the foul

line. The distances between each are different: approximately 60 feet from
home to first base, then 96, 108, and a long 114 feet from third to home.

The rules for running the bases are different too. Technically, I don't
even have to run after hitting the ball; according to the rules, I can hit both
my first and second pitches and just stand there, making it possible to
advance two runners while remaining at bat. If I hit a fly ball and a fielder
catches it, I will be "wounded," not out. (Three outs or eleven woundings
end an inning.)

There are other quirks, too: a triple counts as a home run for scoring
purposes, but the batter gets to stay on third and try to score again. Stealing
is generally not a good idea; anytime a hit is caught, any runner not touching a base is automatically out. If a runner leads off at second and the
pitcher throws to third, the runner is out unless he can physically get back
to touch second before the pitcher's throw is caught by the third baseman.

Here in the Päämajakoulu schoolyard we are hardly playing a professional game, and most of these rules are irrelevant, which is just as well—
it's all I can do to remember which way to run. It's also a burden to know
that I am playing to uphold faculty honor, my honor, the honor of "grown-
ups," the honor of the English language, the honor of Americans. This year,
the year of the Iraq invasion, being an American has been complicated.
In Conversational English classes my students have mustered their best
English, their best understanding of global politics, to ask me why: Why is
America doing this? Why are you doing this? Without consistent access to
English-language news, only dimly aware that the war is even happening,
I am the wrong person to ask. But I am the only American my students
know, and so they assume, surely, I can explain American foreign policy,
and surely, I am brilliant at baseball. In their minds, America is a nation of
warmongers and ballplayers.

The crowd of students has been booing the teachers proudly and pow-
erfully, rooting for their classmates, but I seem to divide their loyalties.
They are used to encouraging me, soothing my embarrassment, watching
me climb back on my skis or stumble through a discussion about the school
cafeteria porridge with their "real" English teacher, who thinks it's hilarious

to test my Finnish in class. They tried to console me when I got so lost during the Official School Skiing Day that the headmaster was dispatched to look for me in the woods. (In my defense, I had been on skis only four times in my life, all of them in the two weeks before the Official School Skiing Day.) They want their team to win the pesäpallo game, but they also want me to do well. Their enthusiasm, their confidence, is palpable: this is baseball, she's American. Finally, something she can do.

"Go, Caitlin!" they yell as I wait for the pitch, and I wonder where they've learned the cheer. Video games, perhaps—a lot of their English is from video games. "Game over!" they occasionally shout at each other on the playground. "Finish him!"

This is the home of Nokia, the neighbor of IKEA and Volvo, a social welfare democracy full of tall, trim, well-educated blondes. Finland's educational system has been ranked the best in the world, its standard of living among the highest. Most of my students look like extras from Children of the Corn, pale and golden-haired and hauntingly wholesome. They love the place they were born with an innocence, a straightforward pride I envy. I check over their sentence-completion exercises: Finland is_____. The most beautiful country in the world. The country with the most beautiful nature. The best country on Earth. A place with excellent four seasons. They are very big on this, the fact that Finland has four seasons; I try to tell them most of the United States does too, except our winter does not last six months, our summer two.

My students speak of "going to Europe" on vacations. When I tell them that to Americans, at least those Americans who could find Finland on a map, they're already in Europe, they shrug. "Sort of," they say. "But not really." This is a country that for hundreds of years was a backwater of the Swedish empire, then a backwater Imperial Russian duchy, then a fledging independent state in the shadow of the Soviet Union. This is a country that has been left to its own devices when it comes to language, cuisine, literature, sports.

Pesäpallo was imported and reinvented by Lauri "Tahko" Pihkala, a Finn studying in the United States who happened to watch a 1907 Red Sox

game. He found American-style baseball frankly boring, but upon his return
to Finland, he noticed how many traditional sports were losing ground
to modern imports. He decided to create a new game, loosely based on a
nineteenth-century Finnish game called Kuningaspallo (Kingball) but named
after American baseball—and more exciting, faster-moving, and more competitive than either. Pesäpallo was officially introduced in 1922, and the
Finnish National Baseball Association (Pesäpalloliito) was formed in 1930.
After a name change or two, the sport settled on pesäpallo, a direct transla-
tion (base-ball) and transcription of how it sounded to Finnish ears: to the
Finnish, the English "b" and "p" sound exactly the same. (Hence my third
grade students' hysterical laughter at the phrase "big pig," and their teacher's
enthusiastic shouting at an exhibition match at Päämjakoulu's sister school in
Britain: "Good bitch! Good bitch!" she praised the English schoolgirls.)

Pesäpallo eventually became known as the kansallispeli, the Finnish
national sport, and at least during the spring and summer the title is earned.
During the winter, ice hockey takes over; losses, particularly to Sweden,
could plunge the entire country into a day of mourning. I never saw pesäpallo inspire such heights of despair or triumph, but it is universally taught
to schoolchildren, and in the warmer months it is played in many small
town and community leagues, as well as in the professional Superpesis
league, which prides itself on its separate-but-equal tournaments for male
and female players.

Outside the country, it's another matter. Baseball has the United States,
Canada, Japan, the Caribbean, and most of the Western hemisphere.
Pesäpällo has Finland, Sweden, Germany, and Australia. There's a team in
New Zealand, too, but it doesn't have the money to compete abroad. The
Pesäpallo World Cup in 2006, held in Munich, had only four participants.
Fortunately for national pride, Finland won the gold. Indeed, there has
been a proposal that in the next World Cup, Finland be allowed to field
twelve separate teams, one from each of its provinces, to increase participa-
tion and create more competition.

As a small country with a pool of potential athletes only five-million
deep, Finland has had to make its peace with almost never being good

at anything on the world stage. I once asked a Finn if the national soccer team had qualified to play in that year's World Cup. He burst out laughing. And yet Finns are ferociously proud of their Formula One race car drivers, their curling team, their ski jumpers, the long distance runner Paavo Nurmi, who has been dead for decades, and a sixth-place finisher at the 2006 European Championships in women's singles figure skating. In 2002 a sprinter named Markus Pöyhönen won his heat and made it into the finals of the men's 100m at the European track and field championships, the first Finn ever to do so. He finished fifth in a field of seven, and the country went wild. This was more than respectable. This was enough to get him on the Finnish version of *Dancing with the Stars*, and to keep the sixth grade female students at Päämajakoulu swooning over celebrity magazine pictures of him for the next nine months.

Pesäpallo is one of few venues for athletic prowess Finns have to themselves, or nearly so. By having their own brand of baseball, they have ensured both that other countries will have to compete on their terms, and that they will never have to compete on those of the United States. But they don't see pesäpallo as a consolation sport; Finns fiercely defend the superiority of pesäpallo to American baseball. They won't even be diplomatic about it. To them, there is no contest. They claim pesäpallo is more entertaining, more physically and intellectually demanding—basically, smarter, fitter, faster, better—than baseball. "Are you tired of watching boring baseball?" demands an international rule booklet. "Do you prefer faster and more tactical batting sports?"

To some extent these claims are demonstrably true—pesäpallo games are shorter, with two periods of four innings each, and the ball stays in motion much more. Finns are proud that pesäpallo doesn't reward power hitters: a ball that goes over the fence is counted as a foul. The goal of a skilled batter is to hit the ball to certain parts of the outfield—where the fielders aren't, yes, but more than that, there are very specific plays that require highly accurate hitting to move all the runners into position. At the game's highest levels, teams have playbooks and plans closer in complexity to American football than baseball.

To present the American side of this argument, I defer to sportswriter Red Smith, who had the (mis)fortune of watching a pesäpallo match when it was an exhibition sport at the 1952 Helsinki Olympics. Pesäpallo's inventor, Pihkala himself, threw out the opening pitch. Smith titled his article "Monstrous Infant": "They played a ball game here last night, and if there's a stone left upon a tomb in Cooperstown today it's an upset.... [The game] was invented by Lauri Pihkala, a professor who wears a hearing aid.... Somebody must have described baseball to him when his battery was dead." Smith thought the game lacked elegance, sense, a coherent strategy, or anything to differentiate it from a bunch of far northern yokels running in zigzag patterns across a field. It is hard to tell, though, whether the game offended Smith's sensibilities simply by being so different from its namesake, or he found it unpleasant to watch, or, perhaps most likely, he simply couldn't get over the most outwardly bizarre aspects of the game. I suppose any true devotee of a sport has a point at which his sensibilities are irrevocably offended. Even Finns look askance at the Swedish brannboll, a version of baseball in which, among other oddities, an unlimited number of players can stay on any one base—the entire batting order, for example, can huddle on first.

Smith also had the luxury of having grown up with the American version of baseball, *the* baseball. But what makes the Finnish sport less legitimate than its precursor? Why is pesäpallo seen as a freakish offshoot of its parent sport, while baseball is given the respect of long tradition and sanctified rules? After all, someone had to come up with baseball, or we'd still be playing "stoolball" on village greens. We just don't know who, despite long-cherished myths like the one about Abner Doubleday's field in Cooperstown. Baseball has a long history and idiosyncratic evolution, as opposed to being the invention of a single man in the 1920s, but baseball is not sacrosanct. Much as Americans complain about the snooze factor in a five-day cricket test match, I never met a Finn who thought American baseball was anything other than the slow-moving dinosaur of the sports world, a woefully unevolved predecessor of his own sport. Even Finns who don't particularly like pesäpallo think it is a sport far superior, in design and execution, to the American version. Surely, if the rest of the world would just sit up and take notice, if pesäpallo boosters had one one-hundredth of one percent of the money and resources of American Major League Baseball, pesäpallo would conquer the world.

Finland doesn't hold out much hope of this happening, but that doesn't stop the Finns from trying to spread the gospel of pesäpallo, or, as it's now known in younger, hipper circles, pesis. There are a few teams playing now in Estonia, Japan, and Switzerland. The next World Cup is in 2009, so the Finnish Society of Auckland might have time to raise the money to send the New Zealand team.

In fact, there is an entire world of baseball offshoots and progenitors, a family of fringe sports played with bats and balls. Pesäpallo is hardly on the farthest fringe; it already has thousands more adherents than British baseball, for example, a sport played in three cities that touts its yearly "international" championship: a match among Cardiff, Wales, and either Liverpool or Newport, England. Pesäpallo has also outlived some of its sister sports: while nineteenth-century Finns were playing kuningaspallo, Russians were playing the closely related lapta, Swedes were playing lang-boll, and Germans were playing schlag-ball. Lapta, Russian baseball, dates all the way back to the fourteenth century, as evidenced by the discovery of seven-hundred-year-old leather balls and wooden bats; the pitcher placement is the same as in pesäpallo (perhaps this is where Pihkala got the idea), but the batter must begin his swing with the bat held between his legs. The game survives as an activity for schoolchildren and an official "Traditional Russian Sport." Schlag-ball is similarly hanging on, and even stoolball is still played, if only in Sussex, England. Langboll, alas, has gone gently into the great sports beyond.

It's hard for Americans to realize this anywhere except a dirt playing field in Russia, or an English city green, or a concrete Finnish schoolyard, but American is the not the only flavor of baseball; it's just the one with the largest reach and the most money, and the only one most Americans are aware of.

And yet Finns, as proud as they are of their homegrown sport, understand that it has a clear kinship with the American version, that

eight-hundred-pound gorilla. Finns see pesäpallo as a starter experience
for foreigners, especially Americans. It is what a Finnish person will try
to teach you to bridge the cultural gap; if the two of you can't talk about
curling, there's baseball. They bring it up when they aren't sure if you're
ready for something like avantouinti, a single verb that means going-swim-
ming-by-jumping-in-a-frozen-lake-through-a-hole-cut-in-the-ice.   Have
you gone avantouinti? Would you like to avantouinti? Did you avantouinti
and get hypothermia and nearly die? The Finns understand that avantouinti is approximately an 8.4 on a ten-point scale of cultural adventurous-
ness and assimilation. Pesäpallo is a 1.2. Pesäpallo is to avantouinti what
karjalanpiirakka is to kalakukko, both of which are specialty Finnish foods.
The former is a rice pastry with butter and the latter is a baked bread bowl
full of lard and fish heads.

Since I arrived in Finland at the beginning of the school year, I didn't
encounter pesäpallo until the start of the new season the following spring.
By that time, I had tried kalakukko and karjalanpiirakka and mämmi, a
delicacy that looks like a lump of tar and is a traditional food for Lent
partly because its laxative effects help purify the body for Easter. I had
also slurped koivunmahla, a traditional spring drink harvested by sticking
spigots in birch trees and drinking what comes out. I'd tried to learn to ski
and had learned both the Finnish word for javelin throwing (keihäänheitto)
and the location of the world's tallest ski jump (Lahti, Central Finland). I'd
attended events, including a Moose Raffle and a First Aid Championship,
been beaten with leafy birch branches in a sauna, and had a Russian border
guard joke about shooting me in the head. By pesäpallo season, I was ready
for anything.

The previous spring, with an English literature B.A. in hand and no
clue what to do with myself, I had applied for exactly two jobs: teaching English in Finland, and being an apprentice pastry chef at a bakery
in Michigan. I didn't speak Finnish, didn't have any Finnish family background—I had stumbled onto the job advertisement online. Why? everyone asked me, both Americans and Finns. Why not? I answered. Eventually
I came up with an answer involving my passionate commitment to teaching

and cultural exchange, but "Why not?" was more honest. I was unprepared and under qualified for the job. I'd made it to my second round of interviews at the bakery when, one morning, the assistant headmaster of a Finnish elementary school was on the phone, telling me Mikkeli was a nice town with only one bear. "I think you will not meet him in the forest. It is not sure that he exists. Maybe you will. But probably not. And if you do you will run away!" This was my job interview: apply for a visa, arrive in August, run from the bear.

My job title is "Assistant Teacher of English," which means various things as the year unfolds. I start out visiting other teachers' lessons: math, science, Finnish, handicrafts, physical education. I'm supposed to engage the students in conversation about anything—numbers, animals, yarn, javelins. I am the school's pet English speaker, the pet American. My job is primarily to be unintimidating, and I trip over my own feet and tongue so often I can't imagine this could really be a problem. By winter, I've graduated to holding my own Conversational English lessons with the older students and teaching the younger ones English songs and games. When a fifth grader tugs on my sleeve one day in the middle of a conversation group and tells me the assistant headmaster/fifth grade teacher wants me to join his phys ed class out in the schoolyard, I worry I've been demoted.

I help haul boxes of equipment out of a shed into the yard that is finally, in late April, free of snow. The kids open the boxes and distribute bats, balls, brown leather mitts. I have heard rumors of Finnish baseball but have never seen a game or the equipment. I allow myself a hint of anticipation. This is not tearing through the forest standing on a pair of someone else's waxed sticks. This is baseball. This I can do.

The teacher tells me he wants me to play, play to win, like I'm one of the eleven-year-olds. He puts me on a team and hands me a glove. For once, he seems to be doing this not as some new way to humiliate me, but because he assumes I will be good enough at the game to provide a productive example for his students. The Finnish winter being as long as it is, there are very few baseball-friendly weeks in the school year, and his students have played only a handful of times in the past few years. No one even asks me if I can play baseball. "Since Finnish baseball is so much easier, you will be very good at this game," he says. "Don't all Americans play baseball?"

For once, I'm glad my father made me play baseball. It was his sport, the one he followed, the one he would have loved to be really good at, the one he would have loved for one of his kids to be good at. My father has two daughters, no sons, and to his credit, the only time I have detected any regret in him over this is when it came to baseball. He had been a rising Little League pitcher, poised to be a large fish in his small hometown pond, when his arm was badly broken in a schoolyard fight. He still can't pull his right arm all the way back, but he could spend weekends pitching softballs to his kids, and he still speaks with embarrassing pride about my single moment of sports glory, which happened when I was nine. I don't remember it, but according to him, I pulled off a double play during a game with my summer softball team. I think it was apparent very early on I had no innate athletic skill, but my father didn't lose heart. Our baseball playing, our occasional tickets to Detroit Tigers games, were reflexive but sincere: this was what fathers did with sons, or daughters; this was what Americans did with each other. Faced with a child who read a lot more books about unicorns than she caught fly balls, my father still thought I should at least be able to play catch, to hit an easy pitch.

In American baseball, that's about all I can do. But as it turns out, I can beat the pants off a bunch of Finnish kids. Finnish baseball gloves are larger and rounder than the American version; so is home plate. The pitching style makes it much easier to hit the ball. A reporter from the Chicago Tribune once asked avid pesäpallo player and Olympic curler Teemu Salo if he thought he could hit a U.S. major league pitch. "I think never," he said. In fact, everything about the Finnish version of the game seems easier. It's like we're playing on the moon, or in some parallel universe. Not only are we all running backwards, swinging at pop-ups, constantly moving, but I'm good. It also doesn't hurt that the opposing team is made up of eleven-year-olds. After my first at bat the kids back way into the outfield every time I'm up. I'm still not a power hitter, so the balls don't foul out by overshooting the edge of the field. I can bring runners home without ever going to first base. The only thing I have to concentrate on is remembering to run towards third, instead of the ingrained instinct to run right. My only slipup is missing an easy grounder in the outfield. "Fuck!" I instinctively shout as the ball rolls past me. I look up at my fifth grade teammates, who grin at me. "Don't tell your teacher," I say. Then the bell rings and I go back inside to talk about fourth grade girls' favorite animals: dolphins, always dolphins.

I never did see a live professional pesäpallo game—only televised ones, flipping through the state-owned channels on weekends. The players compete in small dirt stadiums, more like a high school facility than even a minor league ballpark in the U.S. They wear light helmets something like bicycle helmets, and full-body uniforms covered in advertisements, like the ones worn by race car drivers. It's been harder to find sponsors, though, since a gambling scandal a few years back. Some Superpesis players, frustrated by and struggling on professional players' meager salaries, started betting on and then purposely throwing their games. Like the U.S. MLB strike, the scandal disillusioned fans and drove down attendance.

Although professional pesäpallo is suffering, the amateur version is alive and well. Attendance at the Päämajakoulu staff-student game is universal. A crackling announcement goes out over the PA that I don't fully understand, but I know enough to follow the exodus down the hallway and out into the yard where the children overflow, climbing the wrought iron fence to stand on the sidewalk outside; they aren't making a break for it, just trying to claim a better view. Another teacher spots me and summons me over to the bike racks, where the rest of the staff has congregated. They have heard I am very good at pesäpallo.

"Yeah, against eleven-year-olds," I say.

My coworkers look disapprovingly at my sandals. Today, everyone except me has brought sneakers. Apparently, my grasp of the Finnish language has not improved as drastically as I might like to think. I shrug and tell them it's all right; I'll run and field as best I can. The game has been delayed by a choir performance for the retiring woodshop teacher, so it's already unlikely I'll see much playing time. Like baseball, pesäpallo uses nine men in the field; there are lots more than nine teachers, so we send out our best. I insist I am not among them, and to my relief, they believe me. A sixth grade teacher who also happens to be a star player on a regional soccer team makes the first out in the first inning, but the sixth graders manage several runners on base, and one run. The students are making a good showing, and the crowd is ecstatic.

My nonrenewable contract at Päämajakoulu is up at the end of the school year and I'm not legally eligible to look for work elsewhere. I'd begun applying for teaching jobs in other countries when there was still snow on the ground, when the sun set at two PM, when I thought I'd vomit if the cafeteria served one more tater tot made of shredded beets. But now, with the beautiful spring weather and hundreds of students laughing and cheering in the sunshine, my heart starts to break a little. Not for the Finnish man I am dating—by spring we both know the relationship won't outlive my job contract—but for this country, for the fifth-place sprinter everyone adores, for lard and fish bowls, for drinking the clear blood of a birch tree, for my generous, self-confident students. Finland is the most beautiful country in the world. Finland is the best place on earth. I love them and their moon-baseball, their sport played proudly in four lonely countries. I love them for hitting easy pitches and running backwards and not apologizing for it, for saying this, this is the best kind, the truest kind of baseball.

The teachers get two more outs, and the sixth graders grab gloves and take the field. We lead with our best: the soccer star, the lanky assistant headmaster, the school caretaker. Both sides have been playing fast and loose with the batting order; the heavyset headmaster is allowed to bow out cheerfully while I get shoved up to the plate, even though I haven't fielded. We've scored two runs but have two outs and a single runner on base. The children are disheartened but think they'll have enough time in the next inning to turn the tide. They can afford to cheer for me.

I don't want an American to lose the pesäpallo game for the teachers; I don't want an American to screw up at baseball in front of a bunch of Finnish children. I shoulder the bat and connect with the yellow ball.

It bounces in the outfield and I make it to first/third easily, even with my feet slipping in sandals. Two more batters, two more hits: the woodshop teacher, the long-term substitute for a third grade teacher on maternity leave. The next teacher is thrown out at first as I'm running down the left foul line towards home. The inning ends with the teachers still leading 2–1, and with American honor intact. Our fielders go back out and the next inning begins. Two students make it on base but two more strike out, and before their side can tie the game, the bell rings. The students howl—not only have they lost until next spring, but they have to go inside to class. The teachers have to go back into class too, but we march into the school victorious.

In the staff lounge I check my phone minutes and try to decide whether I can afford to make an international call to my father to tell him I upheld our national reputation in an international exhibition match. I try to figure out how to tell him, if I should tell him, if he will be pleased or offended to learn this: after all his efforts, after being born and bred—every one of us, the athletes and the fans and the clumsy and the dispassionate—to believe that baseball is America's national sport, it is only here on this May morning in Mikkeli, Finland, an hour from the Russian border, three hours from Helsinki, five hours south of the Arctic Circle, running left towards third base, that I am finally the grateful citizen of a baseball nation.

Freddy the Fan

Sean Wilentz

Baseball is nearly incomprehensible without a sense of history. It's hard not to imagine that at the second baseball game ever played, fans and commentators were already looking backward. Here, historian Sean Wilentz applies his research skills to the role of curator—in this case, of an imaginary (for now, at least) Baseball Fans' Hall of Fame. [L. G.]

One-eyed Freddy the Fan seems to attend every game at Yankee Stadium. He's certainly there every time I am. No matter the weather, Freddy wears his team cap and satin team jacket. He carries a freshly executed cardboard sign, with some clever "Freddy Sez" line neatly composed in rounded, handwritten capital letters, commenting on the team's current tribulations or triumphs. And he passes around his signature items, a dented frying pan with a flaking painted shamrock in the middle and a spoon just the right size and heft for the fans to smack a few loud rings out of the good-luck pan.

You may not know about Freddy the Fan unless you are a Yankee fan yourself. His real name is Fred Schuman. A native of the Bronx, he was born (as near as I can tell: I've chatted with Freddy, but mainly about baseball) in the early 1920s. According to his less-than-lavish personal Web site, www.freddysez.com (it is the twenty-first century, remember), he lost his right eye playing stickball on 178th Street when he was nine. His all-time favorite Yankee is Lou Gehrig. He has a regular route through the Stadium: first three innings in the upper deck ("because the fans are so enthusiastic up there"), middle innings in the loge, then finishing off with the suits down-stairs. He used to make his signs at a seniors' center on Gerard Avenue in the Bronx, though I've heard he's recently moved to Manhattan. A lot about Freddy is mysterious. But he's an important man.

• • •

The Yankees' management does not embrace Freddy publicly, or put him on its website. Unlike John Adams, the famous fan in Cleveland who thunders away on a bass drum out in center field, Freddy never shows up on national television during games. The Yankees' radio announcers have not, to my knowledge, once uttered his name. Yet Freddy gets his message across the airwaves as well as the Internet, as the monotone of spoon smacking pan, sometimes adagio, sometimes presto, soars above the crowd's din. It must be a harsh, bizarre sound to uninformed viewers or listeners. The rest of us, Freddy's fellowship, hear the clanks and know Freddy is at the game and making his rounds. In April, the banging is as glorious as the first robin's chirps. For the rest of the season, it is a form of reassurance.

• • •

I recently read in the *Boston Globe* about an intense fan and baseball histo-rian named Peter J. Nash who is trying to get a Baseball Fans' Hall of Fame started in Cooperstown. Why this idea hasn't yet occurred to the official lords of baseball may say a great deal about the lords' priorities. As long as teams have played for money, there have been outstanding fans whose extreme passion, loyalty, and eccentricity set them apart from the average devotee. They are as much a part of baseball lore as Abbott and Costello's "Who's on First?" routine, or Russ Hodges's call of Bobby Thomson's "shot heard 'round the world," or any number of other things featured at the Hall of Fame. The main difference may be that unlike the players, managers, and owners enshrined in the Hall of Fame, Immortal Fans draw no salary for their fervor and ingenuity. They do what they do purely for love. It's long past time for that love to be requited and honored. Permanently.

• • •

The new Fans' wing might start with a solitary display on a glass-enclosed pedestal of one of Hilda Chester's famous brass cowbells. Chester remains, thanks partly to the mystique of the old Brooklyn Dodgers, the most legendary of the great baseball lovers. For thirty years, beginning in the 1920s, she attended nearly every game at Ebbets Field, surviving two heart attacks and decades of annual disappointment until the Dodgers finally won the World Series in 1955. When, two years later, the Dodgers broke all Brooklyn's heart by decamping to Los Angeles, Hilda Chester—with her stringy gray hair, rowdy profanity, cowbell serenades, and unshakable preference for the bleachers (even after Dodgers manager Leo Durocher gave her a lifetime pass to the grandstand)—was nearly as much the face of the team as the cartoonist Willard Mullins's famous gap-toothed Brooklyn bum.

The story (as told in Peter Golenbock's oral history, *Bums*) goes that Durocher, during one of the team's bad stretches, got fed up with an obnoxious, pestering, disgruntled fan and, armed with brass knuckles, punched him out. The fan sued. Hilda, who adored Leo, testified in court for the defense, perjured herself, and saved Durocher's bacon.

"This man called me a cocksucker," she lied, "and Leo came to my defense."

Greater love hath no fan. If the Hall of Fame's archivists could salvage Babe Ruth's locker, surely they can track down one of Hilda's bells.

Just past the Chester display, the Fans' wing's visitors might enter a large room cluttered with showcases and wall displays. A large exhibit would be devoted to the Royal Rooters, originally a band of Roxbury Irishmen that later came to include Brahmin socialites, that from the late 1890s until the end of World War I cheered on, first, the Boston Nationals and, after 1901, the Red Sox. The display could include the sheet music for the song

"Tessie," whose lyrics the Rooters often twisted around to slander opposing teams.

Elsewhere in the room, there might be megaphones from St. Louis and beer cups from Chicago. The floor could be littered with hot dog wrappers and peanut shells (resupplied daily) that crunch underfoot. The True Life Deranged Fan display might have the .22 rifle (or an exact replica of the rifle) with which an obsessed young Cubs supporter, Ruth Ann Steinhagen, shot her idol, first baseman Eddie Waitkus in his hotel room after the Cubs traded him to the Phillies in 1949. ("I'm sorry that Eddie had to suffer so...," Steinhagen said before being judged legally insane. "I had to relieve the tension I have been under the past two weeks.") Waitkus recovered and hit .284 in 1950, helping the Phillies to win the pennant. He then achieved literary immortality as the model for Roy Hobbs in Bernard Malamud's *The Natural*.

There might be a small library of books written by or about baseball fans. Philip Roth's *The Great American Novel* would be there next to Malamud's classic. If possible, the Hall's librarian (working pro bono) will track down the manuscript of Zane Grey's story "Old Well-Well" for display (again, if possible) with some memento of the real-life "Old Well-Well," a leather-lunged New York Giants fan named Frank Wood. Near the books would be two grandstand seats salvaged from the Polo Grounds. Interested readers may use them. But empty, the seats would form the Unfortunate Fans exhibit—dedicated not to those generations of Red Sox and White Sox and Cubs fans who never saw their teams win the Series, but to the great theolo-gian Reinhold Niebuhr and his daughter, now well known among the literatias the editor and author Elisabeth Sifton. On October 3, 1951, Niebuhr took his girl to see the last game of the three-game, pennant-deciding playoff between the Giants and the Dodgers. They left after the eighth inning, with the Dodgers comfortably ahead, 4 to 1. So they missed by minutes seeing Bobby Thomson's legendary "shot heard 'round the world"—possibly the most dramatic moment in baseball history.

In one corner of the room might be the sawed-off top of the flagpole that a Cleveland rooter climbed after the Indians won the 1948 Series, vowing not to come down until they repeated the win. (They didn't, and he did.) On a wall would hang the drum played by the Dodgers' Sym-phoney Band to mock knocked-out visiting pitchers trudging off to the showers. Beneath it would be a stuffed goat, a stand-in to symbolize the still-living curse William "Billy Goat" Sianis placed on the Chicago Cubs when the management ordered Sianis and his goat (whom he had placed in the box seat adjoining his) ejected from Wrigley Field during the fourth game of the 1945 World Series—the last Series, to this date, played in Wrigley. From the ceiling would hang dozens of bedsheet banners, with pride of place given to the first one ever to proclaim, "Let's Go Mets!" And, of course, there would be room set aside, one day— but no day soon—for Freddy "the Fan" Schuman's signs and spoon and frying pan.

As it happens, Freddy may be headed to the Hall of Fame even if the Fans' Wing never gets built. An unofficial Yankee fan website reported a couple of years ago that after receiving some inquiries, the Hall agreed to feature Freddy's wares among its cases of sliding pads and tattered ancient baseball cards.

If the story is true, millions of Yankee haters will blanch at Freddy the Fan being singled out to the exclusion of their own teams' boosters. They will have a point; Yankee haters always have a point. But to complain will be a missed opportunity. Fred Schuman deserves immortality, but so do the dozens of others who came before him and the ones who will come after him. He might prove the lever to upend an injustice that has lasted too long.

The Inherent Human Transgression That Is Umpiring: A Slovene Case Study

Rick Harsch

By natural disposition an anti-authoritarian personality, I can say for sure that my first outburst against an autocrat outside my home was aimed at an umpire on the baseball field. I'm proud to say that in my memory he was in the right and I was simply emulating Leo Durocher. Even at the time I knew in the back of my head I was acting. The number of authority figures I despise has grown over the years, but baseball umpires hold a special place in my spleen. Denkinger is mentioned in my essay, but generally I hold umpires to be a homogeneous group—it's the managers I remember as individuals: their tirades, their refusals to allow umpires to anticipate calls, expand or squeeze strike zones, or simply exist for very long without comeuppance. From Durocher to Earl Weaver to Billy Martin and now Bobby Cox, who is on the verge of setting the most important record in baseball history—for most ejections—these, my allies, stand for my innate individual freedom.

The last thing a self-exiled American wants to do in his foreign home is come off as an ugly American—or so one would think. Although I try to believe this myself (as a writer living in Slovenia), I can't help but think the truth is Americans are ugly.

This should not be taken as an apology, more as something to make my self-aggrandizing stories easier to swallow. For instance, I think it was pretty funny when during a baseball game between the team I manage, Mečarice ("swordfish"), and Zaj ki ("rabbits"), the umpire (the umpire; we only get one per game) told me I had to put out my cigarette and pour out my beer, and I refused to do so on the grounds that Joe Torre—one manager well known here—drinks and smokes during games. Actually, I don't think he does, but I remember Jim Leyland smoked, and probably Lou Piniella, too. Anyway, my tale had the same sort of effect as citing a Supreme Court decision. This unhumble homunculus softened his face, said "oh," in English, "okay," and the game resumed with me drinking and occasionally smoking.

The game resumed, and umpiring resumed, and if you recall that son of a bitch Don Denkinger screwing the Cards out of the Series in 1985, you'll know just what that means. As the game progressed, this Napoleonesque arbiter blew one call after another, until I was obliged by the laws of base-ball to interrupt the game for at least fifteen minutes. The funniest moment came when he got so mad at me he said like a little kid, in English, to my coach, "Tell him I won't speak English to him anymore." So I said to my coach, "Then tell him I won't call him a pizda in English either." I would take a major league fastball to the rib cage to witness his befuddlement one more time. Oh: pizda, a word used commonly by all speakers of Slovene, literally means cunt. I pause to reflect: what could be uglier than to use English in Slovenia to outwit a Slovene man nice enough to speak to me in English given that I'm too dense to learn Slovene? The answer to that is pretty simple: That's no man, that's my umpire.

The Slovene umpire is generally so authoritarian, and his authority is so generally accepted, that it came as a surprise to my own players that I made it a point to engage in at least one savage, prolonged argument per game. What surprised me was that even opposing managers would try to stop me from, as one of them (who should have been wearing a long skirt and thick pantyhose when he said it) put it, "taking away from the integrity of the game." Tell it to Durocher, pizda. (I have since helped change this craven attitude. Just last year a small mob of my teammates chased an umpire to his car after a game, intending to do him bodily harm—the most rabid player was restrained just in the nick of time, and the umpire made his escape. Earlier that year, a player from one of the old guard teams threw a helmet at an umpire, hitting him in the chest protector, a piece of equipment that should be banned.)

In American baseball, one of the arts of managing is knowing when to stage a moment to get thrown out of a game. In Slovenia, the art I nearly perfected as a manager was knowing how to avoid getting thrown out of the game, since the financial penalty that goes along with that was more than my team could afford. But I had to protect the integrity of this great game from the cultural influences of foreigners, even if they were in their own country. What I try to get across is that the baseball field is a country of its own.

This is precisely the point I was making the one time I did, sort of, get thrown out. The umpire, Franko, bless his innumerable imperfections and may he rot in hell, had scolded my pitcher for swearing when he walked a batter. Within a few pitches he swore again, this time because my catcher threw him the ball as he was walking back to the mound and the ball hit him in the ass. I argued that a man who gets hit in the ass by a thrown baseball has every right to curse. I believe what I said was something like "This isn't a fucking church, you fucking moron." And of course Franko told me to watch my language, which was all the more reason to increase the voltage as I further explained that language is neither here nor there on the ball field. Soon he told me I was out of the game. I told him that he could not throw me out of the game because he hadn't given me a warning. He told me I was out of the game. I said he couldn't throw me out without a warning: "Don't you know anything about American baseball, you fucking nun?" And I smoked a cigarette, and then we got three outs and I went out to coach third base, as I do when we're up, and Franko wouldn't allow the game to resume until I got off the field, and I refused, citing constitutional law (improperly, I knew), and the standoff lasted until the manager of the other team, a good enough guy, talked Franko into letting me stay in the game. Only months later, after the fine was paid, did my own players have the guts to admit to me that we had been fined half the norm, since it wasn't clear whether I had been kicked out or not.

Just as the baseball field is not a church, neither is it properly the space to derive insight into the Slovene character, however much one may be tempted. As I said, the baseball field is a country of its own. Here's a good example. We were playing the Yankees of Slovenia in Ljubljana (I'm really not so bad with Slovene and especially Slovene names, but I can't remember this team's real name, because I simply hate them too much and so refer to them only as something like "those assholes"), a game rescheduled to a Sunday night to accommodate some pettiness on their part, meaning we had to drive from the coast ("swordfish," remember), play the game, and then drive back late on that same Sunday night. I love my team, my boys, but baseball in Slovenia was limited to a four-team league for at least twenty years and this was our expansion team's first year and we had no chance against the established teams (though we regularly kick the shit out of the other new team, our natural rival; my first managerial victory was a 41 to 4 rout). The Assholes, in fact, beat us 39 to 1 in my second game as manager, even after an inspirational speech I gave my team, reminding them that though they had got clobbered in their first game, they had the character and natural ability to beat anybody. Turns out, pitching matters as much as they say it does. Imagine one team starting Steve Carlton and the other starting José Canseco. So, 39 to 1. Well, this next game would have been on our territory, but we didn't have a field, so we had to go up there again for a thorough beating. After our sacrifice, we found the Assholes were playing only to get the game over with as fast as possible; once they got the normal eight- or nine-run lead (in the first inning), they started striking out on purpose and not advancing runners on passed balls and that sort of thing. After two innings of this bullshit, I called a meeting at home plate with their manager and the umpire and said we wanted a real game. All agreed, but nevertheless they continued in the same fashion. Finally, in the fourth, I ordered my pitcher to walk the bases loaded when he had two men on. The next batter swung at a ball that went to the backstop, no runners advanced, and so I ordered the pitcher to walk in a run. The batter swung at the first two intentional balls and the inning was over. I pulled my team from the field, informed the umpire that the other team had forfeited, that we therefore had won (the other team's pitcher was throwing a no-hitter, incidentally), and that anyone who felt different could kiss my ass.

The ensuing hijinks illustrate my thesis that the baseball field is a country unto itself, complete with a fully developed sociopolitical system. The guy who most vehemently objected to my decision—being too dense to get how we were being humiliated—was on my team. He was simply out to enjoy a ball game—he was playing for the fun of it!—and was outraged that I had stopped the action prematurely. We may call him the communist. A colleague from the school I am sometimes allowed to work at was on the team at the time, so I said, "Rok, what's your opinion?" "I don't care," he said, "you're the manager." But when he found out we could be fined what would amount to about five dollars per team member, he told me he had changed his mind because "if it affects my wallet I think it's wrong." We may call Rok the capitalist. The biggest pain in the ass about the whole thing was that we had to have a democratic meeting after the game to discuss my unilateral, therefore dictatorial, decision. We may call me the dictator. My closest friends on the team, three of the best players as well, went to get drunk in Ljubljana instead of returning to the coast and would have skipped the meeting anyway. We may call them the anarchists (the people the democratic state most needs, yet, of course, can neither heed nor hear). That leaves the rest of the players, who earnestly discussed the matter to no avail (in that the decision regarding the money was out of their hands and no one would dare depose me). We may call them the everymen, citizen dupes.

I rest my pen. The baseball field could be anywhere: Slovenia, Hungary, Oregon.

Ah, but the outcome of the story. Leaving the field for a moment, we see evidence of Slovenia's Manichean descent and decidedly Balkan character. When I was trying to get a permanent residence visa, the interior minister's coastal representative told me it was impossible—he laughed as he was telling me this—because I needed a work permit, which I couldn't get without a permanent residence visa. "So it is impossible, you see," he said, grinning. Within two weeks I had both the permit and the visa. This is a small country, small enough that even the bureaucrats are humane and what can't be done can certainly be rigged. So, too, with baseball; within a few days everyone in Slovenia's baseball world knew what the insane Mečarice manager had done, agreed I was insane and what I had done was stupid, and so decided our team must have forfeited the game because one of our players was hurt and we didn't have a substitute. No fine was issued, and our team had nothing to do with the perpetrated fiction. As far as I am concerned, we won that game without getting a hit.

• • •

Because my brain has a sort of apperceptual integrity, I am always aware of its tendency to forge ahead despite its uselessness. One way it does this odd noctambulism is by imagining historical figures as umpires. Try it. If you hate umpires on principle, as I do, you'll find that an interesting paradox arises and even someone as loathsome as Nixon—if only his influence had been limited to the ball field—can somehow become a likeable figure (warning: this does not work with Kissinger, who is demonstrably not human).

Take the 2005 playoffs and that dolt who called strike three on the White Sox catcher A. J. Pierzynski yet allowed him to remain safely at first base. How like Nixon the ump was after the game explaining away his screwup. Yet as a Sox fan, how marvelous, how luminous, I find his ineptitude and duplicity. And think of lonely Dick rambling on in an echoing White House—how human to be fooled by Pierzynski's strange about-face and dash. And how Nixonesque to cover up what natural human befuddled behavior had shown through. Imagine whoever you like, and in any circumstances—the game can remove you from life for hours. . . . *The umpire at second, Gandhi, has yet to make the call. . . . It looks like the chief umpire, Bush, has declared the Yankees the winners—Ned, have you ever seen that happen in the first inning with the team down by five? . . . It looked like the tag beat*

DiMaggio's foot, but Garibaldi, known as the fairest of men in blue... This is the first time I've actually seen the umpires lynched, much less the both of them. Sacco made the original call and Vanzetti upheld it... the word we're getting in the booth is that Thucydides overruled him, despite having left the park in shame after blowing the call at third in the fifth...

Who do you think would make a better umpire, Tito or Churchill? Though we must condemn Churchill for his warmongering, his contempt for poor folk the world over, and his astonishingly thorough betrayal of the Poles, among many other things, he would certainly look great behind home plate with his mask off waiting for Earl Weaver to challenge his authority. As for Tito, he's Bobby Cox and Whitey Herzog rolled up into one—not an umpire. This is a particularly Slovene slant on my inutile cogitations, for the very route my team takes to Ljubljana is almost precisely that which Churchill tried to convince Tito to allow the Allies to take during World War II. We drive from Istria, up through the Kras region, through the Ljubljana gap, and get our asses kicked by a team from the capital—week after week. From his cave, surrounded by overwhelming German might—think Herzog pinch-hitting Clint Hurdle against a lefty in the ninth, down by two, Hurdle hitting the one important triple of his life and the Cards winning—Tito put out word that Winston was not to step foot on any soil that was inevitably to be Yugoslav. The reason? If the Allies landed there, the territory would not become Yugoslav. The storm surrounding Trieste and the end result, the London Memorandum, more than bore this out.

I don't apologize for taking up a reader's time with my historical daydreaming, which is an inevitable mix of my American baseball blood and my life in Slovenia. My team, composed of young men with Italian, Slovene, Austrian, Bosnian, Croatian, Serbian, Hungarian, Macedonian, Albanian, and at least seven more types of blood if you count my own, now plays its home games on a borrowed field in Italy, about a forty-five-minute drive from here. The players' family homes are on land formerly occupied by Romans, Huns, Avars, Venetians, Hungarians, Austrians, French, Austro-Hungarians, Italians, Germans, and (some would say) Yugoslavians, that is now called Slovenia. Their traditions are deeply rooted, multifarious, often simple, and often complex; and though for most Slovenes baseball isn't included among them, I am proud that I have added something to the repertoire of these young men.

I have mentioned Franko. Franko made the single worst call I have ever seen in my baseball life. Mirjan Mati, or Gigi, our fastest player, hit a liner into the left center gap and raced around to third for a stand up triple, the ball on the relay throw bouncing about nine feet down the line toward home plate, passing Gigi after he had come to a rest with his hands on his hips. I didn't see or hear Franko's "Out!" call; I was looking at Gigi and saw his bewilderment, which quickly turned into the pacific, wry smile of a man with a mild soul and a finely tuned notion of where events nestle into context. Even I was calm. When Franko saw me simply looking his way he hurried up to say, "I just can't see everything from here," having a Nixonesque moment. A couple innings later, our Billy Martin figure, Zmago Furlani, lined one into left that went over the flysch rock wall but bounced back onto the field after hitting a wooden fence that keeps bullets from a shooting range on the other side from picking us off as we play. I was bemused, even a little warmed, seeing Franko running up the third base line to get a better look at what he was about to call a ground rule double. Allowing my team to riot in protest without me, I went out and retrieved the opposition's left fielder, leading him literally by the arm up to Franko, and when the guy admitted it was over the wall, Franko reversed his call. What a lovable guy our Franko was becoming. In the next half of the inning I was forced to fill in at first base for Zmago, who had twisted an ankle hopping berserk around Franko before the call was changed. We were well ahead of Novo Mesto, our whipping boys, so if principle meant nothing, nothing would have happened; but a rare Novo Mesto run scored because Franko anticipated the call, as I could well see from where I stood, for the throw beat a runner who not only slowed up but didn't have the wit to slide, and was tagged by Gigi with enough space between his foot and home plate for Churchill to march his army of occupation through. You cannot allow an umpire—ever—to get away with anticipating a call. And then better that he simply lie about it. In fact, if he anticipates the call, I don't want to hear him admit it. Well, we were up about twenty-five to two, and it was the last Novo Mesto at bat, and I strolled toward Franko, strolled slowly enough I turned a couple of times toward my boys, and thus saw a most beautiful thing: one here, two or three there, soon all of them, even before I reached Franko, were lying down under the sun, on consecrated baseball grass, having along with me unknowingly conspired in creating a new ritual, one that lasts ten to fifteen minutes, and is undertaken once per Mečarice baseball game in Slovenia.

The Old Man

George Vecsey

The Old Man talks to me every day, in that raspy whisky voice of his. He would clamp his paw on your forearm, like one of those so-called Denver Boots the police put on the tires of illegally parked cars. You could not pry him off.

"Wait a minute," he would bellow. "I'm trying to tell you something."

What was Casey Stengel trying to tell us? Usually, something practical relating to baseball, but often it was about the weirdness of baseball, the intricacies of it, like life itself.

The Old Man used to say, "Every day in baseball you see something you never saw before."

Early in the 2004 season, on national television, Roger Clemens of the Houston Astros was pitching to Barry Bonds of the San Francisco Giants. The broadcasters said it was the first time in baseball history that a pitcher with 300 victories had ever pitched to a slugger with 600 home runs.

Right away I thought: "The Old Man."

It happens a lot. A ball takes a squirrelly path, a player commits a gaffe, and I find myself muttering, "I've never quite seen *that* before."

Strange things happened around Casey and he was alive enough and alert enough to sputter or laugh about them.

Of all the managers and coaches I've been around, Casey Stengel taught me the most. I was part of that motley band Casey called "my writers." Some of his ballplayers were wise enough to learn from him too.

"You knew when he was being funny," said Ron Swoboda, who played one season for Casey with the Mets and still treasured it four decades later. "And you knew when he was serious."

Swoboda was under no illusions, then or now. He was a raw kid with a bit of power, and he was the best Casey had. The Old Man had managed DiMaggio and Berra and Mantle, and now he had a player he called "Suh-boda."

But somehow or other, Casey Stengel, in his four years with the dreadful Mets, performed a more amazing job than he had with the lordly Yankees. For this new franchise he created an image of lovability that has barely eroded decades later.

Managers and coaches are often handed the burden of being role models, doing that job for the rest of society. Molding character was not exactly Casey's goal in life. He was no kindly Mister Chips. He referred to himself as "the slickest manager in baseball"—and he expected others to be slick too.

Ron Swoboda learned that lesson in 1965. He was a husky rookie out of Baltimore, not yet twenty-one years old, bright and outspoken, but in baseball experience still a busher.

In an early-season game in old Busch Stadium in St. Louis, the Mets had a three-run lead in the ninth. Swoboda was playing right field as the rain ended and a strong sun emerged, directly in his eyes.

"The smart thing would have been to call time and get my sunglasses," Swoboda recalled in 2004. "But I figure, 'One more out, I can handle it.' Then Dal Maxvill hits a little flair that either would have been a single or I would have caught it, but I lose sight of it, and I have no clue how to play it, so three runs score and the game is tied.

"I know I screwed up," Swoboda recalled, "and I come up to bat the next inning and I make out and by now I am an emotional bomb. I stomp on my old fiberglass helmet. I'm gonna crush it. But the open end is facing up, and my foot gets caught, and it closes around my foot and I'm jumping around on my other foot."

The description from somebody in the dugout was that Swoboda resembled "a demented chicken."

"Casey comes up the stairs like he's 25," Swoboda recalled, "and he grabs me with his good hand. He had broken his wrist that spring and I figure he's going to hit me with his cast. He's yelling, 'When you screwed up the fly ball, I didn't go into your locker and break your watch, so don't you break the team's equipment!' Then he said, 'Go sit down!'

"You know the movie, *A League of Their Own*, where Tom Hanks says, 'There's no crying in baseball?' Bullshit. I sat there and cried. I figured my career was over."

Only later did Swoboda figure out that Casey had affection for him, the way he did for a few of his brighter young players. He could be tough on the Youth of America, but he was preparing them.

It made him nuts if ballplayers didn't listen. He loved to tell the story about when he was managing the Yankees in 1951 and escorted young Mickey Mantle out to right field before an exhibition in Ebbets Field in Brooklyn. Casey wanted to show Mantle the complexities of the wall, but Mantle mostly stared at him, unable to fathom that his manager had once patrolled this very field.

"He thinks I was born old," Casey muttered to "my writers," who functioned as his Greek chorus. The writers' job was to hum appropriately when he made a good point.

Casey's outlook was based on his experiences. He'd been to Europe and Japan before it was convenient. He was born in the late nineteenth century and he still buzzes in my head early in the twenty-first century.

People said he spoke in Stengelese, a dialect straight out of Lewis Carroll's *Jabberwocky*. Other times he spoke blunt Anglo-Saxon that had earthy folk wisdom to it.

In his monologues, he called other people "Doctor," so we referred to him as "The Doctor." If we debated him, he would frequently say, "You're full of shit and I'll tell you why." He was the first person I remember who used the term "you asshole" as a debating point, without incurring harsh feelings—no easy trick. And when the umpires' decisions and logic went against the Mets in those early gruesome years, Casey used to say, "They screw us because we're horseshit." And he was right. The umpires did, and the Mets were.

He could ramble on, if he wanted to. In 1958, he captivated a Senate hearing into the fairness of baseball's antitrust exemption, filibustering until the senators laughingly begged for mercy.

Casey's testimony is an American classic, right up there with Nixon's Checkers speech and Marilyn Monroe singing "Happy Birthday, Mr. President," well worth seeking out with a simple Google search. Somehow, if you listened long enough, you figured it out.

Charles Dillon Stengel (born July 30, 1890, in Kansas City, Missouri) took a circuitous route to being one of the immortal sports figures in his country. He was a quite decent outfielder in the National League and then he was burdened with the stigma of failure as a manager. In nine horrendous seasons with the Brooklyn Dodgers and Boston Braves, he never once finished in the top half of the eight-team league.

He then managed well enough in the fast Pacific Coast League to earn the Yankees' call in 1949. Joe DiMaggio and many of the older Yankees thought he was a clown, a minor leaguer, but he soon showed he had enough nerve to run the Yankees his way.

"He had his funny moments with the Yankees, but he wasn't this lovable old clown, either," said Swoboda, who later became a broadcaster and a student of his sport, particularly Casey's career.

"He was a tough old bastard," Swoboda added.

Foisted upon the older Yankees, Stengel showed no fear of improvising and tinkering and taking command. He ran a platoon system at some positions like left field, alternating a left-handed hitter like Gene Woodling with the right-handed Hank Bauer. Neither of these crusty warhorses liked being platooned, except when they cashed their World Series check almost every autumn. He even put the great DiMaggio on first base for one game, just to prove he could.

In World Series games, he was not afraid to go a long way with hot relief pitchers like Joe Page, or use one of his best starters, Allie Reynolds, in relief, or bring in an obscure pitcher like Bob Kuzava in a tight situation. He was utterly fearless, and he answered to no one.

His main disciple with the Yankees was a scrappy little infielder named Billy Martin, who had known Stengel back in the Pacific Coast League.

"I love that old man with the ball in his sock," Martin would say, referring to a lump on Casey's ankle, a souvenir from having been hit by a taxi one rainy night in Boston. (One columnist nominated the cabby as the man who did the most for Boston sports that year.)

Martin loved Casey right up to the moment Martin was involved in a brawl in a nightclub, the Copacabana, along with several more valuable Yankees. The Yankees' front office traded Martin away, but Martin blamed Casey and did not talk to him for a decade.

There was very little parental about Casey Stengel. Casey and his wife, Edna Lawson Stengel, did not have children, for reasons only they knew. People did not discuss such things back then. She had been an actress in New York, but they settled near her affluent banking family in Glendale, California. I remember her as willowy, cultured and friendly, a grand old lady in my youthful eyes, and formidable enough to deflate some of Casey's bluster.

I encountered Casey during his last pennant run in 1960. I was twenty years old, just graduating from Hofstra College, and my boss at *Newsday*, Jack Mann, thought it was time for me to cover my first major-league game up at Yankee Stadium.

It was a day game, and by 11 AM, Casey was chattering to the writers in the dugout, blending tales from the olden days with fresh insights into the previous night's game. He was in the process of moving Clete Boyer into the regular lineup at third base, benching the veteran Gil McDougald, and he discussed it at great lengths, with apologies to nobody.

The pregame drill is very different today in the age of the microphone and the camera and the tight security. Joe Torre conducts a useful 15-minute update to the media swarm before the game, seated in the dugout while the Yankee Stadium sound system blares its inanities.

Back then, Casey held court. On my first day covering the Yankees, I was so fascinated with him that I sat in the dugout and gaped, not noticing that I was the only writer left.

Finally Casey turned to me and said, "Young man, you'll have to leave now because otherwise I'll have to put you in the starting lineup." It was about five minutes to game time.

His action revealed the essential Stengel. He could have made me feel like an idiot for staying too long, but he let me off the hook with a joke. He was not like some managers then and now who delight in bullying a newcomer. He saved his best stuff for his bosses, or his stars, or lions of the media like Dick Young or Howard Cosell, or critics like Jackie Robinson.

(Robinson—who had been the favorite player in my Dodger-centric household—criticized Stengel in his Mets years, saying Casey tended to snooze in the dugout. "Tell Robi'son he's Chock Full of Nuts," Stengel blurted, aptly referring to the coffee company Robinson had represented.)

Most of the Yankees kept their distance, judging Casey as one lucky eccentric to be able to manage the Berras, Fords, and Mantles.

Casey would not win a popularity contest in his clubhouse. Clete Boyer will never forget kneeling in the on-deck circle in the second inning of the first game of the 1960 World Series.

Then he heard the Old Man shout, "Hold the gun!" Casey was sending up Dale Long to hit for Boyer because the Yankees had fallen behind, 3-1, and had two runners on base. The Old Man's move was not only unorthodox, it was cold.

The Yankees lost that Series in seven games, and Stengel was blasted for not starting his ace, Whitey Ford, until the third game. Ford wound up pitching two shutouts, in the third and sixth games, and critics said he theoretically could have pitched three times if he had opened the Series.

The Yankees dismissed Casey immediately after the Series. He said he would never again make the mistake of turning seventy.

On his body of work—ten pennants and seven World Championships in twelve seasons with the Yankees—Stengel was now one of the great managers in baseball history. He could have stomped off to California and lived very nicely representing his brother-in-law's banks.

However, he was not ready for the civilian world. He still needed "the baseball business" at least as much as it needed him. He was saving up a last act as manager that was, in its own way, more spectacular than his time with the Yankees.

Casey returned to Yankee Stadium in the fall of 1961 to attend a World Series game with the Cincinnati Reds. I remember the buzz as he strode through the cheering crowd of New Yorkers, his formerly gray hair now shockingly reddish. (Milton Gross of the *New York Post* referred to Casey as "Bixby," the name of a shoe polish of the distant past.)

New York got Casey back in 1962, after the New York Mets had been formed in an expansion draft.

There had been a terrible gap in New York after the Dodgers moved to Los Angeles and the Giants moved to San Francisco after the 1957 season. There was nothing like today's glut of televised games and sports highlight shows to keep up with Mays, Clemente, Aaron, and Robinson.

In 1962, the National League stars were coming back to New York to play the Mets, who included some of the worst culls and rejects from other farm systems. Would haughty New York tolerate a dismal baseball team? That was why the man with the rubbery face and the equally flexible syntax had been brought back from California.

"There was a huge longing for National League ball," Swoboda said. "Casey bought time by taking advantage of this."

Casey's job was to teach baseball, win a game here and there, entertain desperate New Yorkers and sell some tickets. He tried the flim-flam approach at times. Dismissing a young pitcher during spring training of 1962, Casey said the Mets wanted to compete for the pennant and could not afford inexperienced players.

This was pure poppycock. Most of the time, Stengel caustically referred to how "the attendance got trimmed," meaning, in his lexicon, that the paying customers had been shortchanged.

Casey also fought publicly with his general manager, George M. Weiss, who had been his boss with the Yankees and had now rescued him from enforced retirement. Casey probably was grateful. But whenever the frugal Weiss tried to retain a player in whom he had invested a few dollars, Stengel thundered that the player was "a fraud."

I can picture him naked, a tough old bird in his early seventies, his Mets uniform lying discarded on the floor of his office, while he pounded his burly chest and proclaimed the entire franchise was "a fraud."

Casey was doing something no other man in "the baseball business" had ever done—he was managing and performing vaudeville at the same time. He was creating a personality for a bad baseball team in the toughest market in the country. He was inventing the New York Mets on the fly.

"He sacrificed some of his legend to keep the media and the fans from turning on the team," Swoboda said.

At the same time, Casey was talking baseball to the fans, the writers and the players.

"Why wouldn't ya wanna . . . ?" was Casey's Socratic prelude to a lecture about some nuance of his business.

The writers and fans tended to get more out of Casey than many of his players. Casey discovered this one day during batting practice when he was delivering a lecture on the batting technique he called "the butcher boy"—chopping downward to knock the ball through a hole in the infield.

Casey looked around at the blank looks of his own players. Then he spotted one pair of alert, intelligent eyes watching his every move, absorbing his every word.

Unfortunately, those eyes belonged to Maury Wills, the shortstop for the Dodgers, the Mets' opponent later in the day. Wills had already won one World Series in 1959 with his resourcefulness and was not above eavesdropping on Casey's seminar. Needless to say, the Old Man did not run Wills off. He was a baseball man, teaching baseball.

Some Mets appreciated him. One was Richie Ashburn, the feisty old center fielder who ran into walls, fought with umpires, batted .306, and brought out the humorous side of an itinerant first baseman named Marvelous Marv Throneberry, who became the personification of the Mets—inept, but also comical. Ashburn hated to lose, and he understood that the Old Man did too. Nobody blamed him when he bailed for a broadcasting job after one season.

Another player who totally got Casey was Rod Kanehl, a vagabond utility player whom Casey had once noticed years earlier at the Yankees' minor-league complex. Casey kept him around the Mets for three seasons because Kanehl hustled and would play any position (seven, ultimately). Kanehl also took up Casey's standing offer of $50 for getting hit by a pitch with the bases loaded.

A Midwesterner like Stengel, Kanehl felt the same fascination with the big city that Stengel once had. As a young Dodger, Stengel had enticed teammates into the rudimentary subway system, blithely losing them and forcing them to find their way back to their hotel. Kanehl also acted as subway tour guide to other Mets, who called him "The Mole." Kanel absorbed Casey's wisdom; he just didn't have enough talent to execute the lessons.

Casey did not escape criticism. In addition to the old sleeping-in-the-dugout charge—why wouldn't you want to snooze out of sheer escapism?—Casey was said to confuse players' identities. One former Met has said that Casey once ordered "Blanchard" to pinch-hit and that the coaches had to tactfully tell Casey that Johnny Blanchard was still employed across the Harlem River with the Yankees. More likely, Casey just mixed up names. He had two pitchers named Bob Miller that first season, so he called one of them "Nelson," either by design or accident.

A nap or a wrong name didn't matter much. The Mets won 40 games and lost 120 in that first season, with two games mercifully rained out.

Casey was managing the worst team in the history of baseball. "You could look it up," Casey often said, a phrase he either borrowed from Ring Lardner, or Ring Lardner borrowed from him.

One catch phrase for that 1962 Mets team was created by a boisterous raconteur with a gift for language. I am speaking here not of Casey Stengel but of Jimmy Breslin.

A gifted writer from New York, Breslin showed up on assignment from *Sports Illustrated* one hot, humid July weekend of 1962. The Mets threw a seventy-second birthday party for Casey in the Chase-Park Plaza Hotel, then the garden spot of St. Louis. (The headwaiter had once pitched batting practice before Cardinals' games; Casey treated him like an equal, even imitating his pitching form.)

Casey spent the reception standing up, drink in hand, commenting on the multi-ineptitudes of his team. Blessed with youthful kidneys, I stayed by his elbow the entire evening.

A year later, a Breslin book came out, entitled *Can't Anyone Here Play This Game?*, a plea ostensibly uttered by Casey during his long monologue that evening in St. Louis.

Not long afterward, Breslin called me for a phone number or something and at the end I said, "Jimmy, just curious, I was at that party for Casey, never left his side, and I don't remember him ever saying, 'Can't anyone here play this game?'"

Long pause.

"What are you, the FBI?" Breslin asked.

Breslin has since admitted he just might have exercised some creative license. Casey never complained about being misquoted. He would have said it if he had thought of it.

I stuck as close as possible to Casey those years. I wasn't looking for a parent or a mentor but I think I was just wise enough to know I would never meet anybody like him again.

There have been entire volumes devoted to those wonderful early days of Casey and the Mets. (I wrote one myself, long out of print, entitled *Joy in Mudville*.) If I could distill the entire four years into one madcap experience, it would be the night of May 4, 1964, in Milwaukee.

By this time, the Mets were marginally better, partially because Casey had spotted a scrappy second baseman named Ron Hunt in spring training of 1963, and installed him at the top of the lineup. On this nippy night in Milwaukee, Hunt tried to score with two outs in the ninth, but was tagged out at home in a rough collision. Then he and the catcher, Ed Bailey, began to mix it up, as both teams milled around home plate.

In the midst of the scrum, a Milwaukee infielder named Denis Menke felt a pair of powerful arms trying to pry him away from the plate. Menke shrugged the man loose. Then he looked down at his assailant and saw the Mount Rushmore profile of the Mets' manager tangled in a bunch of legs. Menke envisioned the next day's front page: "Menke Kills Casey Stengel," and helped pick up the Old Man, who was still sputtering.

After order was restored, Casey totally denied having been anywhere near the fight. However, a couple of his players raved about the combativeness of the Old Man. Casey's story was discredited when he stripped to take a shower, revealing a few new bruises and scrapes.

After getting tossed around like that, most seventy-three-year-old men might retire to their hotel room and take a long hot bath. Casey went out drinking with his writers. We found some bar, where Casey gave a vivid imitation of a tornado that hit Milwaukee twenty years earlier, his battered body getting blown across the bar room by the imaginary high winds.

When the bar closed, eight of us found a rib joint, which turned out to be the hangout of a motorcycle gang. At first, I was a little concerned we might be in for trouble, until one of the cyclists spotted Casey and came over with his girlfriend, who appeared to be sixteen years old, and respectfully asked for an autograph.

Casey, who had gotten bored with his writers, now engaged the motorcyclists in a debate over whether the Braves were willing to trade their brilliant but aging shortstop, Roy McMillan.

"Now, you want to give me McMillan, who is thirty-three, and we don't know if he can throw. Then who do you want, Hook?"

(Jay Hook was a sweet Northwestern graduate with advanced degrees in physics, who could explain why a curveball curved but could not throw one.)

"Hook has won a lot of games for me and he has a lovely family," Casey told the motorcyclists. "Edna says I can't trade him. Would you like to talk to Edna for me?"

Casey and the cyclists talked baseball for about an hour or so, until the writers began falling asleep on the bar.

The next morning I dragged myself down to the coffee shop around nine o'clock. There was the Old Man, finishing a full breakfast, talking baseball with the customers.

As I think about Casey these days, I am struck by the vast amount of alcohol consumed by him and his traveling chorus. Alcohol had no hold over me but in those days you drank to be sociable. I had not yet figured out that you can sip a club soda and lime rather than a scotch and soda and will feel much better the next morning.

Casey used to say, "Whiskey makes you sick when you're well—and well when you're sick,"

He also had an expression for people who lost their composure when they drank too much: "Whiskey-slick." Even with his amazing constitution, Casey could become garrulous or argumentative, might need a friendly arm to get him from the taxi to the hotel elevator.

Having a lot of friends who are alcoholics, recovering or otherwise, I would say that Casey was nowhere near the state of powerlessness that defines alcoholism. The Old Man surely drank a bit, but at the same time he was skillfully ducking or answering questions from his writers.

He kept up his guard but occasionally you would see a glimpse of emotion. Casey had a great deal of respect for Fred Hutchinson, the burly manager of the Reds, who had once battled the Yankees as a pitcher with the Tigers. I will never forget Casey shuddering when he spotted his friend and rival, emaciated from cancer, being taken around the ballpark on a golf cart in 1964. There was no joking from the Old Man that day. The next year, Hutchinson was dead.

That same spring, Casey broke a wrist when he slipped on a wet patch during an exhibition game. Then, late at night on July 25, 1965, Casey fell and broke his hip and needed an artificial ball inserted in his hip socket. On August 30, he called a press conference to say he would resume managing but would not return the following season. At that conference, he horrified Edna by abruptly crossing one leg over another to demonstrate what a good job the surgeons had done.

"Casey!" she blurted, the way wives will.

They stayed home in Glendale after 1965, although Casey was a fixture every spring training in Florida. My daughter, now a sports columnist with the *Baltimore Sun*, can recall being a little girl, sitting on a bar stool at the old Colonial Inn at St. Petersburg Beach, holding a ginger ale and chatting with that nice old couple, Casey and Edna.

In 1969, Casey was around to celebrate the Mets' improbable World Championship, with Gil Hodges now the manager. Ron Swoboda, the Youth of America, made an epic diving catch in right field to help win one game.

The final years were not kind. One season Casey visited the Mets and confided that Edna was fine—"from the neck down," meaning her wit and reason were gone.

Casey died in 1975 and Edna lived three years longer. I see them every day. My wife has made a large montage of our family photographs and she included a photo of Casey and Edna, circa 1965, in a hansom cab, he doffing a top hat, she chucking him under the chin, a striking mixture of aging prophet and ageless beauty.

To this day, when I am taking an iconoclastic stance in my column, I remember asking the Old Man why he was not afraid.

"I can make a living telling the truth," he would bellow.

I think of him every day.

First Base of Last Resort

Matt Wood

*I started writing this essay to champion first base as a defensive
position and correct the injustice I saw in its characterization as a
dumping ground for aging sluggers and weak fielders. As it developed,
though, I realized I was really writing about how my relationship with
the game had changed. Just as erstwhile superstars shuffle down the
Bill James spectrum as their skills decline, I went from thinking I'd play
baseball forever to accepting the fact that it was time to walk away.
But far from making me bitter or disillusioned, letting go of playing
baseball competitively permitted me to be a better fan. Instead of
sulking about how I couldn't hit a curveball or had missed a ground
ball the previous weekend, I could simply enjoy watching the major
leaguers who did it so well. I've learned by now that all relationships
change over time; friends move apart, new people come into your life.
Baseball has stuck with me, for better or worse.*

In the still-sweltering heat of an early July evening, before the sun went
down and the hard brown June beetles started pelting the infield dust
around my feet, I crouched into my position at first base as the pitcher
made his move toward home plate. I had just finished my junior year of
high school and was playing for the Owen Dunn American Legion team,
Indiana Post #5 in Mt. Vernon. To be picked to play was an honor of sorts;
the post had just re-formed the team after a long absence, and the manager
was a former college coach who drew players from three high schools in
the area.

The right-handed batter hit a ground ball in my direction. It wasn't hit particularly hard, but as it left the bat it had a tight clockwise spin that caused it to slice across the grass toward the baseline. I charged the ball, lowered my glove, and came up empty. The ball trickled through my legs, and the runner reached base safely.

"Nice one, Buckner," I heard from the dugout. I glowered at my teammate Eric, who was sitting near the end of the bench with a smug look on his face. He was referring, of course, to Bill Buckner of the Red Sox, who let a weak grounder by the Mets' Mookie Wilson dribble through his legs in Game Six of the 1986 World Series, allowing the winning run to score and ultimately costing the Sox their first Series win in sixty-eight years. It's still the most infamous play ever made by a first baseman, ruining Buckner's legacy and the defensive expectations of first basemen everywhere. The nickname stuck.

Eric had a knack for getting under my skin. He kept up a constant patter, ribbing me about anything that came to his mind. "Hey, Buckner," he'd say, "is that your sister in the stands? Mind if I ask her out?" or "Why'd you miss that curveball, Buckner, never seen one a them out in the boonies?" I tried my best to ignore him and let my play speak for itself, but a nickname like Buckner doesn't augur happy endings in the baseball world.

First base is a position for aging veterans with bad backs and gimpy knees, the place to hide the worst fielders, the slowest runners, and the weakest arms. It's the place for guys with enough offensive skills to command a place in the batting order but no place on the field. Unlike the other positions, which require specific physical skills—the shortstop must have quick feet and a strong arm; the pitcher, extraordinary arm strength and endurance; the catcher, toughness, brains, and a cannon for an arm—first base is a default position, defined mostly by what its players don't have: namely, the skills required for any other position. A first baseman doesn't even get to touch the ball during the congratulatory toss around the horn after strikeouts; instead he turns his back and smoothes the dirt around the base while the ball goes from third to second, then back to the shortstop, who tosses it to the pitcher.

I started playing first base on my first organized T-ball team in Poseyville, Indiana, in 1982 when I was five years old, and aside from some pitching in Little League and a few emergency fill-in games elsewhere, I've never played anywhere else. I like to think I made the decision because my childhood idol, Don Mattingly from nearby Evansville, played that position, but I know that can't be the case; at the time, Mattingly was having his first cup of coffee with the Yankees, long before he posted the kind of all-star numbers that made kids like me worship him. The truth is, my dad, the team's coach, decided I should play first base because I'm lefthanded, and because in T-ball, where there are no pitchers and catchers, I would get to touch the ball more than anyone else. And though he would never admit it, I suspect my dad knew I would be the slowest kid on the field, even at that early age. (I probably also helped his decision during one of our first practices, when I fielded a ground ball in the freshly mown grass while playing second base. The other kids and dads were yelling at me to make the throw to first, but I just stood there, brushing the grass off the ball before I threw it.) So, as a lefty who couldn't play another infield position and whose plodding feet made me unsuitable for the outfield, I was left with only one option. Like generations of first basemen before me, my position was determined by process of elimination.

Many players change positions throughout their careers, often early in their professional careers when the trained eyes of scouts and minor league coaches spot traits that make them better suited for a new role on the field. Most moves signal the player's versatility and raw athletic skill. Babe Ruth could have been a Hall of Fame pitcher had he not switched to the outfield so his powerful bat could be in the lineup every day. Hank Aaron started his career at second before shifting to the outfield, and more recently, Craig Biggio moved to second base after coming up to the majors as a catcher. Both Aaron and Biggio became good defenders at their new positions, a testament to their utility.

Famed baseball writer Bill James once devised a "defensive spectrum" that rated defensive positions by their level of difficulty. On the far right of this scheme was catcher, which James determined to be the most challenging position. First base was on the opposite end:

1B—LF—RF—3B—CF—2B—SS—C

According to James, players very rarely move from left to right on the spectrum, but can usually move right to left on the scale with relative success, as players like Aaron, Biggio, Robin Yount, Dale Murphy, Cal Ripken, and Alex Rodriguez have. Still, a move to first base, as you might guess from its position in the spectrum, carries a taint of decay, a connotation of demotion or compromise.

Some star players move to first near the end of their careers to minimize wear and tear on their aging bodies. Willie Mays, Ernie Banks, Johnny Bench, and Pete Rose all spent significant time at first in their twilight years. In Bench's case, the move saved him the punishment of playing catcher every day. Mike Piazza made a similar move in 2004, splitting time between first and catcher during an injury-plagued season. Other players land at first after getting pushed out of other positions by superior defensive players. The Cardinals' Albert Pujols played third until the Cardinals acquired Scott Rolen, after which Pujols made his move left along the James spectrum to outfield for two seasons. He settled at first full-time in 2004, and became an excellent defensive first baseman. And in the 2005 off-season, the Dodgers signed Nomar Garciaparra to a one-year contract and announced that he would play first base. Garciaparra was once considered one of the best shortstops in the game while playing for the Red Sox but struggled defensively after being traded to the Cubs, eventually moving to third base at the end of 2005. Little worry for him as he joined the Dodgers, though. He expected to learn to play first base in just three months.

I was oblivious to the long tradition of putting the slowest, clumsiest players at first base when I began my baseball career. In my mind, it was the best position on the field. I was playing first base! The first one! Everyone had to come through me, and almost every ball hit on the infield eventually had to be thrown to me, too. Why shouldn't I be proud to play there? After all, my favorite player, Mattingly, won nine Gold Gloves playing first, second only to Keith Hernandez, who won eleven, six of them playing for the Cardinals, my favorite team.

I started paying attention to defensive technique in Little League, where I learned the basics of fielding grounders and began mastering the art of The Stretch. This move—stretching your glove hand and foot in the direction of the throw in order to catch it sooner and beat the runner—is simple but comes in a surprising number of variations. You have to judge the speed and direction of the throw to know when and where to stretch. Is the ball coming in wide? Will you be able to keep your foot on the bag and make the catch, or should you concede the base to the runner to prevent the ball from going out of play? The Stretch can often require the footwork of a ballerina. A high throw might cause you to reach into the air and pirouette as you tiptoe the bag, or you might have time to jump and make a stab with your toe as you land. You might even end up doing the splits to reach as far forward as possible to beat a speedy runner.

In Little League, where the infielders don't exactly have major league arms, The Stretch, along with its counterpart, The Scoop, often means the difference between an out and an error. The Scoop—catching an errant throw by "scooping" it out of the dirt—is the first baseman's best-known defensive weapon. The official rules of scoring are kind to the first baseman; most throws he can't catch result in an error on the thrower. Still, if he had to practice just one defensive play, a first baseman would perfect The Scoop, not so much because it prevents base runners but because a missed Scoop makes him look so bad. It is such an integral part of the first baseman's repertoire, like a layup for a basketball center, that he is expected to pull out every throw, no matter how bad.

To make The Scoop properly, you should keep your glove low to the ground, watching the ball all the way in and catching it just after it bounces. The degree of difficulty depends on where the ball is thrown, the worst place being straight at your shins. In fact, first basemen wear a special glove made specifically to help them scoop bad throws. Whereas most gloves have five fingers stitched together to approximate a hand, the first base glove resembles a wide, flattened lobster claw. Instead of four fingers, it has a round paddle opposing the thumb that can act like a shovel, scooping up a handful of infield dirt along with a poorly thrown baseball. After the round, padded catcher's mitt, it's the most distinctive glove on the field. I got my first one when I was thirteen and starting to play in Senior League, a new league for junior high kids. I was excited about the glove and how it affirmed my special position on the field, not at all concerned with the irony that the autograph stamped in the pocket of my lefthanded glove was that of Mark McGwire, a righthanded player who had converted to first from the pitching mound and third base.

Despite my fancy glove, however, I was never particularly good at The Scoop. Too many short hops off the inside of my knee had made me skittish. Ignoring the cardinal rule of the game—Don't Be Afraid of the Ball— I would turn my head and swing my glove upward hoping to catch the ball with a flourish. Unsurprisingly, I often missed, and betrayed my slow feet as I ran into foul territory to chase the errant throw.

Runners couldn't lead off the base in Little League, but in Senior League, as would-be Rickey Hendersons took their first few cautious steps off the base, I got to stand behind them and point my glove at the pitcher. There isn't much technique to making pickoff plays, just a catch and a tag, but it is a rare opportunity for one player to legally hit another as hard as he can. I enjoyed pounding the diving runners on the back, answering their complaints by daring them to do the same as I took a three-inch lead the next time I reached base. Holding runners on base was far less fun than I thought it would be, though, because it mostly meant that I was out of position for pitches. On those blistering Indiana summer afternoons, as my perennially bad teams suffered through long at bats by the other team, I tired of running back and forth to the base and ended up missing some of the most routine grounders.

Demoting liabilities to first base is primarily a National League phenomenon, since American League teams can dump their defensive white elephants into the designated hitter slot. The White Sox took the glove out of Frank Thomas's hands, as the Mariners did with Edgar Martinez and the Brewers, Blue Jays, and Twins all did with Paul Molitor. But American League first base purists have to endure the special torment of watching a manager struggle with his lineup in the World Series when the games are played in the National League park, sans DH. In 2004, Terry Francona of the Red Sox opted to bench his team's first baseman and leader, Kevin Millar, so that DH David Ortiz could play there and stay in the lineup for Games 3 and 4 in St. Louis. Ortiz was considered such a bad fielder that some Red Sox fans feared he alone could jeopardize the team's chances of winning the Series. In fact, despite his clutch offensive heroics in the AL Championship Series against the Yankees, Francona pulled Ortiz late in both games for defensive replacement Doug Mientkiewicz. The gamble paid off, as the Red Sox won four straight, squashing my hopes that Ortiz would shed light on the importance of first base defense by making a fatal error, handing a game to my beloved Cardinals and costing Boston the Series, just as a certain outfielder–turned–first baseman did in 1986.

Like any young baseball player, if I could add up all the hours I spent practicing the game, the time I spent perfecting my swing would dwarf what I spent fielding grounders or working on defense. To most kids, including me for a time, hitting was the only fun part of the game, whereas playing defense felt like a necessary evil in between at bats. The longer I played first, though, the more pride I took in my place on the diamond. I loved practicing the arcane footwork around the bag, brandishing my special glove. In high school I started wearing black wristbands—Franklins, just like Mattingly wore—on my forearms just below the elbow, smearing eye black on my cheekbones, and pulling my sweat-stained cap low over my eyes, trying to affect a menacing look to oncoming base runners.

I was lucky enough to make the varsity team as a sophomore in high school, mainly because of my bat and not my glove. I had what the coaches called a "pretty" swing, which I have since learned is a compliment laid on any halfway competent lefthanded hitter. I really was a good hitter, though, perfecting that swing with countless hours of hitting baseballs into a net in my backyard. I was always able to make contact and put the ball into play, not blessed with a lot of power but enough to drive in runs. There was an older first baseman already on the team, so I did my part that year by pinch-hitting and playing late-inning mop-up duty in already-decided games. In practice I perfected The Sweep Tag, an advanced variation of The Stretch in which you come off the bag to catch a ball thrown down the line toward home then sweep your glove at the runner to tag him out as he passes. This play is difficult for two reasons: one, it requires enough agility to catch the ball and twist for the tag without losing your balance, and two, if you're one step off you'll get run over. This happened to me twice, the first just a glancing blow but the second resulting in a violent collision with a player twice my size.

My junior year I was the DH all season. I didn't get much chance to use my Mark McGwire glove that year, either, except for the game in which the coach pulled all the starters and made them run laps for making too many fielding errors. Although I played first every day in practice, after two years of minimal game experience I could feel my defensive skills waning. As a senior I finally played full-time in the field, managing to hold my own around the bag, and in the sectional tournament that year, I made the single greatest defensive play of my career. I was holding a runner on with one out when the batter scorched a line drive toward me. I leapt and snared the ball, landing in nearly a sitting position. The runner had guessed wrongly that the ball was going through and was left stranded between bases. I frog-hopped from the squat and flopped onto first base, doubling up the runner and ending the inning. I remember running back into the dugout, head down, listening to the cheers from our crowd, laughing and blushing as my teammates pounded my back. Later that day I drove home the winning run in the championship game, but the memory of that double play remains just as vivid, a singular moment in which all eyes were on me. That play was something only I, at first base, could have made, and I reveled in it.

I entered my second and final season for Owen Dunn that summer on this high note, hoping to continue at least some part of my high school team's success. The prior summer had been a lesson in humility, our team posting a 5–29 record, losing a majority of those games by the "whitewash rule," in which the game is called when one team is winning by ten runs after seven innings. The summer after my senior year, I drove hundreds of miles in my red Camaro to play in desolate, decaying old farm towns like Fairfield, Illinois, and Petersburg, Indiana, fueled by McDonald's Extra Value Meals and gas station candy. We took a beating again, going 6–31 with just as many blowout losses as in the first season.

I managed to put aside my differences with Eric and the other guys from his school that summer, trying to enjoy what I knew would be the end of my competitive baseball career. Like any kid who has ever swung a bat or broken in a new glove, I had always dreamed I could be the next Don Mattingly, rising to stardom in the major leagues with my sweet swing and Gold Glove. But I was realistic; I knew there was something about the real prospects that I didn't have. I knew it when I played against kids the college and pro scouts in the crowd, with their stopwatches and radar guns, watched instead of me. I knew it when I heard the way a top-notch pitching prospect's fastballs hissed by me when I swung and missed. I knew it when I watched other players hit those towering home runs I never could. I broached the subject of my baseball future with my coach once that season. I was heading to Indiana University in the fall, and I figured he could help me decide if I had a chance at walking on the team. "The first thing they'll do is time you running to first base, so probably no," he said, smiling warmly, sensing I already knew the answer. I nodded, appreciating his candor, and thanked him for confirming my suspicions. He said I could probably catch on with a community college or junior college team, but I didn't want to sacrifice my academic future just to hang on to a pipe dream for a few years longer.

I have one lasting memory from that season, from a game far away from home on a late night in July. We were playing in Switz City, Indiana, just a few miles from where I'd be going to college that fall in Bloomington. Batting in the fifth inning, I swung and connected with that sweet feeling in which you barely feel the ball hit the bat. I watched the ball arc into the night sky toward the gap in right-center. I heard it bounce off the warning track and hit a metal sign on the fence as I rounded first base. I turned to look at the third-base coach as I approached second and he was waving me through. I jogged into third base for a stand up triple, my only triple since my very first base hit in Little League. We won that game by our own whitewash; I squeezed the final out in my Mark McGwire glove. A few weeks later it was officially retired.

My baseball career had a brief resurgence after college. I moved to Chicago for a job after graduation and after a year I felt the itch to play baseball again. I had heard about men's recreational leagues in the city, hardball, not softball or the sixteen-inch rubber ball the coed social leagues used. I found the Midwest Suburban League on the Internet, sent an email, and soon I was a Chicago Pirate. We played on weekends all over the city and suburbs, mostly former above-average high schoolers looking to recapture that spark, to relive the way we felt when we first smelled a brand-new glove. I even bought a new McGwire glove, but things didn't turn out quite like I'd hoped. The league was disorganized; umpires showed up late, the fields were poorly kept, and we had problems scheduling games. The Pirates also weren't such a merry bunch. For every player who was happy just to be lacing up the spikes again, there was an ultracompetitive die-hard who didn't get the message that we were playing in the Midwest Suburban League, not the National or the American. Worse yet, after five years away from the game my skills had atrophied. I missed pitches that I used to drive into the gaps. I swung over curveballs and couldn't catch up with fastballs. I made more errors in the field than normal, and early in the second season I injured my left shoulder and after that I couldn't throw without causing a grinding pain in the socket.

A season and a half of dodging helmets thrown by those overbearing teammates and witnessing my own sad decline on the field sapped my energy to play. We played by a system in which everybody on the team batted and then worked out a platoon rotation among ourselves for playing the field. I usually alternated innings at first base with another player, but as the games wore on during those hot, sticky Saturdays, games in which we were getting drummed just like my American Legion team, I started taking a pass on my turn in the field more and more often. I was tired of getting yelled at by our shortstop for missing The Scoop on throws he bounced ten feet in front of me. I was tired of chasing those same bad throws into foul territory, then jogging the ball back into the infield because I couldn't throw it to second. I had completed my own full shift left on the James spectrum, from potential to futility, without ever changing positions. Some part of me still held onto the idea that if I couldn't play baseball the right way, I didn't want to play at all. One of the friendlier players on my team asked me to help form a new squad the next year, but I turned him down, walking away from the game for good that second season with five games left. I agonized over the decision, fearing I'd regret giving up something that meant so much to me. But to my surprise, the first free weekend after that, I didn't miss it at all.

Ya Gotta Believe

John Thorn

Looking back on a lifetime of watching baseball, as opposed to a very few years of playing it, I have begun to think that the truly interesting action may be in the nation's armchairs. Why do we watch? What do we imagine ourselves to be watching while our minds wander? Does our seeming torpor belie a Mittyesque version of Dionysian transport? What are the roots of rooting? I skim a flat stone across the pond with this essay, but I expect I will have more to say on this subject in the future.

I have written about baseball for more than three decades now. At first I sat in the stands, looking down at the field and writing about what I saw. Then I began to wonder about what might really be going on, hidden from sight yet discernible from the game's statistical residue. Over time, as the fascination of numbers waned, I gravitated to the game's largely unvisited necropolis of ancient worthies and uncharted exploits, the men who grew up with the game in the years before league play.

And there I settled in, hanging out a shingle as a baseball historian despite the title's queasy echoes of real-estate novelist. I investigated how far back this children's romp with bat and ball really went, how it came to be Our Game, and why so many have registered claims to paternity.

Lately, however, I have begun to think that instead of surveying the fields of play for the Great Story of Baseball I might better have looked at the individuals surrounding me in the stands, and their antecedents, who more than any ingenious lad made baseball the national pastime. It was the spectator—not a

Doubleday or a Cartwright, neither a Chadwick nor a Spalding—who transformed baseball from a boys' game into a nation's sport.

Around the time of the Civil War, members of the press used to call the strangely ardent spectators "enthusiasts" or "thirty-third-degree experts concerning the game of ball." (They used to call some of them pickpockets and drunks and rowdies too.) By the early 1880s the baseball-mad were commonly called "cranks" or "bugs," both terms intended to reference chronic and incurable illness, with more than a dash of lunacy. In the *St. Louis Post-Dispatch* of April 18, 1884, an ex-governor of Maryland noted:

> There is a man in the Government Hospital for the Insane who is perfectly sane on every subject except base ball. He knows more about base ball than any other man in America. The authorities have humored him so that he has been able to cover the walls of his large room with intricate schedules of games played since base ball began its career. He has the record of every important club and the individual record of every important player.... He has figured it all out. His sense has gone with it. He is the typical base ball crank.

On the other hand, baseball had also been recognized as an aid to the "moral management of the insane" at the McLean Asylum—then located in Charlestown, Massachusetts, not too far from Fenway Park—and this, one year before Doubleday's purported invention of the game (from *The Friend; a Religious and Literary Journal*, June 23, 1838). When it comes to baseball, evidently, there ain't no sanity clause.

Where the term "fan" came from has long been in dispute, some saying it was short for fanatic—which would be in line with crank and bug—and others seeing it as a truncation of the eighteenth century term "the fancy," a flock of aristocratic fops who enjoyed slumming with the rabble at boxing matches. I am persuaded, however, by Peter Morris's recently expressed notion that "fan" was a term players worked up to deride their bleacher nemeses, and that it was a trope for the endlessly flapping motion of all those cognitively detached tongues.

"Rooter" was not exactly a term of endearment either. Today we may imagine that rooting has something to do with attachment to our team and the nourishment taken from its native soil, but in truth the term derives from the bellowing of cattle, the undifferentiated herd to which otherwise rational individuals willingly surrender their good sense at a ball game.

Whatever one calls the baseball devotee—seam head, stat freak, nerd, and geek are but a few of the recent coinages—the object of the epithet, knowing that his detractors simply do not understand, tends to wear the epithet as a badge of honor. For some fans social maladjustment is indeed a lifelong affliction, meriting empathy and respect, yet for an increasing percentage of others it is temporary and elective: a rented costume and mask, a three-hour license to act badly and get sloshed before the seventh-inning shutdown of the taps. To these revelers the game is irrelevant, and the honorable term "fan" does not describe them.

I have written elsewhere about why we root. Suffice it to say here that it is all about vicarious experience, surrogacy, sublimation, and emulation. When we cheer for our favorites or implore them to win we are doing many other things as well: reenacting archaic rites, reliving past glories, transferring powers from our heroes to ourselves, and, by emulating warfare rather than engaging in it, ensuring the future of the world. In sharing an experience that, like faith, cuts through generational divides, boys learn what it is like to be men and men recall what it was like to be boys. The ballpark, even when visited through electronic media, forms a magic circle for all this metaphysical swirl, which underlies not a staged drama or religious rite, with the preordained outcomes of those performances, but a real-life struggle in which risk is everywhere present.

This is what fans do: they congregate (yes, even when alone in front of the television) to invite change, risk, uncertainty into their lives, confronting danger and loss yet emerging to face another day. Spectating is (at a sublimated level, of course) akin to the experience of gambling or mountain climbing—that is, flirting with suicide. In addition to enjoying the vicarious thrill of an uncertain outcome, fans build belief in themselves for the more significant contests ahead in their own lives. Baseball in America is a sort of faith for the faithless, and its seven virtues are the same as those of religion—faith, hope, charity, fortitude, justice, prudence, and moderation. All these are traits that might sustain a man or a fan.

Adults who come to the game late tend to make rational decisions about which team to embrace, as forty-year-olds might choose a marriage partner; it can be a cold and dispiriting business. A boy, however, selects his team for a range of reasons he only dimly understands at the time, amid a cheerful obliviousness about who is choosing whom. It would not be too much to say that reason does not enter into his choice; it is almost entirely a matter of faith. (This applies to girls too; I talk about boys and men simply for efficacies of style and because I never understood girls or women.) What must be comprehended at the outset, by even the youngest fan, is that a rooting interest is not to be reversed lightly. A youngster who wavers in his allegiance may not amount to much. If his team loses today or tomorrow, or doesn't finish first this year or next, this is a challenge to his faith and endurance, but it must be borne.

A fan's hope is the unreasoning, inexplicable love of Krazy Kat for Ignatz: each blow to the head is merely a love tap, binding the victim ever more closely to the assailant. (At least, some call this hope; others will call it neurosis.) Maintaining faith, an ongoing, in-the-moment process, can be a struggle in the face of misfortune and injustice ("we wuz robbed!"). But hope is forward-looking and, thanks especially to spring training, cyclically renewable.Charity enables the fan to appreciate the human frailty of the players. A child may regard these rented champions for our shires as heroes, but a grown-up fan may not. Disbelief may be suspended, especially in April, but a true baseball fan embraces reality before the end of October forces it upon him. Closers blow saves; infielders make errors on routine plays at awful times; cleanup hitters strike out with men on base. Yes, playing the scapegoat is part of the tribal role for which players sign on. Yes, this is the game you played when you were young, and from a distance it still looks easy. But no, you would not have done better in their place. As an attitude borne in silence, charity is commendable; voiced in defense of a player sorely abused in your presence—now, that is a true virtue.

Fortitude is staying until the game is over, even when your team trails by ten and has lost every game for a week straight and the traffic will be murder. In 1973, the same summer the Mets' Tug McGraw declared, "Ya gotta believe," Yogi Berra famously added, "It ain't over till it's over." Less familiar is the knowledge that Berra left early from Game 3 of the 1951 National League playoff and thus missed Bobby Thomson's home run. Fortitude need not be exercised solo; rally caps, crossed fingers, thunder sticks, whatever fetishes you need to get you through the game—they're all okay. Sure, the players are important, but the outcome of the game depends upon you. Remember that.

Justice is being fair with others, even talk-radio callers, even fantasy baseball bores, even Yankee fans. Look upon these benighted souls with bemusement. Winning isn't everything, and debilitates character. Let them pursue victory heedless of the ruin that awaits them in the next life. Can they gnash their teeth as you can? Certainly not. Right conduct and proper belief, even in the face of provocation, will get you somewhere (though maybe not with girls). As Mark Twain said, "Always do right; this will gratify some people and astonish the rest."

Exercising *prudence* helps one to avoid excesses of optimism. When Tuffy Rhodes hit three home runs on Opening Day of 1994, he did not go on to hit 486 of them that season. Don't extrapolate from today's good fortune. Don't bet on the law of averages. Think twice about getting that tattoo of today's hero. Don't lead cheers from the stands; the Carnival King dies at revel's end. Be calm and serene even when your insides are jumping with joy because your team has come back from three down in the ninth. This will deter gloating by others when your team is the one that blows that three-run lead in the ninth.

(Okay, just kidding on that last virtue. Ya gotta enjoy. And ya gotta suffer. That's the human condition, not simply the arm's-length world of fandom.) So to toll the seventh of fandom's virtues: employ moderation in all things, including moderation. You know that you are not playing shortstop for the

Red Sox, though your emotions are racing as if you were. But face facts—there's no stopping that rush of testosterone or fancied pheromones when your team improbably snatches victory at the last. Winning has its rewards; enjoy them, even while knowing, at the back of your mind somewhere, if you can recall where your mind has gone, that losing is the superior instructor.

For this old boy, with more years behind than ahead, baseball is still at life's core. Not in the same dizzying way as when I was ten years old and my beloved Brooklyn Dodgers left town and, more pointedly, me; not in the same way as when the Mets swept to implausible glory in 1969, filling my heart with joy and my mind with the certainty that anything, yes, anything could happen. No longer in the same warming way as seeing my sons become first players and then fans for life. They are grown now, scattered, yet baseball remains a link for all of us. The game is what we talk about when we want to connect not only with each other in the present but also with our past.

Sport replaces faith for some while enhancing it for others. More importantly for Americans, and more specifically when it comes to baseball, sport constitutes family for the lonely among us, and enlarges it for all of us. Barry Bonds and Ted Williams, Pedro Martinez and Tom Seaver, form extended family at dinner tables; ball games of days gone by are stored like holiday snapshots.

Still baseball, after all these years.

Overhustle

Lee Gutkind

Art Williams wasn't exactly nervous before those games in which he worked behind the plate. His hands didn't tremble, his knees didn't quake, butterflies didn't dance in the pit of his stomach, light-headedness never set in. But still, there was something different going on, not within him as much as around him, nothing he could see or feel, nothing a doctor could diagnose, nothing biological that a microscope could dissect into tiny, flitting, bacteriological particles, nothing his loved ones could fathom, but all the same, there was something, a feeling, a dream, a gnawing, doubting, tickling, fog-warped, unsettling sensation.

Being a black man in a white man's world was hard; being an umpire, an official in a game of skill and chance, a lawman in a game where your every judgment could very well influence, if not decide, the fate of a man's career, the size of his paycheck, the weight of an entire team's purse—that was even more difficult. But to combine those two problems, to be the first black umpire in the National League and the only black umpire in all of the major leagues to be a black official in a game that has been and will continue to be supported by white owners, white management, and white spectators—that was to be, at least potentially, a misfit supreme. That was to be in a position of terrible vulnerability.

Art Williams did the best he could, both on and off the field, and as he grew older and more experienced, he felt himself increasingly capable of dealing with what he confronted as an umpire in the major leagues. Yet there were times, most especially every fourth game when it was his turn to call the plate, that a momentary uneasiness set in. This was an umpire's most difficult and tiresome job. This was the time in which all eyes were unavoidably on him.

Early that evening in the umpires' room at Jarry Park in Montreal, Williams stripped down to his shorts, carried the boxes of new baseballs and the can of Delaware River mud into the bathroom, and sat down near the sink. Colosi, Harvey, and Wendelstedt were in the dressing room talking quietly, but Williams turned his back and concentrated on rubbing the black briny mud into the smooth white balls. Usually he listened with eagerness to the advice and the easy-going banter of his more experienced companions, but today he felt tired of baseball and didn't want to hear what anybody had to say.

He glanced up at the mirror. The whites of his eyes were yellowish this evening and his cheeks and the smooth skin above his brow seemed wrinkled and sorrowful.

Yesterday night had been an excruciatingly bad night for Williams, his worst of the year as an umpire. He had been working first base and doing what he considered to be a competent job when fleet-footed Montreal shortstop, Tim Foli, hit a slow ground ball to third. It looked like it would be a close play, but Williams was on it, stepping into the slot to the right and at a forty-five degree angle from first base, dropping down on one knee to watch when the ball slapped the glove and the runner's foot touched the base. The ball beat the runner by nearly half a step, and Williams jumped, whirled around, raised his right fist and yelled, "Out!"

Then, for a split second, he was confused. The fans were cheering, and his fancy movement on the out call left him somewhat off-balance. He might have lost sight of the play, he wasn't sure, but the next thing he knew, the ball was rolling on the ground. His fist, signaling out, still hung like a black hammer in air as he lifted his eyes and ran the play back on the screen of his mind. Had Foli knocked the ball out of the first baseman's glove? Interference? He thought so. "Out!" he bellowed again.

"He dropped the ball! The first baseman dropped the ball!" Foli croaked, jumping on his haunches like a frog.

"No, he's crazy!" yelled first baseman Dick Dietz, motioning at Foli. "He grabbed the ball. He grabbed it!"

"You're wrong, goddamn it!" first base coach Walt Hriniak bellowed into Williams's face, so close that Williams could taste the warm tobacco juice on his breath. "You're wrong, wrong, wrong!"

The three men crowded around the lone umpire, barking and shouting, jumping up and down like angry dogs. Williams regarded them momentarily, then blinked his eyes shut for an instant, remembering Doug Harvey's words. "I'm telling you, son, you can't let them double team you, triple team you, quadruple team you. That's what they like to do. They like to get you so damn confused you look and feel like a fool. You tell them like I always tell them: 'One man, I'll talk to one man only. I'll talk to one man or no man at all.'"

But Williams knew he had hesitated too long, losing the advantage of his authority. He stood there, paralyzed on that spot of grass and dirt, realizing that perhaps only fifteen seconds had passed, and knowing also, through experience, that too much time had gone by for him to effectively take command of the situation. With his stomach feeling as if it had sunk to his ankles, Williams swallowed and accepted the dreaded situation.

"What are you going to do?" yelled Foli. "I was safe. I had it made, goddamn it, I had it made. I was safe!"

"Out!" shouted Dietz, jumping in front of Foli.

"Safe! Safe! Safe! Safe!" Hriniak jawed, pushing Dietz out of the way.

Williams composed himself and opened his mouth with the intention of clearing the field, when Hriniak suddenly stepped forward and bumped him. Whether accidentally or on purpose, it was hard to tell, but instinctively, without stopping to breathe deeply and gather up his frazzled nerves, Williams pushed the man back hard. "You're gone," he yelled, pointing to the dugout, "get out of here!"

"You pushed me, you ..." Hriniak rushed forward and bumped him again. This time it was no accident but Williams held his ground and his temper. "You're gone! You're gone! Get out! Get out!" His arm shot out once more toward the dugout.

Simultaneously, Harvey, Wendelstedt, and Expo manager, Gene Mauch, reached first base and pulled the men apart, but Williams knew the damage had been done. Whatever the player or coach might do, however they acted, the umpire had to control himself and, in so doing, control the situation. It was an indisputable rule: an official maintained order with respect. He should never exercise authority physically. Besides, the argument had started at least partially because he, the umpire, had turned his back on the play. Rule number two broken: never lose sight of the situation you are judging.

After the game, when Wendelstedt and Colosi were in the shower, Harvey said to Williams, who was sitting dejectedly in his sweat-soaked blue uniform, hanging his head in disgust: "You can't ever allow yourself to become off-balance on a play. You've got to plant both feet and keep your eyes on the play until you're sure the play has concluded. You can't get overconfident, Art. It takes eight years in the major leagues to make a good umpire, Art, and you haven't been in for even two.

"I know you just made one mistake, two mistakes, but we're not supposed to make any mistakes. I know it doesn't make sense, but it's true. Umpires are human. Umpires do make mistakes. We're not supposed to make mistakes, but we do, and we suffer for it afterwards. A man who begins his career as an umpire must be perfect, then improve significantly every day after that. That's the kind of ideals we have to live up to."

Harvey walked over and put his arm on Williams's shoulder. "Why don't you take your shower," he said.

That night Williams paced his room, periodically reading and watching television, attempting again and again to compose exactly the right words to use in explaining the incident when he called League president Chub Feeney the following morning. Williams wasn't worried that Feeney would fire him. It hadn't been that bad a mistake, and Feeney was a good and fair man. But it was embarrassing to admit to anyone—especially the president of the National League—that he had broken two ironclad and elementary umpiring rules.

Of course, Feeney wasn't the man who had hired him. Fred Fleig, the National League secretary and supervisor of umpires, was the one who had called him, after only two and a half years of minor league ball, to ask if he thought he could work in the majors. He remembered that night very well. In fact, lying there in that dark room, mounds of pillows hunched up behind his back, blankly staring at a late night television show, Williams saw flashes of his past come back to him in vivid, darting images.

• • •

In 1953 Art Williams became the first black player to be signed by the Detroit Tigers organization, receiving a one hundred dollar bonus, a figure that became standard for black players. Directly out of high school, he was assigned to the Tigers' Class A farm team in his home town of Bakersfield; he posted an 11–6 record. The next year he was offered a contract for AAA ball in Buffalo, New York, but the Tigers refused him enough money to bring his wife. So Williams declined the offer and was consequently sent to the Tigers' Class A organization in Idaho Falls, Idaho. He pitched well there for the first half of the season until he hurt his arm. Despite his physical troubles, he chalked up a 9–3 record that 'year.

But as the only black player in the entire Detroit Tiger organization, an organization that even today doesn't go out of its way to court black athletes, and coming up with a sore arm so early in his career, Williams felt his prospects for the future were significantly diminished. He turned down an offer to play A league ball in Augusta, Georgia, the following year on the advice of his father. Like all black men who grew up in the South, the elder Williams knew that Georgia was no place in 1954 for a young black man who wanted an opportunity to make the big leagues. The senior Williams felt there was no way his son could spend a season in the Southern League, pitching in Alabama, Georgia, and Florida and return to his family both spiritually and physically healthy.

So instead, Williams signed that year with the Wanetka Tigers in the now defunct Class C California League, and, on the advice of Tiger scout Joe Gordon, agreed to pitch a game every other day. "This is the only way you're going to prove to our management," Gordon told the young pitcher, "that your arm is strong enough for big league ball."

Whether the advice was faulty or downright cruel, Williams still isn't completely certain twenty years later. Maybe he really didn't possess what a black man needed in those days to make the majors; then a black man had to be virtually twice as good a player, sheer superstar material, in fact, to harbor any serious hope of ascending the major league ladder. Whatever, Williams wore out his arm while pitching as many games as possible for the next two years. He won twice as many as he lost, but never once received any indication he was being scouted and considered for advancement in the Detroit or any other pro baseball organization. He returned home at the end of the 1957 season and quietly and unobtrusively retired from the game.

He was so disappointed that he swore to his wife, Shirley, that he would never again involve himself in baseball. He would never watch a game, in fact, if he could help it. He tucked his memories of those years—the odor of neatsfoot oil rubbed into cowhide, the smell of sweat clinging to dry, hot dust, the crack of a bat and the slap of a ball, the thudding of a mitt, the scrape of steel spikes against concrete runways, the splat of tobacco juice against splintering dugout walls, the banter of teammates and, most especially, the roaring gratification of a crowd—he tucked those thoughts back into the deepest corners of his mind. He did so with a quiet shrug and an offhand sheepish smile, without any sign of bitterness toward the game or the people who very well might have impeded his progress. Art Williams had always been and would always be a man who took his punches without showing anger outwardly; he was able to mask his pain with a grin.

A second child was now on the way and so Shirley was no longer able to both continue to nurse full time and care for their growing family. Williams turned to an employment where colored men almost seem to maintain a monopoly: he went to work for the Bakersfield Sanitation Department.

Today, as Williams travels in the first class sections of airplanes and hires porters to carry his baggage into fancy hotels, he often thinks of his years hefting the garbage of both the rich and poor of Bakersfield. Today, no one has to crawl into a truck and stand kneedeep in filth like you used to have to do, he reflects. There are automatic compactors and, most important, there are union contracts. It gave Art Williams more than a little satisfaction to read that the sanitation workers in San Francisco had recently been awarded a contract guaranteeing them a little less than twenty thousand dollars a year. It rather tickled him to see white faces popping up on the garbage trucks around the country as he walked the streets of National League cities. Did that mean that collecting garbage now had its own measure of dignity? Or was it merely that Old Whitey disregarded his dignity when it came to making a hefty piece of change? He pondered the question with a smile.

Williams was soon promoted to supervisor in the Bakersfield Sanitation Department, and he worked for the next twelve years overseeing anywhere from 120 to 150 men. His family grew until he had four children, and for extra cash he took a part-time job with the Bakersfield Recreation Department supervising evening activities at a playground near his home. He also started attending classes part-time at Bakersfield Junior College and began refereeing high school basketball. For seven full years he kept his peace with, and his isolation from, baseball. He wouldn't watch it on television. He refused to join his friends for the 120 mile, two-and-a-half-hour trip to Los Angeles to see the Dodgers play ball. It hurt too much to be confronted with what might have been.

But when his eldest son, Art Jr., began playing little league baseball, Williams agreed to umpire some of the games. Before he really realized what was happening to his life, Williams quickly moved up into high school and college contests. Within two years he was the most skillful and sought-after umpire in amateur baseball in the state. As a former pitcher working behind the plate, Williams could easily follow a breaking ball with his eye from the moment it left the pitcher's hand to the instant it struck the catcher's glove. Often, just by watching the motions of the pitcher, Williams could anticipate what kind of pitch to look for even before the ball was released. On the field, his sense of the game deriving from his past years enabled him to take off in the obvious direction of the play almost as soon as the batter made contact with the ball.

All of the old feelings, all of the smells and sounds, the excitement and the satisfaction of competition came back to Williams in those next few years. It was like the continuation of an old love affair for the now thirty-eight-year-old father of four children. In the winter of 1969, with his wife's reluctant blessing, Williams enrolled in the major league's Umpire Development Program and spent six weeks attending classes and learning his trade in St. Petersburg, Florida, under the direction of former AAA Class minor league umpire Barney Deary.

Even then the federal government, armed with comparatively new civil rights legislation, was beginning to poke with suspicion into the hiring practices of National and American League officials. With justification. Close to half of all the athletes playing baseball in the major leagues were members of minority groups, yet there was only one black umpire, Emmett Ashford, in the American League, and he was planning to retire the following year. The situation had changed significantly since Art Williams had been selected to break the color barrier for the Detroit Tigers in 1953, but in 1969 he was again a pioneer having to prove that a black man was at least as good as, perhaps even better, than a white man. Now he was to plunge into the strange white world of law and order, of enforcing rules in a game which, two decades ago, only white men were good enough to play.

"I got a call from the National League office in San Francisco," says a major league umpire who had been working as an instructor for the Umpire Development Program in St. Petersburg that winter. "They wanted to know if there were any good black candidates and asked me to pick the best so that they could be sure he got a job. Not that these blacks mightn't have gotten jobs anyway, but there were about two hundred candidates that year for thirty or forty jobs, and they wanted to be sure a black got hired. Well, I picked Williams. He was maybe the best black candidate we had that year—maybe the best we ever had—but what I liked about him was, well, he was respectful. I mean, you could talk to him because he was respectful. Some of them coloreds are, well, uncouth."

Williams was hired by the Class D Pioneer League in Southern Florida that year for $525 a month for seven months, including expenses. Simultaneously, he relinquished his position with the Bakersfield Sanitation Department which had netted him eleven thousand dollars annually. Shirley was forced to go back to work that year and for the next four years, but Art was certain of his ability to make it into the big leagues.

He was elevated to the Class A Midwest League in 1970 and traveled for the season with another black umpire, Harold Van, who had been in baseball for a number of years and was, at the time, a National League prospect. Van, unfortunately never reached the proficiency in his calls required of major league umpires.

One evening in Appleton, Wisconsin, after a particularly difficult game, a tall, broad-shouldered, gray-haired, middle-aged man came into the umpires' room and engaged Van in a quiet conversation. Williams showered and dressed, then lingered in the passageway waiting for Van.

The stranger and Van entered the passageway some time later, stopping in front of Williams.

"What's your name, son?" the man asked gruffly. Williams told him.

"Well, I think you did a fine job out there tonight. Just keep on hustling."

"Goddamn," said Van later, "you got yourself a fan. That man don't know what the word 'compliment' means, but he handed one out to you, sure as hell."

"Who is he?"

"Why, that's Fred Fleig, the supervisor of umpires in the National League—the man who does the hiring and firing."

"Well goddamn," said Williams.

That night he called to tell Shirley. He felt like a real giant that night.

Williams worked hard for the rest of that season, harder perhaps than at any time before in his whole life. He had a sense of deep confidence that if he could hang on and perform with a hustling, well-concentrated efficiency, he would accomplish his long-sought objective of reaching the major leagues. Many times he reflected on the silliness of the whole idea. Here he was, a thirty-eight-year-old father of four, attempting to chart a new course in life by officiating a game for boys. Often he was wrenched by the thought that he was abdicating his responsibilities as a father and husband; his wife had had to assume the role of both parents and worse, she had had to become a semi-provider. Most frightening was that Shirley's long letters communicated a constrained fear of impending financial disaster, even with both their salaries taken into account. Slowly, but ever so surely and certainly, the savings account reserve on which they had counted when Art relinquished his sanitation job was dwindling. Each month, they were forced to dip into the well more than they had planned and now the bucket was nearly scraping bottom. At that point his telephone service had been cancelled twice for nonpayment of the bill.

Although his salary had increased to six hundred dollars a month for the seven months of the season with his promotion to the Midwest League, Williams had to withhold some of that money for winter financial obligations and for the obviously important traveling expenses during the season. Often during that long summer, Williams would spend his nights curled and cramped in the back seat of his car, washing and shaving at local gas stations to save a few dollars to send back home. He had never had a more difficult, heartbreaking, ego-deflating year. On the other hand, he couldn't deny his happiness and satisfaction at being awarded a second chance to fulfill his boyhood dreams. He returned home at the end of that season with no fear, no dread, no second thoughts about his future. He returned home with a triumphant feeling of confidence and accomplishment.

Since major league ball clubs invite so many extra players to their spring training camps and divide their teams into two sub teams (A and B), the American and National League offices require a number of minor league umpires to help officiate. Williams was included in this group of two dozen in January, 1971. The letter came directly from Fred Fleig.

Of course, there were two dozen of these young umpires and at most there might be two major league umpiring slots open each year; moreover, not all or even many of these men had a chance of ever being selected anyway. Some had worked spring training games four or five times in the past and had already been judged by the major league umpires with whom they worked to be too old, too slow, too fat, or too inefficient to cut it in the big leagues. Williams was the only black prospect and he had advanced quickly in his two years of professional ball.

He officiated twenty-six B team ballgames that spring while most of the major league umpires worked the A team contests, but what he remembered most of that month he spent in Arizona was his meeting with a man who was to become his confidant, a source of strength and of knowledge when he ascended to the major leagues.

Doug Harvey, tall, deeply tanned, white-haired, was working the plate in a game between the Padres and the Giants, and Williams, who had finished his game earlier in the day, was sitting on the sidelines watching him. He liked Harvey's style, the way he steadied himself on one knee and leaned way over the catcher's shoulder to see the ball. Of all the umpires Williams had studied, Harvey seemed to get closer to the plate and to be able to stay with the pitch much longer than anyone else. This was perhaps the most difficult part of being a successful umpire: the ability to ignore outside influences and internal pressures and to maintain absolute concentration on the game and only the game, including each individual play and pitch. Williams had never seen anyone more in control of himself and of the situation around him than Doug Harvey. It was as if the man put himself into a deep and totally consuming spell, as if time and space, heat, wind, and thirst were immaterial; as if the entire universe consisted only of a bat, a ball, a game.

Near the end of the game, however, between the eighth and ninth inning, Harvey abruptly turned from his position behind the plate and walked toward Williams. "You're Art Williams," he said, offering his hand.

"Nice to know you." The two men smiled at each other and shook hands.

"Look, I've got a problem. I just bought a house back in San Diego and I've got to make a plane in forty-five minutes to get back home to sign the papers and close the deal. I wonder if you could take over for me behind the plate?"

"You want me to call the plate for you? With Willie Mays coming up?"

"The pitches don't come in no different to Mays than anybody else. You call your own game and it doesn't matter who's swinging."

Art Williams never forgot Doug Harvey's kindness and his consummate skill behind the plate and when it was time to request a crew for his first year in the majors, he told Fred Fleig it wouldn't matter with whom he worked, as long as one of the men was Doug Harvey.

For the first five weeks of the 1971 season, Williams was elevated to the Class AA Texas League. But when veteran National League umpire, Tony Vinson, had a heart attack, Larry McSherry of the AAA International League was promoted to the major leagues and Williams subsequently moved up another notch, assuming McSherry's position. He remained in the International League that year, working the playoffs, and then returning both to major league spring training and to the International League in 1972. Again, he was selected to work the playoffs, an honor bestowed only on the best umpires in the league. Since this particular year the playoffs were to be held in Hawaii, as a celebration Williams was planning to take Shirley. He knew she deserved a vacation after helping to support their big family for three straight years.

• • •

The phone jangled in the small frame house in the south side of Bakersfield, California, that day, only twelve hours before Art and Shirley were scheduled to leave for Hawaii on their first vacation in four years. Shirley, then black-haired and slender, was in the kitchen. She listened until her husband picked up the phone, then cranked on the water, and began to scrub the maple syrup and pancake remains from the grimy breakfast dishes.

In a while, Art came in and stood in the doorway, watching his wife in silence, her bare black arms elbow-deep in bubbly white dishwater. He was smiling but when he spoke, he hung his head and covered part of his face with a towel. "Damn," he said softly, shaking his head. Then, when his wife did not respond, he said it again louder—"Damn!"

"What now?" asked Shirley, lifting a glittering plate from the bubbly water and running her thumb against it until it squeaked.

"That was Mr. Fleig," said Williams somberly.

Shirley turned to watch her husband. "And..." she said cautiously, sensing something, probably something bad, by the way her generally open and enthusiastic husband was speaking.

"Well, something has changed," said Williams, shaking his head and rubbing his face with the towel.

"What's changed?" said Shirley.

"I hate to tell you this."

"Well, you have to tell me sometime. Now what's the trouble? Is something wrong?"

"We're not going to Hawaii," said Williams softly, shaking his head again and again.

"Why? What's happened?"

"You don't want to know."

"Of course I want to know. Now tell me what's going on."

"We're not going to Hawaii," said Williams, pausing. "We're not going to Hawaii," he said again, slowly. "Because ..." he paused. "Starting tomorrow ..." he paused again.

"C'mon! Starting tomorrow, what?"

"Because starting tomorrow," Williams shouted, throwing the towel into the air, lifting his wife high by the waist and twirling her around the room, scattering dirty water and light silvery soap bubbles in every direction, "starting tomorrow I'll be in the major leagues!"

• • •

Art Williams suddenly found himself chuckling as he lay in his rumpled bed in the Sherbrooke Motor Hotel in Montreal watching the morning light quietly curl in through the cracks in the curtains. Thankfully, he had endured the darkness and the boredom by thinking his way through the night. He washed and shaved quickly, then looked at his watch, shrugged, and went down to the coffee shop for breakfast. He consumed an order of pancakes and two orders of sausage, washed down by four or five cups of bitter-tasting coffee. Afterwards, as he headed back to his room, he patted his stomach, wishing he hadn't eaten so much. It was becoming increasingly difficult to control his weight lately. This year alone he had picked up more than ten pounds.

Back in his room his heart beat heavily as he recited the number of the National League office to the operator. As he listened to the phone ringing, he was still attempting to conjure up an adequate explanation for yesterday's two very embarrassing and hard-to-excuse errors. Turning his back on a play and pushing a player were mistakes on the level of an electrician testing an appliance he had forgotten to plug in. Sure, he knew that neither Fleig or Feeney would do anything drastic to him. It was the embarrassment of confessing to his absolutely inexplicable errors. The operator told Williams no one seemed to be answering.

Williams looked at his watch, thumbed through his wallet, and read the operator Feeney's home number.

"Hello?"

He heard Feeney's voice, somewhat groggy and distant.

"Chub?" Williams tried to sound cheerful. "This is Art Williams. I'm in Montreal. How are things in San Francisco?"

"Who?"

"Art Williams. I'm in Montreal with Doug Harvey's crew."

"Well, what do you want?"

Had Feeney already heard about the game? Williams couldn't quite understand the reason for Feeney's instant irritation. He took a deep breath. "I wanted to explain to you, I mean, I wanted to tell you about what happened in last night's game."

"Do you know what time it is?" Feeney demanded.

Williams glanced at his watch and, at the same time, felt a sinking, queasy; bottomless feeling in his stomach. "Why, it's nine o'clock, Chub."

"It may be nine o'clock in Montreal, young man," said Feeney loudly, "but in California it's still the middle of the night!"

• • •

Today, sitting on a stool in front of the sink in the umpires' room in Jarry Park in Montreal, his eyes avoiding an all too accurate mirror, the big black man splattered saliva and mud on the last baseball to be tossed into the cowhide bag. Sighing, he kneaded the mud into the ball with a silent fury, betrayed only by the grim set of his leathery lips.

"I'm telling you," he heard Wendelstedt in the next room, "there are no finer looking women in the world than those found right here in Montreal. You know how some women come to ballparks in other towns? In baggy pants and blue jeans, their hair blowing in a hundred different directions? Sometimes I look up in the stands and see these chicks munching on popcorn, smoking, their faces covered with rouge, and I say to myself, 'The monsters have invaded!' Later on I discover the truth. It's only ladies' day.

"Then I come to Montreal, which is probably where beautiful women were invented. I mean, they got furs on, fancy dresses, high-heeled shoes. When they go to the ballpark, they look sharp, the way women ought to look."

"So," said Harvey, "what's the point?"

"Harry don't ever talk to make a point," said Colosi, "Harry just talks."

"So I'm telling you, this happened to me last year," said Wendelstedt."Are you listening to this, Art?" he queried, rising and walking slowly over to the door between the dressing room and the bathroom in his underpants.

Williams nodded, his back still turned.

"I'm working third base this particular night, see, and there's this broad, the most beautiful broad I've ever seen, sitting in the front box seat directly in line with the base. I'm tellin' ya, I've never seen anyone more gorgeous in my life. She's tall, and her long blonde hair, hair that's almost golden like the sun it's so shiny yellow, is swept into an absolutely meticulous bun. And that's not all," said Wendelstedt, shaking his head and lifting his eyes, "I swear, never in my life have I seen legs as long and curvaceous and smooth and white. Were I to give this chick a name, it would be Eve."

Wendelstedt paused for a deep breath to elongate suspense; he began to pace barefoot around the room. "This woman has also got the most appealing breasts I have ever seen. These were some tits, not too big, but luxurious, full and shaped perfectly. All I could think of when she leaned over the railing and I saw what I saw was cream puffs. Standing there, I wanted to bury my face in all that sweetness and goo for a month.

"You may well be sitting there and thinking I'm describing Miss America—or Miss Canada in this particular case," said Wendelstedt, "but if you'da seen her ass . . . 'Oh my God in heaven,' you'd say, 'better than Miss America, better even than Miss World.' I'm telling ya, this had to be Miss Universe, Miss Galaxy, Miss Solar System, she was so goddamn gorgeous. She was so beautiful that she was absolutely out of this world."

"Yeah, but Harry, hey Harry," said Colosi. "What did she look like?"

Harvey chuckled. Wendelstedt set his lips tight, made his face go red, and stared at Colosi momentarily before continuing. "The thing I remember about that night was the Expos were getting whipped something terrible. Something like ten to two after a few innings. A real massacre. And you know Montreal fans. They want to slit the throats of anybody scores a run against their Learn. But not this woman. She kept ogling me, staring at me, puckering up her lips at me as the game went on. And she let me see every part of her body and every morsel of clothes she was wearing. Which wasn't much. She got up and walked back and forth to the ladies' room, I'll betcha a hundred times, just so I could see her ass in that hiked-up black satin miniskirt. I'll tell ya, her ass swayed so much, I was getting seasick watching.

"I had a couple of pretty tough calls to make in that game, and they all happened to go against the Expos, but she didn't seem to mind. Sometimes you can stand around at third base three, four games in a row and nothing seems to happen. But on this night I was really getting the heat."

"Isn't that always the case?" asked Harvey. "Sometimes you go through a whole season without nothing to look at. Other times you get slam-bangers every time you stick your nose out on the field."

"In about the sixth inning," Wendelstedt momentarily raised his voice to regain the floor, "she took off her mink stole. That's right! She had on a silver mink stole, and the blouse she wore under that stole—or should I say the blouse she didn't wear under that stole—was virtually non-existent.

"Then, and I'm telling you, this is true, as sure as I'm standing here, she leaned her tits over the railing and started to call me. 'Vendelstedt, hey Vendelstedt,'" Wendelstedt mimicked in his finest imitation French accent. "Cum 'ere, Vendelstedt. Cum 'ere.'

"Course I ain't about to stop the game to go talk to a chick no matter what the chick looks like—but I'm telling you she was getting me so worked up I thought I was going to have a heart attack. Every time I went down the line with a foul ball I could feel myself—I couldn't stop myself-taking wider and wider circles along the sidelines near the railing so I could watch her more closely before returning to my position.

"'Hey Vendelstedt, Vendelstedt, cum 'ere.' She wasn't yelling or anything like that, but speaking in this nice little, sexy French voice. I'm sure only a few people besides me could hear.

"I was going crazy," said Wendelstedt, sighing and lowering his voice to a more confidential tone. "My wanger was so hard that a line drive to the crotch woulda cracked it in half. It was so big and stretched out it was crawling up my stomach and halfway to my throat. If I woulda pissed, I could have hit the sky.

"So after the game," said Wendelstedt, raising his voice once again, "instead of going into the dugout, I walked halfway to the sidelines just to see what she would do. And she was still sitting there, waiting for me. I'm not kidding! Just sitting and waiting. I went closer and she motioned me over with her finger." He stuck out his forefinger and bent it five or six times.

"'Vendelstedt, cum 'ere.'" Now Wendelstedt was whispering sexily and puckering his lips. "'Ho Vendelstedt! Vendelstedt! Cum 'ere!' She was just cooing," said Wendelstedt. "I'm not kidding! And I kept coming closer and closer, and she started making these sexy signs with her lips like she wanted to tell me a secret, so I leaned my ear over till it was almost touching her lips. I could smell her perfume and I could feel the warmth of her skin. Ohhhhh boy," Wendelstedt moaned.

"Then she said," said Wendelstedt, "and her voice didn't change one little bit when she said it . . . 'Vendelstedt, oh, Vendel stedt, Vendelstcdt. YOU COCKSUCKER! YOU EAT SHEET!'

"That's exactly what she told me," said Wendelstedt, throwing up his arms, feigning helplessness. "I'm telling you, there is no other umpire in the history of baseball that takes more abuse than me. That's exactly what she said. I'm telling you the God's truth."

Wendelstedt pulled his tight-fitting T-shirt up past his shoulders and dragged it over his head. He picked up a ballpoint pen from his suit jacket and carried the T-shirt and the pen into the bathroom, tightly closing the door of the stall. "How you doing, Art my boy?" he boomed.

"Just fine, Harry, just fine," Williams said, unable to match the joviality of his partner.

Williams went into the dressing room and sat down in the chair in front of his large black suitcase, staring absent mindedly and still somewhat dejectedly at his neatly pressed blue uniform.

"What I want to know is," said Harvey, splattering a chunk of tobacco juice into a cardboard box by his chair, "would you rather take the clap home to your wife or leave with it after you've been with her? Tell me that, Nick."

"I'd rather take a black man fishing," said Colosi, winking secretly in Williams's direction.

"What the hell does that mean?"

"I like to use 'shiners' for bait."

"If I had it to do all over again," Wendelstedt's deep voice boomed from his stall in the bathroom, "I'd rather be a black umpire."

Wendelstedt waited, but Williams didn't much feel like making a reply.

"If I were a black umpire," said Wendelstedt, "then I wouldn't have to wash my hands after rubbing up the balls with mud."

"Sometimes," said Harvey, "when I'm working the plate and I look out at Art standing behind second base, I swear I can't tell where his uniform leaves off and his face and hands begin."

Williams managed to shrug his shoulders and smile weakly, then he sighed and began the long process of dressing and preparing for a game behind the plate. First he dug into his suitcase until he found the bottoms to a pair of long gray knit underwear. He held the underwear, its legs dangling in his lap, up to the light. This was the same underwear he had worn for his first major league plate assignment almost two years ago. He had, in fact, worn these same long johns for each plate appearance since that time, but today he felt as if he were in need of a new good luck charm. Or no good luck charm. For some reason he thought it best to confront this plate job wholly on his own. He rolled the underwear into a loose ball, brought it back nearly to his face, then set shot it in the large wide mouth of the corrugated metal trash can. The underwear unrolled in the air and slid into the trash can, legs tiredly flapping like soggy, weathered streamers.

"Well, did you see that?" said Harvey. "It's about time."

"I never minded what the underwear looked like," said Colosi, "but he hasn't washed them since I've known him."

"If I did that," said Williams softly, "then the luck would have all been washed out."

"What you ought to do," said Harvey, "if you need a good luck charm, is drill a hole in your nose and insert a ring or a bone in it."

"I'll tell you what else he ought to do," Wendelstedt hollered."I think he ought to get a haircut."

"Good idea," said Harvey, "I don't want no goddamn Afros on my crew."

"If Art got a haircut, we'd all be rich," said Colosi. "We could open up a Brillo factory with what he cut off."

• • •

With a deep breath Williams stifled a steely-eyed grimace, then turned to face Harvey and Colosi with a shy but satisfactory smile. This had only taken a quick second. With forty-two years' practice; he was a master at masking his irritation.

"Most of the time I laugh with Nick and Harry and Doug when they make jokes about my color or race because I think what they say is funny. I'm not so proud that I can't laugh at myself once in a while," Williams has said. "I laugh also because I trust them. There are other guys in this league—other umpires—who make racial comments and mean it. They believe that whites are different than blacks, better than blacks, but luckily, I'm in a crew with people who, I truly believe, feel that all men are equal.

"Sometimes I laugh when I don't think things are particularly funny," he says. "I think it's often better not to start trouble. I don't want people talking about me behind my back, saying I can't take a joke. Because I *can* take a joke, I can take a joke just as good, maybe better, than anybody.

"Now, up to this point, no one on this crew has ever gotten personal with me. If they do they'll be sorry for it, I can assure you of that.

"What I like about this crew is that we're all ribbing each other. I don't rib anybody, actually, but everybody is throwing jokes in all different directions. Nick is a greaser. Doug is an Indian squaw. Harry is the Nazi racist pig. I like that. It brings things out in the open and relaxes me. I get a real good feeling inside of me when all of us are laughing together.

"There are other umpire crews in this league," says Williams, "who aren't as close as us. They stay in separate hotels, eat dinners alone, and travel to the ballpark and from town to town individually. That's not right. Living with one another day after day you get to know how each man shines his shoes, what kind of clothes he wears, when he needs a haircut. It's like being in a family. It helps time pass. It's something like a security blanket to me, I guess."

Thinking of his days in the minor leagues, both as a player and an umpire, he could almost feel those mustard-soaked hot dogs and stale peanuts anchored permanently in the pit of his stomach; he remembered the embarrassment and shame of having his telephone service disconnected for lack of payment and, when it was paid at home, not having enough money in his pocket to make a long distance call to the family. Williams stared at his neatly pressed blue uniform and his black, freshly polished shoes with the toes so shiny they looked like satin. He pictured the comfortable roll of five and ten dollar bills in his trouser pocket, and he savored the pleasure he would take tonight in calling home after the ballgame, the security of having credit cards and of having more than enough money in his checking account to cover his debts. I have earned these comforts, he said to himself. I have earned the authority of my position. I have earned the respect of other umpires and players. I like it when people give me special attention in hotels and in restaurants when they find out who I am. I like it when the little black boys wait for me outside of the ballpark, thrust a gritty, stubby pencil in my hand, and ask me to sign my name. I like it, I've earned it, I deserve it. God knows, I worked and prayed for this chance since 1953. Since long before that.

"Overhustle," says Art Williams, flashing a big, open-mouthed grin. "Although I'm sure other people have thought of it and used it, that's a word I've made up on my own. Overhustle," he says again, still smiling. "It perfectly describes my outlook on life, the way I conduct myself on the field, off the field, on the road, or at home.

"I don't want nobody to talk about me in this league, you see, because the way things are, with me the first and only black umpire, if they talk about me, they talk about my race. That's the way people are. I don't want nobody talking about me. That's the one thing I would hate, so I work real hard until I'm sure people know that I'm just one of the guys, 'cause that's exactly what I want to be.

"In everything I do, everywhere I go, in all of my life, I overhustle. That's the word. A ball's hit down the right field or left field line or into center field, I run like the wind, faster than any umpire, 'cause I don't want anyone to be able to say I'm lazy, that blacks are lazy.

"When I'm supposed to meet somebody at six-thirty, I get there at six-twenty because I don't want anyone to say that I'm always late, that blacks are always late.

"When it comes to sharing a taxi fare or picking up a tab in a restaurant, I always try to buy more than my share, two beers to everyone else's one, because I don't want anyone to say I'm cheap, or that blacks are cheap.

"I overhustle. I want to carry my load and I want everyone in the whole goddamn league, in the whole country, to know I'm doing it. That's what I want.

"Even when I'm home, I try to make an extra effort to carry double my load, to do things specifically to please my family. After a long road trip, I'm tired. I might have worked three or four doubleheaders in a row, or twenty games in twenty days in seven different cities, but I always try to remind myself that my wife has certain rights too. I want to sleep. Oh, sometimes

I want to sleep so badly that while I'm sitting and watching television and talking to my kids, I dream about being asleep. . . . Then, after the kids go to bed, I take my wife out. She deserves a little fun too, and it's my responsibility to do the best I can.

"You better believe I overhustle," says Art Williams, shaking his head and gesturing with his arms. He is smiling so openly that even the sternest of interrogators would want to smile with him. Then suddenly Williams's grin fades and his eyes become hard and stern.

"There are a lot of umpires in the minor leagues, and right up here in the majors, who are jealous of me because I'm black and have gotten a few breaks because of it. But they don't know, don't realize, that I've also lost out on many opportunities earlier in life for the same blackness. They don't understand, furthermore, that I can't help my color one way or another. I am what I am.

"I resent being called a 'token black' by reporters," he says. "I get that all the time. 'Don't you feel uncomfortable, or how does it feel to be the token black umpire in the major leagues?' they ask me.

"'I'm not a token anything,' I tell them. 'I'm an umpire. It's pure and simple as that.'

"They smile and nod, but they never write my answer down. I guess my honesty doesn't have any news value."

Williams denies that black men in baseball are like gladiators performing for a white crowd. He believes that baseball is a game for white and black alike, wholeheartedly equal—as equal as unconscious prejudice will permit, that is.

"Sometimes I call a black player out on a close play and they look up at me, surprised. They are actually surprised," he says, shaking his head in astonishment, "and they say to me, 'Hey brother, you could have given me a break.'

"Well, I don't like that. They ain't doing me any good and they ain't doing my race any good. They are jeopardizing my authority, my position, and my job. On the field, I ain't nobody's brother. They're players and I'm an umpire, and it don't go no farther than that.

"In a way," says Williams, "umpires and black people have been lifted out of the same mold. We're both outcasts. We both find comfort and friendship only with our own kind.

"People don't understand that umpires as well as blacks have human feelings and normal functions. Most people don't think there's anything underneath our uniforms. We're just faces, masks, ghosts in blue. They don't understand that we eat and sleep, we feel pain and love, we shit and piss and fart like most everybody else. We're human beings. Black and white. In uniforms and street clothes. Flesh and blood and bone."

• • •

He unwrapped a fresh set of underwear, tossed the cellophane wrapping toward the corrugated metal can, then stood and dragged the elasticized cotton material up his muscular legs and over his athletic supporter. Although it was to be a warm and muggy night, Williams sat back down and pulled on a pair of knee-high woolen socks, then strapped on a pair of catcher's shin guards made of shiny blue heavy-duty plastic. Umpires wear such undergarments for a number of sensible reasons. First, the long underwear will not only soak up the heavy perspiration flowing freely under the heat attracting blue uniforms, but will also prevent large quantities of dust from sweeping up their loosely fit-ting pant legs. The socks and the underwear also help avoid potential chafing caused by the tightly drawn straps of the shin guards. In addition, the triple layer of material serves as a cushion in case an umpire is struck by a ball or bat, or is spiked behind the calf or around his relatively unprotected thigh.

Over the underwear, Williams pulled on his pants. He slipped into a pair of black, plain-toed oxfords, laced them tightly, and got to his feet. His shoes had half-inch, nail-like but dull-tipped spikes protruding from the soles and heels, similar to those on golf shoes. The shoes had an elongated, leather-wrapped steel tongue, which extended from the base of the toe and over the laces, and climbed up the bottom part of the ankle, meeting the lower portion of the shin guard. Most umpires purchase these shoes from retailers specializing in coal miner's gear.

He pulled his padded chest protector down from the top shelf of his cubbyhole, its heavy-duty plastic shoulder pads clattering, straps dangling, and paused for a second. "Shirts or jackets tonight, Chief?"

"Jackets."

Williams nodded, buckled his chest protector over his undershirt, slipped on a short-sleeved, light blue shirt over the protector, then pulled on his navy blue suit coat. Williams looked as if he were wearing a 1940s-style zoot suit.

Preparing for a game behind the plate, American League umpires dress themselves essentially the same way, except that the American League umpires use a larger, highly-inflated outside, or over-the-uniform, chest protector called a "balloon."

"Balloons are fairly easy to use," explains Doug Harvey. "There are two straps that go over your shoulders and slide down your arm, so when you relax, the balloon hangs loosely in front of you. This protector is light and provides a fair amount of mobility. There's a slot or indentation at the top of the protector. When calling strikes behind the plate you bend over as far as you can behind the catcher, lining the protector straight up and down, parallel to the catcher's back. Then you put your neck into that indentation and peer over the catcher's shoulder. It's basically an awkward position to get used to. It's almost like you're bending down, craning your neck upward, all the while holding a mattress up in front of you."

The balloon provides an umpire with much more protection than the National League protector against a wild pitch or sharply hit foul ball. It is not only longer, wider, and more thickly padded, but it can be lifted to protect the face or lowered to protect the upper thighs. On the other hand, it is fairly unwieldy and, to a certain extent, reduces an umpire's mobility.

Minor league umpires still have the option of using either the inside or outside protector. "I worked my first five years in the minors using the balloon," says Colosi. "I had been told some time before that the American League was interested in me, so naturally I tried to familiarize myself as thoroughly as possible with the way they liked to do things. All of a sudden, a year and a half before I made the majors, I discovered that the National League had purchased my contract, so I made a fast switch. Most young umpires will do that. They might use both the first couple of years—if they can afford to buy two chest protectors—but as soon as they receive any indication one particular league is more interested in them than the other, then they'll switch. Naturally, they'll do anything in their power to ingratiate themselves."

"What most people don't realize," says Doug Harvey, "is that the differences in the protectors significantly change the game. The National League umpire, with his inside protector, leans way over the catcher's shoulder. He can see the plate better and, consequently, call a much more accurate pitch.

"Because of the two different protectors, the strike zone is different from league to league. Because we're closer to the pitch in the National League, we'll call a low strike, maybe as much as an inch below the kneecap. We'll also go an inch or so below the pectorals on the chest."

Colosi nodded. "On the other hand, the American League umpire is standing further away from the pitch, behind the catcher rather than over him. He can see the high pitch good, but he can't see the low pitch too well. What happens is that the American League low strike might be as much as two or three or even four inches above the kneecap. An American League umpire could also call a high strike at the neck."

Says Harvey: "Which doesn't necessarily mean there is anything wrong with this. The strike zone may be a little different from league to league, but it's not any bigger or smaller in either league. The size of the strike zone is the same.

"I keep trying to tell Art Williams," Harvey continues, "that the most important thing for an umpire to remember is to maintain consistency. Consistency is the most important part of our job. As long as an umpire calls the same strike zone all the time in each league, then it doesn't matter too much if it's six inches higher or six inches lower. The batter can eventually adjust to it. As long as the batter knows where the strike zone is going to be, he'll be able to hit that ball.

"Of course," says Harvey, leaning forward and chawing rapidly, "we have what we call the 'twilight zone' in baseball. What I mean is, how accurate can we be? The rule book says we're supposed to call the strike at the knee. Does that mean the top of the knee or the bottom of the knee? Does that mean the top of the ball or the bottom of the ball? What happens if he misses the plate with a curve ball by a bare microscopic inch? If he's that close, we try to give the pitcher the benefit of the doubt. The idea in baseball is to try to open up that strike zone as much as possible and make the batter hit the ball. That's baseball. If we were 100 percent rigid, we'd average ten walks a game.

"Still," says Harvey, "an umpire's utmost consideration is consistency. If a pitcher's wild, if he's throwing the ball up and down and over and under the batter, the umpire won't give him the strike when a pitch just so happens to come an inch away from the corner of the plate. He's got to be able to get it there all of the time."

"Pitchers who invariably have trouble with their control," says Colosi, "are bitching at us all the time because we won't give them a break. We won't give them a break because they lack consistency. You give them a break on a couple of pitches and pretty soon they're fighting for a pitch nearly a foot off the plate."

"I've been having trouble with (Cardinal pitcher) Bob Gibson," Harvey explains, "since 1961 when I met him in the Puerto Rican League. Now, Gibson seems to think that the plate has four-inch corners. I told him, 'The home plate is seventeen inches wide. If I give you four-inch corners, that makes it twenty-five inches wide. That's not the way the game was written.'

"Gibson has been bitching about this to me for thirteen years, and he's getting more and more argumentative as he gets older and less effective. Even his catcher one time, Ted Simmons, told him to 'fuck off.' Simmons makes his money as a hitter. He's smart. He knows that the bigger the strike zone the more difficult it's going to be for him to get on base. Why should we turn baseball into a pitcher's game?"

Says Colosi: "What makes me really mad is the reaction of the fans, or the players in the dugout, or the hypos in the press box. They think they can call the game as good as we can from where they are. Half the time, they're watching the catcher's glove. They don't understand that we couldn't give a shit less where the catcher catches the ball because we're watching how and where the ball crosses the plate. You take a pitcher with a good overhand fastball. The ball crosses the plate at the batter's knees, so we call it a strike. But the catcher receives the ball at the ankles, so to the fans or reporters it might look like a ball."

"Or how about a curve ball that breaks and hits the front corner of the plate?" asks Harvey. "By the time it reaches the catcher, it could be two feet outside, but in the meantime it nicked the plate and is consequently called a strike. It doesn't matter where the batter stands or where the catcher receives the ball. All I care about, all any umpire should care about, is where the ball crosses the plate. That's when the judgment is made."

Harvey lifted his rubber-soled oxfords onto a stool and began to tighten the laces. Looking in the mirror, Colosi carefully placed a blue, brimmed baseball cap on his head. Williams dragged his face mask and blue hat down slowly from the upper shelf. Harvey then looked at Colosi and Williams. "Where the hell is Harry?" he said.

· · ·

Suddenly, Wendelstedt whooped, crashed through the toilet stall door, leaped in the air, twisted around and landed in the main room with a bare-footed thud. He had shed his underwear, but stood in the middle of that room, staring sheepishly at his partners, and wearing a T-shirt on which he had drawn a large and elaborate swastika in blue ballpoint ink. Neatly lettered above the swastika were the words, "Super Kraut."

"Super Kraut!" he yelled, pounding his chest with his gigantic fist, then goose-stepping round and round the room. "Look! Up in the sky! It's a bird! It's a plane! It's Super Kraut! Super Kraut! Super Kraut!" Harvey, Colosi, and Williams watched as the big man twirled and paraded, bare-assed and barefooted, from one corner of the room to the other, again and again. They began to snicker and chuckle as Wendelstedt continued to perform, then finally they exploded in great gusts of laughter as Harry Wendelstedt, as straight-faced, apple-cheeked, and imperturbable as ever, put on his clothes, his light blue, short-sleeved shirt, his navy blue pants, und his suit jacket. He laced his black, ripple-soled oxfords and led his crew somberly out onto the field.

The players looked at the umpires strangely, then began winking at one another, but none would ever quite understand why these usually mean-jowled, grim-lipped men periodically chuckled and giggled, smiled, and suddenly guffawed through the game. Nor would the fans ever know, or even imagine, that one of the men on the field, wearing the blue suit of authority of that great and uniquely American game of baseball, was wearing a Nazi swastika over his heart, even though it was a joke.

• • •

Art Williams felt the fog and the weight above his eyes lift as he walked slowly out onto the field. He blinked his eyes and a delightful shiver of relief seemed to dance up his back. He accepted the lineups from both managers with an authoritative and enthusiastic nod, checked his digital ball strike counter, and loaded up his pockets with five newly rubbed baseballs. He stood erect and respectful through the Canadian and American national anthems, staring up at the two flags flapping silently side by side. With a great deal of satisfaction, as the dying music still reverberated in the dusty rafters of the ballpark, he turned to the visiting team's dugout, raised his arm up in a sharp, snapping manner, and yelled, "PLAY BALL!"

My Glove

Katherine A. Powers

*I was born in Minnesota but spent half of my childhood in Ireland.
In both countries, baseball occupied a private chamber of my heart
and imagination. It was my private joy, which no one could make me
surrender, not by taking me away from the game's native soil, and not
by suggesting, as my parents did, that it was not for girls. My first paid-
for published work was a roundup review of baseball books, and so
I can say without exaggeration that this greatest of games gave me
my career as a writer.*

My oldest personal possession is my baseball glove, which I bought for eight dollars at Woolworth's in St. Cloud, Minnesota, in 1960, when I was almost thirteen. It was a "modern" glove in that it had shape, unlike the ancient specimens I came across in my grandfather's house that looked as if they'd been fashioned for trolls and exhumed from a bog, or my uncle's first baseman's mitt, a folding horseshoe crab. My glove had—has, I should say—a good deal of rawhide lacing, including four knots tied off on the back of the webbing. Its many seams are beaded, its metal eyelets number twenty-five. It has two leather pulls, one to snug up the thumb, the other to tighten the wrist strap, which is felt-backed for comfort and secured by a metal button that says:

TRADE
H.K
MARK

The strap's black nylon label boasts a "W," which might stand for "Wilson," except it doesn't. The label also says "Made in Japan" and something else I can no longer read. It could be "Professional Model," because that is what is inscribed in the leather of the glove's "little" finger (its largest). The glove's inside surface sports another beguiling "W," as well as "Style 2681" and "[illegible] Set Pocket." I can't remember what sort of "Set Pocket" it was. Deep, I'd say. The inscription has been flattened out of existence by almost fifty years of service.

I bought this wonderful thing secretly because my father had met the few remarks I'd made about "thinking of getting a glove" with his rote response: "You don't want that." (Other things I "didn't want" were blue jeans, a bicycle, a penknife, a fishing pole, a permanent wave, and a pet of any sort.) A baseball glove? What would I do with it? Who would I play with? Boys at school? I was a girl. Didn't I know that? And what was I going to play with? Not a hard ball: we were not having anything to do with hard balls. That's how people got killed and their teeth knocked out and the next thing you knew there'd be a broken window and "I'll be out there doing my act with the putty knife."

For a week or so I fraternized with my new glove on the sly. Behind the closed door of the room I shared with my younger sister—silenced by death threats—I cradled my glove and pushed my face in it, inhaling the deep, fertile leather smell it pumped out along with pheromones, I'm sure. I kneaded it, shaped it, and slammed a ball—a brand-new baseball—in it. Outside the house, around the corner, out of sight, I found a clandestine battery mate, the wall of a brick college dormitory that had no windows on the lowest story. The glove activated all the baseball boilerplate I had amassed from incessant baseball book reading. Confronting the wall, I flicked off the sign, looked in for another, slapped the glove against my thigh, wound up, and poured one in. Sometimes (if the wall was hitting) I cupped my knee with my glove, waiting for the batter to try to punch one through. I snagged the ball, pounced on it, speared it, whipped it home.

I walked around (out of sight of the house) with the glove tucked under my arm, wishing I could shove it in my back pocket like boys did in books, but of course my pants, when I was allowed to wear pants, had no pockets because my mother had made them, as she made practically all of our clothes. I wished I knew where to get neat's-foot oil, not available at Woolworth's, but no one I could confide in knew anything about that. Another thing I could not do, I might as well confess, was spit in my glove. I could direct the occasional spitting noise at the pocket, yes. But shoot a gob of spit right in there and work it in like you read about? No, I couldn't.

I brought the glove to school, placing it beside me on the old-fashioned bench seat, on top of my books—just like the boys did. In that distant day, or perhaps only in that parochial school, the boys and the girls were not allowed to play sports together at recess, and none of the girls had gloves. But we did play softball and my glove had no problem at all handling the larger sphere. It could handle anything.

Soon enough, unable to keep my love object to myself, I came clean with my parents. Fairly clean, at least: I kept the hard ball under wraps, nestling a tennis ball into the glove's pocket in a prissily responsible manner. I told my father I thought I better tell him I'd gotten a baseball glove. It was a really good one, even though I happened to have bought it at Woolworth's and even though it was made in Japan. I said it was a Wilson and I did not use a hard ball. He looked the glove over, said something unkind about "Made in Japan," and pointed out it wasn't a Wilson. He massaged it with his thumbs, sort of churning them around in the glove, which is what he always did when weighing in on leather quality—one of his specialties. The leather seemed okay, he allowed, but he said he didn't see why the glove had to look the way it did. He whapped his fist in it a few times and then took it with both hands and bent it back and forth as if to reprimand it for the affectation of its deep pocket and slightly curved webbing. He entered briefly into the subject, familiar to all baseball-book readers, of infielders sitting on their gloves to keep them flat so they could turn the ball over fast. I said I knew about that.

He said, "Is this the best you can do for a ball?" I told him that actually I had bought a baseball, but that I only used it against the side of the brick dormitory—you know the wall that doesn't have any windows low down you could accidentally hit. He said that's how you ruin a good ball, scuff it up, leather gets all nicked. I said that was true.

• • •

The next big phase of life for my glove came the following year, 1961, with the advent in Minnesota of the Twins. My two brothers, then six and eight, became infected with the baseball bug, though in their own particular way, which, for the most part, did not include playing ball, and certainly not with other boys. This was not really their fault because our parents did not like the idea of their children associating with other people's children, especially with boys, who might piss against a tree, as had happened once. My mother had said, "That puts the kibosh on playing with boys." Instead, my brothers collected baseball cards—not too many, though, because my mother had declared the gum that came with them to be "verboten." One of the boys collected statistics, just collected them and wrote them down. My parents got him a rubber stamp with his name on it followed by the title, "Statistician."

Still, my father, who had been an athlete in high school, felt the urge to toss the old pill around with his sons and teach them the rudiments of the game. Fear of the annihilating ball persisted, however, and, after much deliberation and weighing of consequences, he procured a hardish rubber ball whose destructive power was less terrible than a baseball's, or at least that was the idea. He also got the boys gloves, managing to find suitably archaic versions, possibly from the Goodwill, one of his haunts—though, given the intimate, even germy, nature of a baseball glove, inside and out, maybe they were new. My mother made the boys baseball suits. Being the same sort of person as my father when it came to authentic quality, she made them of genuine woolen flannel, just the thing for Minnesota's ferocious summers of heat and humidity. She made them big so the boys could grow into them and they'd last for years.

So once a week my father, my two brothers, and I got in the Studebaker and drove across the river to the park where hardly anyone went, where there were no baseball diamonds to attract other people's children—and played ball. What ensued beside the brown-flowing Mississippi, among the leafy knolls, and upon the undulating greensward, so unsuited to ball playing as most people understand it, is not really mine to describe. I can only say that it had no resemblance to *The Natural* and its scene of prelapsarian baseball. My father called it his "time on the cross"—as he called most family affairs.

I brought my glove to Metropolitan Stadium to see the Twins that year. I sat in the grandstand with my father and his friends, well out of reach of the lethal horse hide, wearing the clothes my mother had made for such occasions: pleated skirt and middy blouse. My glove was in my lap, like a handbag.

• • •

The first few years of my glove's long life were filled with bathos. I rarely found satisfactory human beings to play with, and my relationship with the wall ended when one of the dormitory residents complained about the sound the ball made hitting the building. Then we moved to Ireland. My glove came too. I introduced it to various Irish people who ridiculed it, calling it another instance of American softness in sports—football players wearing armor, baseball players wearing padded gloves. They rolled out the familiar, self-regarding comparisons between American football and rugby, between baseball and hurling (a vicious game played with whirling sticks and a preternaturally hard ball that might have come from my father's nightmares). I looked at my glove and was overwhelmed with homesickness.

Years passed in a generally unfruitful fashion for my glove and me. I moved to London with it and worked long hours as a barmaid. I had no chance of getting to know anyone who wanted to play ball, at least not when they were sober. My glove rarely made it out of my seabag. I learned later that there had been a regular Sunday pickup game of baseball or softball somewhere in London while I was there. That just made me feel bad: I had missed yet another chance for a different, more baseball-rich life.

Finally, in 1972, my glove and I returned to this country for good, to Massachusetts. This is when we both really came into ourselves and began to live. I finally got some neat's-foot oil. I found people to play ball with. I found, too, for the first time, that it is an unfeeling world out there for the glove owner. I finally had to write my initials on my glove's wrist strap with indelible ink because some people can't seem to distinguish between their own and other people's gloves. They start trotting off or, worse, driving away with them. When they don't have their own gloves—having lost them through negligence—they use your glove when your team is at bat. They haul away on its leather pulls. They stuff their big hands in the glove and yank the thing off when they're done. Because they have chunky fingers, the inner lining gets pulled out, so now you have to find a little stick or something to poke it back in. It would make you weep, or throw up. I never saw anyone spit in my glove—I can't think anyone would actually do that to another person's glove. But people do leave a lot of sweat behind. Sometimes you don't even feel like putting your glove back on, and you wonder whether real baseball players ever, somehow, wash out the insides of their gloves.

• • •

After a couple of years being back in this country playing ball, a terrible temptation came over me. I can hardly bear to write this down: I thought I might buy a new glove. But when I went to look at the up-to-date models, I was shocked. They looked so big, much bigger than mine, and overweening. They had latticework, hinges, supernumerary integuments and rigging, and all sorts of trademark graffiti stamped all over them, like "Flex-o-matic" and other things too stupid to remember. The fingers of some models extended all the way down the rear of the glove to the wrist, like the back of a lute or a huge leather seashell. They looked like they played a different game or were pieces of furniture. And they were horribly expensive, soaring into the two-figure range. What did it mean? Were gloves getting bigger to compensate for cars getting smaller?

I shelved the new-glove project for years, until, possessing no daughters, I bought gloves for my sons. By that time, the 1970s and its version of style were only a bad memory, and I found elegant gloves, at reasonable prices, that had at least a modicum of my glove's natural grace.

My glove still has an ancient, raddled grace. Sweat, I suppose, has fused the inner lining to the body of the glove. It could not turn inside out if it wanted to. In fact, it's sort of scraggy in there except in the first finger, which is still smooth from my keeping my finger outside, against the back of the glove, where it has created an abraded hollow. The heel of the glove is ripped where the wrist-strap pull has been yanked too hard, too often, and you can see the padding, looking something like alpaca. When I put my face in my glove I can smell our shared history. The leather's intoxicating odor isn't as urgent as it once was. It is mixed with the cold, mildewy aroma of Ireland and my seabag. There is a biscuity waft of ancient sweat and the muddiness of far-flung playing fields, and, for some reason, an ineffable, but unmistakable, fragrance of books.

Spring Training Lights

Jake Young

Like many people, when I think "summer," I think "baseball." I'm not sure whether that's the baseball of my youth—playing catch with my neighbor, Patrick, barefoot, losing balls over the bluff, a BoSox matinee on the radio, the play-by-play drifting out to us through the screens of his house's covered porch—or if it's the baseball of today, which offers steroid investigations, fat contracts, year-round updates, expanded leagues, "fantasy" teams, a wild card, and interleague play. This essay attempts to reconcile the two versions of baseball, past and present. I think every fan tries to make the two compatible. And the baseball of old, sepia-toned, usually carries the day.

It's the bottom of the seventh inning, no one on, no one out, and the Oakland Athletics' Mark Ellis hits a broken-bat bloop into shallow left-center off Arizona Diamondbacks reliever Jorge Julio. The second baseman takes an angle. The shortstop, Augie Ojeda, number 11, gets a good jump on the ball. He tracks it over his shoulder, running in a straight path under the ball's trajectory in the lights. He is short for a ballplayer, barely 5–8, but he has good, rapid turnover in his stride as he tracks the bloop; he's got a chance. He gives a hurried signal to ward off the second baseman (who won't make it anyway). It will be a tough catch for Ojeda: being human, susceptible to the drawbacks of bilateral symmetry, he'll have trouble catching a ball that traces his direct path, the ball drawing a bead in line with the fielder's head, the fielder having to cock his head back at a precipitous angle to catch the ball. Baseball players have to make catches like this; so do football players. You watch it: the fielder or receiver runs with his head turned nearly 180 degrees, Adam's apple protruding, hands cradled in front of his chest as if in supplication, as if willing the ball into his mitt or hands, then begins to bend in response to the ball's flight.

There is no wind, the night a still ninety degrees, the Arizona state flag—at half-mast due to the death of Bowie Kuhn, Major League Baseball's commissioner from 1969 to 1984—limp against its pole. If Augie Ojeda doesn't run down the ball, it won't be called an error: Ellis's bloop would fall in for a single and there would be a man on first to lead off the inning. Even so, Ojeda's sprint draws the crowd's attention, a held breath or two. With shallow bloops, there is always a moment when the ball seems to hang in the air, timeless, suspended.

It's March, and the ghost of Willie Mays—who made a famous over-the-shoulder basket-catch in the 1954 World Series—has been invoked during spring training. In the Polo Grounds' abyssal center field (the clubhouse in center field—the distance required of a ball to be counted as a home run—was once measured at 505 feet away from home plate), Mays robbed the Cleveland Indians' Vic Wertz of a 460- foot potential triple (the Polo Grounds allowed for triples; Mays once hit twenty of them in a single sea-son). After "the Catch"—and less well remembered—Mays wheeled and flipped the ball three hundred yards to third base, falling away off his back foot, to prevent the runners on first and second from moving. Mays's play—an over-the-shoulder catch not unlike the one that could take place right here and now at Arizona Municipal Stadium (better known as "Muni")—recalls "The Big Green Bathtub" of the Polo Grounds, the stadium with a full house of history: home to both the Babe and the Mets and the football Giants (1925–1955) and the Jets (formerly the Titans, 1960–1963), but whose longest and most memorable tenant was the New York (baseball) Giants (1911–1957).

Ojeda's attempt at an over-the-shoulder catch is a convergence of his-tory and memory and something else, something much more literal and earthbound. Of Mays, who recorded the first home run at Muni for the San Francisco Giants after the team moved in 1957. Of the player, Augie

Ojeda, who recalls the time of another Augie (March, the Adventures of whom were published in 1951). Of March, that time of year when guys like Ojeda are just trying to make the cut. And then of the ten light poles circumscribing Muni that have presided over not one but two fields, the Polo Grounds from 1940 to 1963, then Phoenix Muni, where they have stood and baked and lit hundreds of night games since. Here they are, transmigrated cross-country to the desert, taking their retirement early, mimicking the migration pattern of thousands of other old-timers on their way west to the desert, where the spare climate might help them eke out a few more years.

The Polo Grounds' light poles were basically evicted from Manhattan, the stadium's demolition scheduled to bring the grandstands (where the light poles were perched) to the ground. On April 11, 1964, the first crews of the Wrecking Corporation of America showed up at the stadium at West 156th–157th Streets and 8th Avenue wielding jackhammers and wearing shiny steel helmets and T-shirts with "Giants" written across the chest and numbers emblazoned on the sleeves (the corporation's manager and vice president, Harry Avirom, a Dodgers fan, wore the number "1"). It would take the sixty-man crew four months to bring the stadium to the ground.

That first day was all smiles and photo ops. Truth be told, the Polo Grounds' demise had dragged on for six years, causing litigation in courts between the city and the Coogan family (the Polo Grounds was nestled in the lee of Coogan's Bluff, which became one of many Polo Grounds sobriquets). The Mets' Polo Grounds finale, September 18, 1963, was the stadium's third, the first being for the Giants when they left in '57, the second for the Mets in '62, before they knew that Shea Stadium's construction had delays and their debut in Queens would be pushed back to '64. That was the attitude as the Polo Grounds came down: let's get this show on the road.

The center field bleachers and clubhouses—right about where Mays made "the Catch"—were the first to go, to allow trucks and cranes to enter the ballpark. Crew members who were Dodgers fans joked about how long they'd wanted to bring the Polo Grounds down (Ebbets Field had been

demolished in 1960; the same wrecking ball was used on both stadiums).
When Dodgers fan Stephen McNair approached the left field fence beneath
Section 33, over which Bobby Thomson launched the line drive home run
better known as "the shot heard 'round the world" at 4:11 PM on October
3rd, 1951, he marked it off and vowed, "I'm going to take that place down
myself."

You see, Thomson's three-run homer had knocked the Dodgers out
of the World Series and brought the Giants in. (Russ Hodges's call is the
most famous in sports history: "Brooklyn leads it, 4–2. Hartung down
the line at third, not taking any chances. Lockman without too big of a
lead at second, but he'll be running like the wind if Thomson hits one.
Branca throws. There's a long drive. It's gonna be, I believe ..." Hodges
then repeats "The Giants win the pennant!" five times.) The game was the
third of a best-of-three playoff, each team taking its home field in the first
two. On August 11 of that year (1951), the Giants had been trailing the
Dodgers by a seemingly insurmountable thirteen and a half games. Leo
Durocher, formerly the Dodgers' manager, led the Giants to a stretch run
of thirty-seven wins against only seven losses in the team's final forty-four
games, tying the Dodgers for first place and the right to go to the World
Series. That the Giants would lose the World Series to the Yankees was
no matter; they'd already achieved the impossible. (What kind of avarice
demands more grace when grace has already been achieved? For example,
even if the Red Sox had not beaten the St. Louis Cardinals in the 2004
World Series to break the Curse of the Bambino, their comeback from a
3-0 series deficit against the Yankees in the ALCS would have been a legend in itself.) So when that ball took flight at 4:11 PM that afternoon, no
Giants fan living wanted to see it come down; it meant a heck of a lot to
them that it didn't.

With McNair at the ready with his sledgehammer, about to demol-
ish the left field fence for the New York City Housing Commission (and
Dodgers fans everywhere), the foreman, Abe Gach, called over to McNair.

"No, you don't," he shouted. "Be gentle over there. History was made
there."

It wasn't reported whether Gach was a Giants fan or not.

It's the only home night game of the Oakland A's spring training, the lamps of the Polo Grounds' light poles brightening the night. (The A's schedule only one night game during spring training, for the sake of visiting fans who want to soak up sun.) I'm watching the game from a vacant press box with James Vujs (pronounced "voice"), the stadium manager of Phoenix Muni. He's an employee of the city, not the A's. These are his "three outs," which usually occur towards the end of the game when his two-way radio goes quiet and he gets the chance to take in an inning.

For the game's other fifty-one outs, the other eight or eight and a half innings of play, Vujs walks constantly, treads ground from one end of the stadium to the other. His work uniform consists of khakis and a polo shirt. He has a permanent sheen of sweat on his brow, his hair short and combed over. Every March, he goes through two pairs of dress shoes—one a pair of black loafers, the other a pair of brown lace-ups—handling the small hiccups and distractions and slipups and snafus that are a product of nearly nine thousand people occupying the same enclosed space at once.

Hiram Bocachica is batting for the A's now. The lights have illuminated a hovering cloud of smoke slowly drifting over the field from the barbecue behind the left field stands, the cloud appearing eerily purple, casting a spooky feeling over the stadium. The home team A's have rallied for two runs in the seventh to close the gap in the score to 8–3, Diamondbacks. Julio delivers a pitch that looks outside from the box. The umpire calls strike three, and the stadium fills with halfhearted booing.

"Spring training strike," Vujs says.

The rally and the inning are over, the game sped along by the bad call. Vujs has taken in his "three outs," and it is time to leave the box and go back to work.

Vujs is in his seventh year at the stadium and, with his team of five men, he makes certain the operation of the stadium during game time runs like inning-work. (His time doesn't run by the clock, it runs by the inning. He doesn't clock out from work; you could say he innings out.) Here, at Muni, his job is minimizing risk—prophylaxis, predamage damage control.

Because this is the only night game of spring training, Vujs has had to deal with more snafus than usual. Twenty minutes before the first pitch, mistimed sprinklers went off in front of the Rock House, nearly dousing people by the Speed Pitch attraction on the concourse. Then, while Vujs was checking out a vomit spill near the gate, his boss, Rob Harmon, who manages both Muni and Maryvale, the stadium across Phoenix and the spring training home of the Brewers, phoned him on his cell.

"James. Do you keep a pregame checklist of things that need to get done?"

"Sure," Vujs said uncertainly. "In my head, sure."

"Well, why don't you run down that 'checklist' and see whether or not 'Bridge Lights' is checked off. 'Cause I'm looking right at 'em and they aren't on."

After the call, Vujs immediately disappeared underneath the spiral ramp up to the bridge, where the locked circuit breaker box is.

Vujs's goal is to have a flawless March. For one month a year, the stadium must run smoothly, perfectly. In this regard, Vujs is not unlike the ballplayers in the field: he is docked for errors, but there is no statistic recognizing his tireless efforts to ensure that bad things don't happen.

• • •

The ten light poles of Phoenix Muni support 162 lamps (as opposed to the 400 they carried at the 54,000-seat Polo Grounds), 18 of which are 400-watt security fixtures trained on the stands for pedestrian traffic, Vujs's territory. The security lamps, arranged in threes, aimed down as opposed to across and outfitted with Nema Type-6 Reflectors, look like bluebells drooping from the light poles' stems. The fixtures are mounted on ballasts that aim the lamps and control and modulate the amount of electricity flowing to each lamp.

The other 154 fixtures engage 15-megawatt (1,500,000 watts, about equivalent to the power of thirty thousand conventional lightbulbs at once) lamps, serried into banks of double-tiered seven-lamp rows on six of the eight standards. These lamps appear more confident in their arrangement, aimed across the field. The other two poles, to either side of home plate and aimed across the infield, carry three stacks of lamps, the top bank holding a row of seven, with two neatly stacked rows of six lamps below. There are eight lamp towers total mounted on the ten poles: the left- and right field concourse poles are joined in pairs, and the individual poles are connected together by a steel "Z" a third of the way up.

Augie Ojeda attempts his catch in shallow left-center. According to Muni's aiming diagram, this is an area beyond the exact spot where 15- megawatt lamp number 12 is aimed, a limbo when it comes to the stadium's light field. For a professional ballpark, 150–200 foot-candles is considered standard coverage, with the infield generally 20 to 30 foot-candles brighter than the outfield. The way the lights are aimed at the field is similar to the way the fielders themselves are positioned. Bloops into the shallow fields correspond to unpatrolled zones, limbos, gaps, shadows between the lights. The territories on the field that lie farthest from immediate policing are then its frontiers. The stadium's aiming diagram shows this clearly enough, an empty, uncovered space in shallow left and right, slight, barely noticeable dimples in the stadium's light surface like dark patches on the moon. The map resembles a blueprint, and the T-shaped crossing of the aimed lamps' beams in the outfield is what fielders have by way of illumination, enough to ensure that there is no Bermuda Triangle (unless the ball gets "lost in the lights," or the glare) on the field.

While Ojeda chases down the bloop, navigates the lull in the stadium's light field, I question how history slips into these dark patches, these interstices of light. Do events similarly "bloop" off the radar beyond the infield, or are they recognized immediately as "history in the making"? Or are these questions moot now? Has history left Muni altogether, left spring training behind, these light poles no longer custodians of a stage prone to history but retired, like a police officer acting as a security guard? Does it matter what happens in the dregs of lamp number 12's light? At first blush—no one on, no one out, and with "spring training" called strikes—whether Ojeda stabs the ball short of the ground with his glove seems irrelevant: there is no playoff now, not even a regular season box score at stake.

Taking a closer look, however, something is offered up: context. By baseball standards, Ojeda is no spring chicken: he turned thirty-two in December and has been around the big leagues. Now, his fielding must "back up" his pitcher, Jorge Julio. But, two and a half years earlier, on the night of September 7th, 2004, Julio, then the Baltimore Orioles' closer, in an act of frustration after yielding a go-ahead (and eventual game-winning) home run to Minnesota Twin Michael Cuddyer, issued a "brush back" pitch to the next hitter, who happened to be none other than a seldom-played "journey-man," a Twin utility infielder named Augie Ojeda. Julio was ejected from the game and three days later suspended four games by Major League Baseball. Catching Julio that night was Oriole Javy Lopez, who said afterwards of the nasty pitch, which by all appearances was an attempt to bean Ojeda: "One thing I do know: if he hit him with a pitch, it would have killed him."

It would be Julio's last month as the Orioles' closer; the following year he was replaced by B. J. Ryan and demoted to middle relief. Up to that point, 2004 had been a productive season for Julio: for the year, he converted 22 of 26 save chances on a mediocre Orioles team. Now, Julio and Ojeda, after several stops each along the way, have ended up on the same squad trying together—in a coordinated (and in this case, considering Ojeda's tracking of the ball, potentially collaborative) effort—to make "the bigs" once again in March of 2007.

On the bloop, Ojeda's job is to put every ounce of energy in his body into helping Julio have one fewer base runner to face, one fewer out to earn, to preserve the perfect outing of the teammate who, two years prior, had tried to take off his head with a baseball at the distance of sixty feet, six inches. And the reality is: the thought—the memory—probably never enters Ojeda's head.

So much for history.

• • •

During the day the lights are off, of course, their lamps milky, cloudy. I sit in the right field bleachers away from several shouting kids tearing across the seats beneath Muni's signature concrete, accordion-roof grandstand. The poles are painted garish silver, though the upper part of some of the poles is smudged with red, rust washed down by rain from the bilevel maintenance catwalks—referred to as "baskets"—appended behind the banks of light fixtures. Blackbirds' choruses can be heard from the palo-verde and mesquite trees around the stadium. Papago Park's giant red rock buttes that look as if they belong on Mars crop up, surreal, beyond the light standards in the outfield. The metal bleachers tick around me like a hundred car engines just cut. Overhead, airplanes descend in their final approach to Sky Harbor. A single sparrow hops between the bleachers, scavenging.

The bases of the steel poles are riveted with huge screws around which giant hexagonal nuts have been wound to hold them in place, clamping them to the ground. The poles are hollow and one hundred feet high. On the base is an emblem: "Union Metal MFG. Co. Canton, OHIO. U.S.A." A steel-sheathed conduit runs down the pole, encasing the electrical wiring. In the left- and right-field bleachers are the two banks of lights each supported by two poles instead of one and rising from the concourse seats. Each of the ten poles is saddled with ballast boxes around the front; rungs extend outward from the poles to allow for maintenance work. The double poles are fused by the Z-shaped metal connection, and each of these double concourse poles is mounted with speakers. The double poles also support the netting that runs all the way behind home plate. The two left field poles are ringed halfway up by a circular cluster of cell phone antennae like choke collars, not uncommon on high points in small towns or cities. The left field and left-center poles' clusters are owned by different companies. When another company wanted to lease pole space for the right-center pole, Vujs finally drew the line and said no, as if he were done leasing out tree house space. The companies on the two left field poles do their work at 3 AM so as not to disturb any of the stadium's daytime activities.

Vujs has hired Fluoresco Lighting & Signs as the company in charge of making sure his lights are operating at full capacity come March, that not one of the 162 lamps will fail to strike. From the press box at the night game, when Vujs thinks he sees a dull lamp in the standard on the left-center pole, he frowns. But later it turns out the lamp was just aimed directly down along the warning track.

Fluoresco began in Tucson in 1961 and now maintains many stadiums, both professional and municipal, across the American West. No one at the company has climbed "the poles from New York" in a number of years, though if there's a person on earth for whom the Polo Grounds' light poles are real (perhaps too much so), it's probably Ted Frisbee. Frisbee has climbed every one of the poles at Muni, relamped the ballpark at one time, and "put on all the heads at third base and home plate." Perhaps that's why he's a little reluctant to speak about them. For him, at bottom, it's a matter of trust.

Like most pole climbers, Frisbee is lanky, with the requisite wingspan to reach the rungs. He is in his mid-fifties with black hair slicked back, showing gray at the edges. He still has the 1970s look and smells of cigarette smoke. His work uniform consists of a short-sleeved, pin-striped mechanic's shirt with a cursive red "Ted" stitched over his breast pocket. He is unexpectedly soft-spoken.

What Frisbee—affectionately described by Fluoresco's service manager, Tim Ocker, as the "old dog of this world"—remembers as the distinguishing characteristic of the old Polo Grounds light poles are their "double stage" catwalks. One catwalk is layered on top of the other to allow for the servicing of both tiers of lights, and there is a trapdoor between the two. He remembers he once retrofitted the poles with new fixtures. He remembers that the fixtures in the corners of the catwalk are harder to get to, especially when he was given a shorter cord. (Instead of the safety harnesses more common now, Frisbee worked simply with a belt around his waist tethered by this cord to the catwalk.) He remembers that the poles at home plate and at third still ran the original 1,500-watt quartz lamps (the rest had changed over already to metal halide), which provide a whiter light and unlike halides don't need time to warm up, firing instantly, though they are more expensive and not as durable. He remembers traversing the double poles, "going across" when he probably shouldn't have, from one to the other. He was able to complete this dangerous and tricky maneuver because, though he doesn't remember the exact span between the double poles, he has those trademark long arms and legs of a climber. ("I could do it," he says.) He remembers how, like bridges and skyscrapers, the poles would sway in the wind at the top ("with the clouds and the planes flying over you"). Being atop one of the two double poles, with the arm going across the center, seemed especially precarious when the other pole would sway, not in unison with the pole he was working on.

"You're on one and seeing kind of like this stuff . . ." he says, mimicking the swaying with a gesture, his palms facing each other and doing an out-of-rhythm rumba.

The reason he had to climb the old Polo Grounds poles was because Amtech, the company he then worked for as a full-time climber, had limited equipment: its tallest crane was fifty-five feet high. Meaning, he'd have to climb the rest of the way—forty-five feet—up to the catwalks.

He doesn't remember how many years ago it was—or the exact date—nor does he remember which pole it was, but his days as a climber ended some fifteen to twenty years ago. He stopped climbing not because he couldn't, but because he wouldn't. (He mostly shies away from ballparks now.)

He was working alone that day. It may have been in preparation for a Pink Floyd concert, which he claims is the last time he worked on the lights at Muni. (Pink Floyd only played Muni twice, April 25 and 26 of 1988; Frisbee's work was probably at least a week or so in advance of those dates.) At first, he laughs when recalling that day, before telling me why he stopped climbing. He is coy about disclosing his story, laughing as if to say, "Why the hell did I—much less anyone else—ever do that?

"It's something you don't do all the time," he tells me. "You have to kind of get used to it again. You have to build up a little nerve."

His job that day was to turn off the breakers. There were no safety harnesses then, he reminds me, just that belt hooked to a rope he'd run from the railing of the enclosed catwalk. "I fell through the trapdoor," he says, running a hand through his slicked hair and letting it land on his shoulder blades, as if pinching them together. "I was up on the top stage. I didn't close the trapdoor and fell through to the next level. I had that so-called safety belt thing on and that left me dangling. There's a ladder that climbs up to the next one. When I went through, I just tore up my whole side. There was nobody else out there."

He'd fallen from the top stage to the bottom—a distance of about six feet.

"But I was tied off on the top, so when I dropped down, I wasn't touching at the bottom. I had to, you know, grab hold of the ladder section of it, and . . . I had to climb all the way down. There was nobody there."

Without stricter safety standards, Frisbee says he "just wouldn't continue. . . . It was just . . . something I just said, 'No, I don't need to do this crap anymore. I don't mind doing this line of work but . . .'"

I ask him if he liked climbing. He leans back in his chair, his hands folded in his lap.

"Not necessarily. Like I said, if you do it all the time, it's one thing. You've got to trust your piece of equipment. I had no idea when I grab that rung if it ain't going to come off in my hand, you know. . . . You don't know who put it together, or what happens throughout the years. So. Back then, they didn't have a safety cable. It was just a pole and the rungs."

Now, Fluoresco's workers maintain the stadium concourse's poles using a "knuckle boom," a crane Vujs describes as moving forwards and backwards and bending and turning like an inchworm. The "boom" is a 135-foot articulating crane that allows maintenance workers to avoid obstacles—in this case, the stands, the crane positioned along the concourse. A bucket truck (containing a hoist) runs along the dirt of the warning track to maintain the outfield poles. One of the challenges the old poles present is that the ballast boxes are on the front of the poles, which makes them difficult to get to because of the pegs extending from the sides, making for a long reach. Compounding this difficulty is that the ballasts are heavy and about the size of a pound cake. The concourse's double poles are also a challenge because the grass of the field cannot be disturbed. Vujs tells me the light poles have preserved some magic, brought some luck with them. To his eye, not one foul ball has ever hit them.

• • •

Despite the protracted demolition, six days before the first sledgehammers struck Thomson's famous fence, a small advertisement appeared in the *New York Times* from the Wrecking Corporation of America: among items available from other demolition sites ("SELLING OUT: Entire Power Plant Equipment formerly NIAGARAMOHAWK- HERKIMER, NEW YORK STATION or RAYMOND STREET JAIL, Brooklyn, New York SELLING: Usable granite, various sizes; Fencing, gratings and other usable items") was listed "DEMOLISHING— POLO GROUNDS, Ball Park, New York City SELLING: Approximately 54,000 seats; 100—flag poles; 1—Scoreboard; 8—Tower Lights."

Avirom, the manager, had pledged to pick the Polo Grounds "clean as a bone." He said the four hundred lamps that were left in the eight steel light towers would be sold, as would the steel piping, as would the "sacred" sod (a two-square-foot section of which, from center field, the Giants had taken with them to San Francisco in 1957). The phone number to call was MU 2-7595.

Avirom said some seats and the Giants' bench would go to the Baseball Hall of Fame in Cooperstown, New York. He concluded that the "cats and dogs who live here will be able to take care of themselves." The light poles, on the other hand, were transported—most likely a long load by train, with the baskets, catwalks, and the lighting fixtures torn off—cross-country to Arizona.

• • •

James Vujs is constantly minimizing hazards and risk; concourse minutiae are his areas of expertise. He controls placement and forces movement all over the stadium floor. Since he works hand-in-hand with the A's spring

training staff, some of whom are directly involved with the corporate sponsors, occasionally he can make the staff members look good by playing the
role of the bad guy. This good cop/bad cop routine—removing corporate
bigwigs from places on his property where they aren't allowed—seems to be
one aspect of the job Vujs enjoys. A spring training sponsor's tent support
pole is precariously close to the queue at the concession stands, and Vujs
delegates one of his men to have the tent moved. Another sponsor's table is
clogging pedestrian traffic at the gate; Vujs instructs them to relocate.

Tonight, the biggest sponsor is an ABC *Dancing with the Stars* promotion. Models in purple bikinis and sheer, gauzy, tutu-like outfits are
traipsing around the concourse accompanied by ridiculous-looking mascots
dressed in giant gold star costumes. They create a regal entourage of gold
and purple and seem to think they can go wherever they want. First, Vujs
and I see them down on the field. During the game, the girls are posing
with men from the crowd on top of the dugouts. I find myself hoping the
entourage does something wrong to provoke Vujs's "bad cop" routine, to
see Vujs mano a mano with the "stars," but apparently in his view their
grandstanding is okay.

Power cords are another potential problem for Vujs. Many of the sponsors' tables require power, and Vujs is in charge of making sure the cords
are laid so as to avoid any potential injuries to the stadium's guests. His
trick is to run the cords along the bases of walls and in the seams of the
concrete, covered with silver duct tape. These are security measures, more
ways of minimizing risk and increasing safety, of preventing accidents from
happening.

He tells me all of this as we stand under the concourse's double light
pole along the right field foul line. He is showing me how he has run the
power cords along the shortest distance possible while at the same time minimizing risk down the handicap walkway ramp from the seats. Above us the
power running through the lights makes a droning sound, a lower-pitched,
sustained version of the sound a fly makes when it buzzes in your ear.

When shadows cross the infield, an hour or so before sunset, the lights
are turned on via two switches—one for the light poles on each side of the

field—back behind the scoreboard in center field. Muni's lamps are metal halide (HID) and require about ten minutes to fully kindle, the way street-lights begin dim and then take time to warm up.

Once, Vujs had shut down the lights for a fireworks display beyond the outfield during the seventh-inning stretch. When the show was over, the lights didn't rekindle immediately. For ten minutes the stadium remained in darkness, the slow halide lamps glowing like dim moons. For this rea-son, many stadiums now have both HID and quartz fixtures, the former taking time to kindle, the latter striking immediately.

• • •

The lamps at Muni are outfitted with glare shields, visors, and dampeners for every one of the 162 lamps. The lamps look a little like they have on ball caps, the NemaSpring-type reflector a bill extended out over the light. The more precision with which the lights are aimed, the less glare: Muni's lamps have advanced directional accoutrements. The lighting system was devised by Musco Lighting in Oskaloosa, Iowa. The old-fashioned way to aim lights was at night, with before and after readings taken on the field to ensure proper coverage.

But now, says Gary Gryder, Fluoresco's vice president of corporate sales and marketing, the process of re-aiming the lights, which happens almost every year, has become a little more high tech:

"Generally there is a red dot that's on the fixture itself right in the mid-dle where there's an aiming spot, and you can only see it when it's aimed properly. So you stand on the field with a pair of binoculars and the guy [on the pole] just kind of moves it around until you can see it. And then you tell him it's good, and you tighten it down."

This seems right—that a person standing on the field would need bin-oculars to make sure that the lamps were aimed right, that the spaces illu-minated by looking back, by history, would have to be precisely aimed, dependent on some strange red spot, some glimmer, in the full glare of 1,500,000-watt metal halide lamps. It's no small wonder that the guy on the field doesn't go blind, and then I wonder about historians—all that looking back. The person doesn't even need to be a historian; someone merely nostalgic would do. Gravity tamps down the ball's flights, the Polo Grounds is demolished, but the nostalgically inclined person—and there are many— keeps propping those balls back up into the air, remembering Mays's "Catch" and Thomson's "Shot," buoying the balls and refusing to let them touch the ground. And I think to myself, for a fleeting second, this is what these light poles are about, if only for a moment: once upon a time they brought light to one of baseball's great stages. Occasionally, they stood in for the sun.

• • •

Augie Ojeda is quick enough to get under the bloop fly. He keeps the mitt close to his chest; he knows he won't have to reach. The cognitive ability allowing a fielder to track a ball, an instinctual gauge for distance and trajectory that might even be faster than a computer and can trace the arc of a ball in its first inches off the bat, this combination of knowledge and acumen gathered from tracking hundreds of fly balls, blended with this instant analysis of the ball's trajectory and how to avoid the glare of the stadium lights—this is what Augie Ojeda has going for him.

Maybe that's what allows him, scurrying out to shallow left, to make "the catch." Open mitt against chest, the ball drops in barely over his shoulder, a basket catch before he flops to the ground from the effort of his run.

Don Delillo's epic, *Underworld* (1996), recalls the Polo Grounds' other famous moment, "the Shot," using Thomson's home run ball as its central structural motif. This is a place where the Polo Grounds remains standing, one could argue. The novel's first forty-nine pages are devoted to Cotter Martin's retrieval of the ball that fateful afternoon. Delillo writes, "[Martin] hears the crescendoing last chords of the national anthem and sees the great open horseshoe of the grandstand and that unfolding vision of the grass that always seems to mean he has stepped outside his life. . . . It is the excitement of a revealed thing."

I think about the things I idealize, my flights of fancy, how my imagination occasionally makes somethings out of nothings. How I often willfully dream, instead of letting dreams come to me; how I prefer them that way.

• • •

One gameless night, the lights are on, though no one is home. They can be seen blazing from the 202 Loop Freeway, at first clearly visible and then spotted through the horizon-scrapers of a new Tempe office park. From a greater distance, they can be seen merely as a small dome of light rising from the desert, pushing up from the ground to the sky. There is the stadium, deserted, light banks bright, as hard to look at as eight distinct (and halide) suns; the field is green, Bermuda grass viridescent like a lime green highlighter. There is no sound but a leaf blower, one of Vujs's men (by several degrees of separation; the man is actually hired out by contract) tidying up the parking lot from the day game.

I'm reminded of pictures I've seen on the Internet of the Polo Grounds' light standards in their original positions, perched on the green wraparound grandstand of the park. Roger Angell wrote of entering the Polo Grounds: "You came slowly down the John T. Brush [the Giants' original owner in the 1910s] stairs to the cool of the evening, looking down at the flags and the tiers of brilliant floodlights on the stands and, beyond them, at the softer shimmer of lights on the Harlem River." I think of the pictures posted on the Internet of the lights, the poles decorated with some four hundred smaller lamps, tiered on four horizontal shelves, looking, from a distance, like birds ranked on power lines against the sky or, up close, a dizzying wind chime collection.

There are entire online communities devoted to discussion of the old Polo Grounds. The physical site in Manhattan has long since been converted into four thirty-floor apartment buildings that accommodate 1,614 families. A Willie Mays playground, a pool of asphalt featuring four basketball backboards, occupies the place where center field once was.

When the last major league baseball game was played at the Polo Grounds on September 18, 1963, only 1,752 fans gathered to watch the

Mets, the lowest draw the Mets had had in their two years of existence. The Jets played football at the Polo Grounds until December 14, 1963, their last game there a 19–10 loss to the Bills. (The old stadium's football history, though less storied, offers several memorable moments: the appearance of the Bears' Red Grange in 1924 that put professional football on the map and the famous Giants-Bears sneaker game in 1935 when the Giants changed their cleats at halftime because of the muddy turf and dominated the second half.)

The Mets moved the following season from the Polo Grounds to Shea Stadium in Flushing Meadows. Their first night game was greeted the next day in the *Times* with the headline "Shea's Lights Make Brilliant Debut." Comments from fans ranged from "Everything just seems to be clearer" to "It makes the game more interesting" to "Best light I've ever seen" to "It's definitely the brightest park in the majors." The players complained, saying they couldn't look directly into the lights but had to turn their heads. Mets shortstop Al Moran said, "There's a little bit of a bluish glare . . . and I imagine we'll have an advantage when we get used to it." The "new" light came from a "circular necklace" of 884 mercury-vapor lamps blended with 820 incandescent quartz lamps to avoid a "blue-out." Moran concluded, "There are no shadows at all. . . . It's so clear, you can see an ant crawling across the grass." (Shea Stadium was replaced as the Mets' home by Citi Field for Opening Day, 2009.)

But members of the online community, particularly members of baseball-fever.com and its forums immersed in the nitty-gritty specifics (a form of nostalgic rigor, perhaps), remain more interested in Polo Grounds' baseball. One discussion debates whether, after the $250,000 1962 renovation before the Mets (temporarily) moved in, the grandstand was repainted green or painted blue. The posts go back and forth on the subject, old men debating the vividness of their memories in relative anonymity. The last post, written on January 17, 2007, at 9:25 PM by someone with the screen name Elvis, underneath which his sig says, "That's the way it is"— the post that put the issue to bed, so to speak—reads: "I believe that the Polo Grounds was indeed repainted in the early '60s, but that the 'ballpark green' wasn't replaced by blue, but rather this color, which is a more bluish-green, but still more green than blue."

• • •

In 1982, the Giants relocated their spring training to Scottsdale and the lights remained behind when the A's took over the stadium. The lamps are seldom used, less than five hundred hours a year; the stadium, once spring training is over, remains mostly idle through the year's other eleven months, a lengthy, inningless off-season. When Muni was built in 1964, the sports editor of the *Arizona Republic* called it a "million dollar grass farm."

By June, when I look down on the stadium from a plane, desert dust has overrun Muni's seats down each foul line, nature's attempt to lay claim to the stadium's land. Only the seats under the accordion-roofed grandstand remain distinctly blue, sheltered from the wind. The practice facility directly adjacent to Muni—another identical diamond with identical outfield grass and dimensions—gives the cluster the appearance of houses or hotels piling up on the same property in Monopoly: the new Arizona Avenue.

The D-backs placed Jorge Julio on waivers the last week of spring training. He was picked up by the Marlins, where he registered an ERA over ten before being traded to the Colorado Rockies, where, at the halfway point of the season, he has enjoyed some success. (ESPN.com blogger Nate Ravitz unsympathetically describes Julio's resurgence as "like a scab that keeps growing back.")

By the 2007 All-Star break, Augie Ojeda has been back in the bigs for a month. For his entire career since he was drafted by the Orioles in the thirteenth round of the 1996 amateur draft (only four of the thirty players selected in that draft stanza ever played in a big league game), he has shuttled between the minors and the majors. Entering the season, he had appeared in 178 career big league games—just over one complete season's worth in eleven years of professional baseball. But this season things are looking up. He goes into the break with a .382 batting average that has raised his career average to .232. Of his 13 hits in 34 major league at bats this season, one was his sixth career home run.

Ojeda has even gained a reputation. The scribes who refer to themselves online as the "Diamondhacks" have this to say about Ojeda: "If Honus Wagner had a 'Minime,' this guy is it." And Ojeda has made his spectacular over-the-shoulder catches routine. On MLB.com, his list of highlights from the regular season includes an "over the shoulder" video download.

The catch comes from a June 23AŁ home interleague game against— you guessed it—the Baltimore Orioles (the team that drafted him, nearly killed him, and against which he practically patents his spectacular play). There is one out, a man on third. Clad in the D-backs' new black shirt, Ojeda—retaining number 11—tracks a bloop over his shoulder. The bloop slices sharply, and Ojeda bends with the ball. He makes the catch, his legs sliding out from under him. He jumps up and—like the immortal Mays highlight—fires the ball back to hold any runners.

The Baseball Pastoral

Jeff Greenfield

Over the years, working as a commentator and political analyst
for ABC, CNN, PBS, and now CBS, Jeff Greenfield has reported
on baseball stories, interviewing the likes of Hank Aaron and
baseball commissioner Bud Selig. In the stands, however, he
abandons journalistic impartiality, and is, this essay makes clear,
a born and bred Yankees fan. [L. G.]

There's a scene in *City Slickers* where Billy Crystal, in the midst of the midlife crisis that has taken him out West, recalls with near-reverence his first visit to Yankee Stadium: his first glimpse of the field as he and his father emerge from the tunnel, the brilliant blue sky, the blinding white of the uniforms, the rich green grass.

That scene hit me with special force because I had written almost exactly the same scene in a widely unread book I'd published nearly twenty years before *City Slickers* hit the screens. Plagiarism? Hardly. Coincidence? Much more than that. If my friends and contemporaries are any clue, this is something close to a collective memory as pervasive and as powerful as a memory of a first love, or first glimpse of Paris at night. It is so powerful, in fact, that it survives the most earnest, heartfelt, painful efforts of the belles-lettres crowd to pound the game over the head with Meaning.

I've had my own innings at infusing Great Thoughts; decades ago I proudly concluded that the reason baseball was the classic American pastime was that it paid joint homage to our two historic eras: the outfield, unbounded by the strict dimensions that apply to other sports, was our tribute to our agricultural roots. The batting order and method of scoring, on the other hand, were rigidly linear; unlike any other sport's players, batters had to proceed in exact order, and the movement around the bases was modeled on the assembly line, and thus, this aspect of the game saluted our industrial era.

I know, I know. At least I have the solace of knowing I am not alone in my ventures into the portentous: I've seen otherwise admirable writers produce enough hot air to melt the polar ice caps with talk of "the agora" and the mythological dimensions of players past—a tendency Philip Roth not-so-subtly skewered in *The Great American Novel*, his account of the nonexistent Patriot League of the 1940s, in which he named his characters, such as Gil Gamesh and Tris Mesgistus, after mythic figures.

I now define the game's hold on me in more personal, less cosmic terms. At its simplest, many of my most powerful memories are rooted in the ballpark. And the reason may be laughably simple: I can trace those memories back further than almost any other part of my life. And, with just a couple of exceptions, they are memories of the *same* ballpark.

My father first took me to Yankee Stadium when I was five years old, well over half a century ago. It was a game against the St. Louis Browns, a game so bizarre the late sportswriter Tom Meany once chronicled it as one of the weirdest he'd never seen. The final score was 20–2. All *three* Yankee catchers—Yogi Berra, Charlie Silvera, and future manager Ralph Houk—were beaned by opposing pitchers. (I believe outfielder Hank Bauer wound up as the final catcher, but I could be wrong). I'm pretty sure Joe DiMaggio hit a bases-loaded ground-rule double into the bleachers. I *know* my father kept telling me, "You know, this isn't really like most baseball games."

For the next several years, trips to the Stadium became a regular father-son outing, always following the same ritual. My father was a highly punctual man, and back in the 1950s, there were far more general admission seats than there are now, so an early arrival meant a choice of excellent upper-deck seats behind home plate. We sometimes arrived at the Stadium as the grounds crew was setting up the cage for batting practice, which was fine with us; it left plenty of time for me to memorize the statistics that filled the sports pages of the Sunday *New York Times*, while devouring the tuna-on-white sandwiches my mother had prepared. (On a warm summer day the oil slick that formed on the brown paper bag was enough to chill the heart of any self-respecting environmentalist.)

My father was a good and kind man, but like most men of his time, was not comfortable sharing his feelings, and I'm pretty sure I would have found any effort on his part more than a little strange. But we talked a lot of baseball on those Sunday afternoons. He was a passionate Brooklyn Dodgers fan, probably because he'd spent a lot of his childhood in Brooklyn and his parents owned a candy store near Ebbets Field, where some of the Dodgers used to drop in on their way to work. (I don't know how many times he told me about the day Pee Wee Reese, off to join the navy in World War II, bought enough "good luck" candy bars to get him through the war. Apparently they did the trick.) So we'd argue the merits of Reese versus Rizzuto, Berra versus Campanella, even Duke Snider versus DiMaggio.

And even when World Series time came around, we'd wind up at the Stadium, if only in the bleachers. I don't know how hard it was to get tickets in those days, but I knew he was determined to get us in the ballpark. They may not have been the best seats in the house, but we were there for the fifth game of the 1953 World Series, an incredible eleven-inning 6–5 Dodger victory highlighted by spectacular late-inning, home-run-saving catches by Dodger outfielders.

Over the years, the memories of these games, and of the games I attended with my friends when I grew old enough, formed as solid a core of my past as any experiences I ever had. No matter how long ago they were, they come back to me every time I'm at the Stadium. For instance, there has not been a game in the last forty years when I haven't looked out to right field, where the tiara-like façade used to be, and remembered a 1956 game when Mickey Mantle hit a ball that kept rising, and rising—until a cheer from the fans in right field, like nothing I have heard before or since, exploded throughout the park. The ball had hit a mere eighteen inches below the top of the roof—the closest any player has ever come to hitting a fair ball out of the park during a ball game. (This was the first game Billy

Crystal ever attended, a story he tells in his brilliant one-man show, "700 Sundays." When I met Crystal backstage, I remembered that I'd saved the scorecard from that game for thirty years; I'm still sorry I threw it out. On the other hand, I'm glad I stopped keeping score somewhere in my middle forties; you get to see a lot more of the game when you're not noting down the hieroglyphics required for accurate record keeping.)

When my children came along, the memories grew to stretch back and forth across the generations. When my daughter Casey was about nine, I got three tickets to a box seat next to the visiting team's dugout, and brought Casey and my father to the game. When the three of us walked out of the tunnel into the stands, I found myself close to tears. A few minutes later, I was struck by less pleasant memories when my father, who has always believed in Behaving the Right Way, became progressively more annoyed by the young fans crowding the railing in front of him looking for autographs or baseballs, even though the game was about an hour away from starting. (The apple doesn't fall far from the tree; to this day, I channel his spirit when the yahoos in front of me decide to jump up every time a Yankee pitcher gets two strikes on the opposing batter.)

My son, David, came into sports-fanhood in the late 1980s and early '90s when both the Yankees and the Mets were struggling. Basketball was his passion—we'll pass over his blessedly brief flirtation with pro wrestling, except to note that my paternal devotion was such that I took him, in person, to two WWF events at Madison Square Garden, and planned to tell anyone who recognized me that we were on our way to a porn store. Baseball, for Dave, was too slow, too stately.

And then something happened: maybe it was the onset of wisdom. Maybe it was that the Yankees began to win. But suddenly, he became a fan; and by the time he was ten, he'd learned to appreciate not just the game, but also its history. When he'd swing a bat in our yard on weekends, my job—apart from pitching to him—was to announce the lineup of major league All-Stars, past and present. I knew the history had taken when he began to ape the distinctive swing of Stan Musial, or reenact Babe Ruth's "I'm calling my shot" gesture from the 1932 World Series.

In our years at the Stadium, Dave and I have collected more than our share of memories. In 2001, we were part of the dispirited crowd that was preparing to leave in anticipation of a devastating Game Four loss to the Arizona Diamondbacks. The Yankees were two runs down with two out in the ninth and a runner on first. We had put on our coats, but Dave had long since become a firm adherent of the game ain't-over-till-the-last-man's-out school of thought. When Tino Martinez slammed a game-tying homer off reliever Byung-Hyun Kim, the roar of the crowd was otherworldly; when Derek Jeter won the game with a two-out homer in the tenth, I told Dave he'd likely never experience anything so dramatic ever again. And my prediction held true: for twenty-four hours. The next night, the Yankees were two runs down with two out in the ninth, and a runner on second.

"Put on your coat, Dave," I said.

"We're not leaving," he said.

"No, of course not, but if you put on your coat, Brosius'll tie the game up with a homer."

We did—and he did. As much as I remember the sound of Yankee Stadium slowly leaving the gravitational pull of the earth, I also wanted Dave to see reliever Byung-Hyun Kim on the mound, sinking to his knees in utter despair. When you're in the midst of exultation, it's good to remember someone else is in pain.

We learned that lesson well—not just when Arizona won the next two games and the Series back in Phoenix, but in the coming years. In 2002, I paid an extortionate amount of money so Dave and I could attend Game Six of the Series against the Florida Marlins. Inning after inning, as young Josh Beckett shut the Yankees down, the fans began cheering again, certain that the magic of 2001 would repeat. When the game—and the Series—finally ended, after a masterful shutout, the silence was as profound as any sound I've ever heard.

Two years later, we were in the best seats in the house—the gift of a very well-connected sports figure—for Game Seven of the American League Championship Series. Surely God would not let the Boston Red Sox fall behind three games to none, and then actually win. Dave and I swapped tales of the great Sox foldos of the past: Enos Slaughter's trip around the bases in 1946, Bucky Bleeping Dent's home run in the '78 playoffs, Buckner's bobble of a Mookie Wilson ground ball at Shea in '86, Pedro's collapse in '03. Heck, we'd been at that classic twelve-inning Red Sox–Yankees game in July, when Derek Jeter had flown head first into the stands to catch a critical short fly ball.

Our euphoria lasted all the way into the top half of the first inning, when David Ortiz hit a two-run homer with two outs. An inning later, with the bases loaded, Johnny Damon stepped up to the plate. From our splendid seats in the first row just behind home plate, I remember watching Kevin Brown let the pitch go and muttering, "look out!" just before Damon hit the grand slam home run that effectively ended the game, giving us a fine seat for the longest funeral in Yankee Stadium history.

And in a funny way, I'm as happy Dave and I were witnesses to the losses as I am that we saw those incredible back-to-back comebacks in 2001. It doesn't require any pompous fatherly instructions to figure out what you take away from games like those.

Those trips to the Stadium bond us in ways the scoreboard doesn't report. Dave is something of a sports polymath, and I get a kick out of watching him engage other fans in conversation. When he overhears fans exchanging massive amounts of blatant misinformation, there is a glint in his eye as he stores the howlers away for later examination. He even indulges my memories of Mantle and Berra, and Vic Raschi and Allie Reynolds—up to a point. And there are times when I've brought Dave along on reporting gigs for ABC and now CNN, not just because I thought he'd get a kick out of being on the field, but because he's simply better than I am at recognizing the players I might want to interview.

And on my office wall is a picture, more than twenty years old, of a summer softball group I'm part of that got to play a softball game at Yankee Stadium, thanks to Tom Brokaw. Dave is on my shoulders, and I'm getting ready to play in my first and last Stadium appearance. I dribbled a soft ground ball down the third-base line, and beat the throw to first. As I tell it, I have a 1.000 batting average at the Stadium, and if my listeners imagine me slamming a ball into the power alley—shades of Jerry Coleman winning the pennant against the Red Sox in 1949—I am not about to disabuse them.

On the Ball

Roger Angell

Roger Angell began writing about baseball in 1962, when New Yorker editor William Shawn sent him to Florida to cover spring training. He still writes about baseball for the magazine and has been called "the poet laureate of baseball" and "the best baseball writer ever." As to why baseball is the subject of so much writing, Angell speculated, in a 2003 interview with Robert Birnbaum, that "most of the sports that get lengthy books written about them are fairly lengthy themselves.... And God knows there is a lot of time in baseball. You can sit there and take notes and watch the field and have an idea once in a while." [L. G.]

Summer 1976

It weighs just over five ounces and measures between 2.86 and 2.94 inches in diameter. It is made of a composition-cork nucleus encased in two thin layers of rubber, one black and one red, surrounded by 121 yards of tightly wrapped blue-gray wool yarn, 45 yards of white wool yarn, 53 more yards of blue-gray wool yarn, 150 yards of fine cotton yarn, a coat of rubber cement, and a cowhide (formerly horsehide) exterior, which is held together with 216 slightly raised red cotton stitches. Printed certifications, endorsements, and outdoor advertising spherically attest to its authenticity. Like most institutions, it is considered inferior in its present form to its ancient archetypes, and in this case the complaint is probably justified; on occasion in recent years it has actually been known to come apart under the demands of its brief but rigorous active career. Baseballs are assembled and handstitched in Taiwan (before this year the work was done in Haiti, and before 1973 in Chicopee, Massachusetts), and contemporary pitchers claim that there is a tangible variation in the size and feel of the balls that now come into play in a single game; a true peewee is treasured by hurlers, and its departure from the premises, by fair means or foul, is secretly mourned. But never mind: any baseball is beautiful. No other small package comes as close to the ideal in design and utility. It is a perfect object for a man's hand. Pick it up and it instantly suggests its purpose; it is meant to be thrown a considerable distance—thrown hard and with precision. Its feel and heft are the beginning of the sport's critical dimensions; if it were a fraction of an inch larger or smaller, a few centigrams heavier or lighter, the game of baseball would be utterly different. Hold a baseball in your hand. As it happens, this one is not brand-new. Here, just to one side of the curved surgical welt of stitches, there is a pale-green grass smudge, darkening on one edge almost to black— the mark of an old infield play, a tough grounder now lost in memory. Feel the ball, turn it over in your hand; hold it across the seam or the other way, with the seam just to the side of your middle finger. Speculation stirs. You want to get outdoors and throw this spare and sensual object to somebody or, at the very least, watch somebody else throw it. The game has begun.

Thinking about the ball and its attributes seems to refresh our appreciation of this game. A couple of years ago, I began to wonder why it was that pitchers, taken as a group, seemed to be so much livelier and more garrulous than hitters. I considered the possibility of some obscure physiological linkage (the discobologlottal syndrome) and the more obvious occupational discrepancies (pitchers have a lot more spare time than other players), but then it came to me that a pitcher is the only man in baseball who can properly look on the ball as being his instrument, his accomplice. He is the only player who is granted the privilege of making offensive plans, and once the game begins he is (in concert with his catcher) the only man on the field who knows what is meant to happen next. Everything in baseball begins with the pitch, and every other part of the game—hitting, fielding, and throwing—is reflexive and defensive. (The hitters on a ball team are referred to as the "offense," but almost three-quarters of the time this is an absolute misnomer.) The batter tapping the dirt off his spikes and now stepping into the box looks sour and glum, and who can blame him, for the ball has somehow been granted in perpetuity to the wrong people. It is already an object of suspicion and hatred, and the reflex that allows him occasionally to deflect that tiny onrushing dot with his bat, and sometimes even to relaunch it violently in the opposite direction, is such a miraculous response of eye and body as to remain virtually inexplicable, even to him. There are a few dugout flannelmouths (Ted Williams, Harry Walker, Pete Rose) who can talk convincingly about the art of hitting, but, like most arts, it does not in the end seem communicable. Pitching is different. It is a craft ("the crafty portsider . . .") and is thus within reach.

The smiling pitcher begins not only with the advantage of holding his fate in his own hands, or hand, but with the knowledge that every advantage of physics and psychology seems to be on his side. A great number of surprising and unpleasant things can be done to the ball as it is delivered from the grasp of a two-hundred-pound optimist, and the first of these is simply to transform it into a projectile. Most pitchers seem hesitant to say so, but if you press them a little they will admit that the prime ingredient in their intense personal struggle with the batter is probably fear. A few pitchers in the majors have thrived without a real fastball—junk men like Eddie Lopat and Mike Cuellar, superior control artists like Bobby Shantz and Randy Jones, knuckleballers like Hoyt Wilhelm and Charlie Hough—but almost everyone else has had to hump up and throw at least an occasional no-nonsense hard one, which crosses the plate at eighty-five miles per hour, or better, and thus causes the hitter to—well, to *think* a little. The fastball sets up all the other pitches in the hurler's repertoire—the curve, the slider, the sinker, and so on—but its other purpose is to intimidate. Great fastballers like Bob Gibson, Jim Bunning, Sandy Koufax, and Nolan Ryan have always run up high strikeout figures because their money pitch was almost untouchable, but their deeper measures of success—twenty-victory seasons and low earned run averages—were due to the fact that none of the hitters they faced, not even the best of them, was immune to the thought of what a ninety-mph missile could do to a man if it struck him. They had been ever so slightly distracted, and distraction is bad for hitting. The intention of the pitcher has almost nothing to do with this; very few pitches are delivered with intent to maim. The bad dream, however, will not go away. Walter Johnson, the greatest fireballer of them all, had almost absolute control, but he is said to have worried constantly about what might happen if one of his pitches got away from him. Good hitters know all this and resolutely don't think about it (a good hitter is a man who can keep his back foot firmly planted in the box even while the rest of him is pulling back or bailing out on an inside fastball), but even these icy customers are less settled in their minds than they would like to be, just because the man out there on the mound is hiding that cannon behind his hip. Hitters, of course, do not call this fear. The word is "respect."

It should not be inferred, of course, that major league pitchers are wholly averse to hitting batters, or *almost* hitting batters. A fastball up around the Adam's apple not only is a first-class distracter, as noted, but also discourages a hitter from habitually leaning forward in order to put more of his bat on a dipping curve or a slider over the outer rim of the plate. The truth of the matter is that pitchers and batters are engaged in a permanent private duel over their property rights to the plate, and a tough, proud hurler who senses that the man now in the batter's box has recently had the better of things will often respond in the most direct manner possible, with a hummer to the ribs. Allie Reynolds, Sal Maglie, Don Drysdale, Early Wynn, and Bob Gibson were cold-eyed lawmen of this stripe, and the practice has by no means vanished, in spite of strictures and deplorings from the high chambers of baseball. Early this year, Lynn McGlothen, of the Cards, routinely plunked the Mets' Del Unser, who had lately been feasting on his pitches, and then violated the ancient protocol in these matters by admitting intent. Dock Ellis, now a Yankee but then a Pirate, decided early in the 1974 season that the Cincinnati Reds had somehow established dominance over his club, and he determined to set things right in his own way. (This incident is described at length in a lively new baseball book, *Dock Ellis in the Country of Baseball*, by Donald Hall.) The first Cincinnati batter of the game was Pete Rose, and the first pitch from Ellis was at his head—"not actually to *hit* him," Ellis said later, but as a "*message* to let him know that he was going to be hit." He then hit Rose in the side. The next pitch hit the next Red batter, Joe Morgan, in the kidney. The third batter was Dan Driessen, who took Ellis's second pitch in the back. With the bases loaded, Dock now threw four pitches at Tony Perez (one behind his back), but missed with all of them, walking in a run. He then missed Johnny Bench (and the plate) twice, whereupon Pirate manager Danny Murtaugh came out to the mound, stared at Ellis with silent surmise, and beckoned for a new pitcher.

Hitters can accept this sort of fugue, even if they don't exactly enjoy it, but what they do admittedly detest is a young and scatter-armed smoke-thrower, the true wild man. One famous aborigine was Steve Dalkowski, an Oriole farmhand of the late 1950s and early '60s who set records for strikeouts and jumpy batters wherever he played. In one typical stay with a Class D league, he threw 121 strikeouts and gave up 129 walks and 39 wild pitches, all in the span of 62 innings. Dalkowski never made it to the majors, but, being a legend, he is secure for the ages. "Once I saw him work a game in the Appalachian League," a gravel-voiced retired coach said to me not long ago, "and nothing was hit *forward* for seven innings—not even a foul ball." An attempt was once made to clock Dalkowski on a record-ing device, but his eventual mark of 93.5 mph was discounted, since he threw for forty minutes before steering a pitch into the machine's recording zone.

Better-known names in these annals of anxiety are Rex Barney, a briefly flaring Brooklyn nova of the 1940s, who once threw a no-hit game but eventually walked and wild-pitched his way out of baseball; Ryne Duren, the extremely fast and extremely nearsighted reliever for the Yankees and other American League clubs in the '50s and '60s, whose traditional initial warm-up pitch on his being summoned to the mound was a twelve-foot-high fastball to the foul screen; and a pair of rookies named Sandy Koufax and Bob Feller. Koufax, to be sure, eventually became a superb control art-ist, but it took him seven years before he got his great stuff entirely together, and there were times when it seemed certain that he would be known only as another Rex Barney. Sandy recalls that when he first brought his boyish assortment of fiery sailers and bouncing rockets to spring-training camp he had difficulty getting in any mound work, because whenever he picked up his glove all the available catchers would suddenly remember pressing appointments in some distant part of the compound. Feller had almost a career-long struggle with *his* control, and four times managed to lead his league simultaneously in walks and in strikeouts. His first appearance against another major-league club came in an exhibition game against the Cardinals in the summer of 1936, when he was seventeen years old; he entered the game in the fourth inning, and eventually struck out eight batters in three innings, but when his searing fastball missed the plate it had the batters jumping around in the box like roasting popcorn. Frank Frisch, the St. Louis player-manager, carefully observed Feller's first three or four deliveries and then walked down to the end of the dugout, picked up a pencil, and removed himself from the Cardinal lineup.

• • •

The chronically depressed outlook of major-league batters was pushed to the edge of paranoia in the 1950s by the sudden and utterly unexpected arrival of the slider, or the Pitcher's Friend. The slider is an easy pitch to throw and a hard one to hit. It is delivered with the same motion as the fastball, but with the pitcher's wrist rotated approximately ninety degrees (to the right for a righthander, to the left for a southpaw), which has the effect of placing the delivering forefinger and middle finger slightly off center on the ball. The positions of hand, wrist, and arm are almost identical with those that produce a good spiral forward pass with a football. The result is an apparent three-quarter-speed fastball that suddenly changes its mind and direction. It doesn't break much—in its early days it was slightly known as the "nickel curve"—but a couple of inches of lateral movement at the plateward end of the ball's brief sixty-foot-six-inch journey can make for an epidemic of pop-ups, foul balls, and harmless grounders. "Epidemic" is not an exaggeration. The slider was the prime agent responsible for the sickening and decline of major-league batting averages in the two decades after the Second World War, which culminated in a combined average of .237 for the two leagues in 1968. A subsequent crash program of immunization and prevention by the authorities produced from the laboratory a smaller strike zone and a lowering of the pitcher's mound by five inches, but the hitters, while saved from extermination, have never regained their state of rosy-cheeked, pre-slider good health.

For me, the true mystery of the slider is not its flight path but the circumstances of its discovery. Professional baseball got under way in the 1870s, and during all the ensuing summers uncounted thousands of young would-be Mathewsons and Seavers spent their afternoons flinging the ball in every conceivable fashion as they searched for magic fadeaways and flutter balls that would take them to Cooperstown. Why did eighty years pass before anybody noticed that a slight cocking of the wrist would be sufficient to usher in the pitchers' Golden Age? Where were Tom Swift and Frank Merriwell? What happened to American Know-How? This is almost a national disgrace. The mystery is deepened by the fact that—to my knowledge, at least—no particular pitcher or pitching coach is given credit for the discovery and propagation of the slider. Bob Lemon, who may be the first man to have pitched his way into the Hall of Fame with a slider, says he learned the pitch from Mel Harder, who was an elder mound statesman with the Indians when Lemon came up to that club, in 1946. I have also heard some old-timers say that George Blaeholder was throwing a pretty fair slider for the St. Louis Browns way back in the 1920s. But none of these worthies ever claimed to be the Johnny Appleseed of the pitch. The thing seemed to generate itself—a weed in the bull pen which overran the field. The slider has made baseball more difficult for the fan as well as for the batter. Since its action is late and minimal, and since its delivery does not require the easily recognizable arm-snap by the pitcher that heralds the true curve, the slider can be spotted only by an attentive spectator seated very close to home plate. A curve thrown by famous old pretzel-benders like Tommy Bridges and Sal Maglie really used to *curve*; you could see the thing break even if you were way out in the top deck of Section 31. Most fans, however, do not admit the loss. The contemporary bleacher critic, having watched a doll-size distant slugger swing mightily and tap the ball down to second on four bounces, smiles and enters the out in his scorecard. "Slider," he announces, and everybody nods wisely in agreement.

• • •

The mystery of the knuckleball is ancient and honored. Its practitioners cheerfully admit that they do not understand why the pitch behaves the way it does; nor do they know, or care much, which particular lepidopteran path it will follow on its way past the batter's infuriated swipe. They merely prop the ball on their fingertips (not, in actual fact, on the knuckles) and launch it more or less in the fashion of a paper airplane, and then, most of the time, finish the delivery with a faceward motion of the glove, thus hiding a grin. Now science has confirmed the phenomenon. Writing in *The American Journal of Physics*, Eric Sawyer and Robert G. Watts, of Tulane University, recently reported that wind-tunnel tests showed that a slowly spinning baseball is subject to forces capable of making it swerve a foot or more between the pitcher's mound and the plate. The secret, they say, appears to be the raised seams of the ball, which cause a "roughness pattern" and an uneven flow of air, resulting in a "nonsymmetric lateral force distribution and . . . a net force in one direction or another."

Like many other backyard baseball stars, I have taught myself to throw a knuckleball that moves with so little rotation that one can almost pick out the signature of Charles S. Feeney in midair; the pitch, however, has shown disappointingly few symptoms of last-minute fluttering and has so far proved to be wonderfully catchable or hittable, mostly by my wife. Now, at last, I understand the problem. In their researches, Sawyer and Watts learned that an entirely spinless knuckler is *not* subject to varying forces, and thus does not dive or veer. The ideal knuckler, they say, completes about a quarter of a revolution on its way to the plate. The speed of the pitch, moreover, is not critical because "the magnitude of the lateral force increases approximately as the square of the velocity," which means that the total lateral movement is "independent of the speed of the pitch."

All this has been perfectly understood (if less politely defined) by any catcher who has been the battery mate of a star knuckleballer, and has thus spent six or seven innings groveling in the dirt in imitation of a bulldog cornering a nest of field mice. Modern catchers have the assistance of outsized gloves (which lately have begun to approach the diameter of tea trays), and so enjoy a considerable advantage over some of their ancient predecessors in capturing the knuckler. In the middle 1940s, the receivers for the Washington Senators had to deal with a pitching staff that included *four* knuckleball specialists—Dutch Leonard, Johnny Niggeling, Mickey Haefner, and Roger Wolff. Among the ill-equipped Washington catchers who tried to fend off almost daily mid-afternoon clouds of deranged butterflies were Rick Ferrell and Jake Early; Early eventually was called up to serve in the armed forces—perhaps the most willing inductee of his day.

• • •

The spitball was once again officially outlawed from baseball in 1974, and maybe this time the prohibition will work. This was the third, and by far the most severe, edict directed at the unsanitary and extremely effective delivery, for it permits an umpire to call an instantaneous ball on any pitch that even looks like a spitter as it crosses the plate. No evidence is required; no appeal by the pitcher to higher powers is permissible. A subsequent spitball or imitation thereof results in the expulsion of the pitcher from the premises, *instanter*, and an ensuing fine. Harsh measures indeed, but surely sufficient, we may suppose, to keep this repellent and unfair practice out of baseball's shining mansion forever. Surely, and yet... Professional pitchers have an abiding fondness for any down-breaking delivery, legal or illegal, that will get the job done, and nothing, they tell me, does the job more effectively or more entertainingly than a dollop of saliva or slippery-elm juice, or a little bitty dab of lubricating jelly, applied to the pitching fingers.

The ball, which is sent off half wet and half dry, like a dilatory schoolboy, hurries innocently toward the gate and its grimfaced guardians, and at the last second darts under the turnstile. Pitchers, moreover, have before them the inspiring recent example of Gaylord Perry, whose rumored but unverified Faginesque machinations with K-Y Jelly won him a Cy Young Award in 1972 and led inevitably to the demand for harsher methods of law enforcement. Rumor has similarly indicted other highly successful performers, like Don Drysdale, Whitey Ford, and Bill Singer. Preacher Roe, upon retiring from the Dodgers in 1954, after an extended useful tenure on the mound at Ebbets Field, published a splendidly unrepentant confession in which he gave away a number of trade secrets. His favorite undryer, as I recall, was a full pack of Juicy Fruit gum, and he loaded up by straightening the bill of his cap between pitches and passing his fingers momentarily in front of his face—now also illegal, alas.

It may be perceived that my sympathies, which lately seemed to lie so rightly on the side of the poor overmatched hitters, have unaccountably swung the other way. I admit this indefensible lapse simply because I find the spitter so enjoyable for its deviousness and skulking disrespect. I don't suppose we should again make it a fully legal pitch (it was first placed outside the pale in 1920), but I would enjoy a return to the era when the spitter was treated simply as a misdemeanor and we could all laugh ourselves silly at the sight of a large, outraged umpire suddenly calling in a suspected wetback for inspection (and the pitcher, of course, *rolling* the ball to him across the grass) and then glaring impotently out at the innocent ("Who—*me?*") perpetrator on the mound. Baseball is a hard, rules-dominated game, and it should have more room in it for a little cheerful cheating.

• • •

All these speculations, and we have not yet taken the ball out of the hands of its first friend, the pitcher. And yet there is always something more. We might suddenly realize, for instance, that baseball is the only team sport in which the scoring is not done with the ball. In hockey, football, soccer, basketball, lacrosse, and the rest of them, the ball or its equivalent actually scores or is responsible for the points that determine the winner. In baseball, the score is made by the base runner—by the man down there, just crossing the plate—while the ball, in most cases, is a long way off, doing something quite different. It's a strange business, this unique double life going on in front of us, and it tells us a lot about this unique game. A few years ago, there was a suddenly popular thesis put forward in some sports columns and light-heavyweight editorial pages which proposed that the immense recent popularity of professional football could be explained by the fact that the computer-like complexity of its plays, the clotted and anonymous masses of its players, and the intense violence of its action constituted a perfect Sunday parable of contemporary urban society. It is a pretty argument, and perhaps even true, especially since it is hard not to notice that so many professional football games, in spite of their noise and chaos, are deadeningly repetitious, predictable, and banal. I prefer the emotions and suggestions to be found in the other sport. I don't think anyone can watch many baseball games without becoming aware of the fact that the ball, for all its immense energy and unpredictability, very rarely escapes the control of the players. It is released again and again—pitched and caught, struck along the ground or sent high in the air—but almost always, almost instantly, it is recaptured and returned to control and safety and harmlessness. Nothing is altered, nothing has been allowed to happen. This orderliness and constraint are among the prime attractions of the sport; a handful of men, we discover, can police a great green country, forestalling unimaginable disasters. A slovenly, error-filled game can sometimes be exciting, but it never seems serious, and is thus never truly satisfying, for the metaphor of safety—of danger subdued by skill and courage—has been lost. Too much civilization, however, is deadly—in this game, a deadly bore. A deeper need is stifled. The ball looks impetuous and dangerous, but we perceive that in fact it lives in a slow, guarded world of order, vigilance, and rules. Nothing can ever happen here. And then once again the ball is pitched—sent on its quick, planned errand. The bat flashes, there is a new, louder sound, and suddenly we see the ball streaking wild through the air and then bounding along distant and untouched in the sweet green grass. We leap up, thousands of us, and shout for its joyful flight—free, set free, free at last.

Contributors

Roger Angell is a writer and fiction editor for the *New Yorker*. His baseball books include *The Summer Game*, *Late Innings*, *Season Ticket*, *Once More Around the Park*, *Game Time*, and *Five Seasons: A Baseball Companion*. His most recent book is *Let Me Finish*, a collection of essays. He is the 2014 winner of the Baseball Hall of Fame's J. G. Taylor Spink Award for meritorious contributions to baseball writing.

Kevin Baker is the author of four novels, including the *City of Fire* trilogy: *Dreamland*, *Paradise Alley*, and *Strivers Row*. He is currently at work on a nonfiction book about the history of New York City baseball.

Philip F. Deaver is the thirteenth winner of the Flannery O'Connor Award. He has held fellowships from the National Endowment for the Arts and Bread Loaf. His short fiction has appeared in *Prize Stories: The O. Henry Awards* and has been recognized in *Best American Short Stories* and *The Pushcart Prize*. His poems are collected in *How Men Pray* (Anhinga Press). In recent years, he has also published memoir and creative nonfiction in the literary magazines and edited a book of creative nonfiction essays on baseball, entitled *Scoring from Second: Writers on Baseball* (University of Nebraska Press). He is a professor of English and permanent writer-in-residence at Rollins College, Winter Park, Florida, and teaches on the fiction faculty in the Spalding University brief residency MFA program in Louisville, Kentucky.

Frank Deford is the author of fifteen books and two screenplays. He is a senior writer for *Sports Illustrated,* a commentator for NPR, and a correspondent for HBO's *Real Sports with Bryant Gumbel*.

Stefan Fatsis is the author of the New York Times bestseller *Word Freak: Heartbreak, Triumph, Genius, and Obsession in the World of Competitive Scrabble Players*; *A Few Seconds of Panic: A Sportswriter Plays in the NFL*; and *Wild and Outside: How a Renegade Minor League Revived the Spirit of Baseball in America's Heartland*. He talks about sports on NPR's "All Things Considered" and on the Slate podcast "Hang Up and Listen."

Diana Friedman's fiction and essays have appeared in a variety of journals and magazines, including *Newsweek, The Baltimore Sun, Flyway: Journal of Writing and Environment, The Huffington Post, Sport Literate, Bethesda Magazine* and *Whole Earth Review*. Her work has received multiple awards, including the Alexander Patterson Cappon Fiction Prize, and has been shortlisted at *Glimmer Train, Hunger Mountain* and *Red Hen Press*. She cut her baseball teeth on the dirt fields of Central Park, during compulsory reenactments of the 1969 World Series with her brothers, and at Sunday pick-up games in Amagansett. While not as star-studded as the Hamptons artist-writer game, the Friedman family matches were equally unruly and competitive. Friedman lives outside of Washington D.C. Her work is available online at www.dianafriedmanwriter.com.

A. Bartlett Giamatti (1938-1989) a decorated scholar, started out at Yale as a professor of comparative literature. In, 1978 he became president of Yale University. From there, he become president of Major League Baseball's National League, and was appointed the commissioner of Major League Baseball. His academic love was Renaissance literature, but his passion was baseball and the Boston Red Sox. Mr. Giamatti was raised in South

Hadley, Massachusetts, adjacent to the campus of Mount Holyoke College, where his father, Valentine, a world famous Dante scholar, also taught Italian. Mr. Giamatti also authored several books, including *Take Time for Paradise: Americans and Their Games* and *A Great and Glorious Game: Baseball Writings of A. Bartlett Giamatti*.

Jeff Greenfield is a thirty-year network news veteran, with stints at ABC, CNN, CBS and PBS. His work earned him five Emmys. He is also an author of thirteen books, including the alternate histories: *Then Everything Changed* and *If Kennedy Lived*. He lives in Santa Barbara and New York City.

Lee Gutkind is the founding editor of *Creative Nonfiction* and prize-winning author or editor of more than two dozen books, including *The Best Seat in Baseball, But You Have to Stand!: The Game as Umpires See It*. He is Distinguished Writer in Residence in the Consortium for Science, Policy & Outcomes at Arizona State University and a professor, School for the Future of Innovation in Society.

Rick Harsch is the author of several novels, one of which is taught at the University of Tasmania in a course on American film and literature. All of his published novels were translated into French by a publishing house that went bankrupt soon after. He lives in Izola, on the Mediterranean coast of Slovenia, is married to a woman named Sasikala, who has no interest in baseball, has a son named Arjun, who throws harder at age three and a half than Greg Maddux, and a daughter named Bhairavi, who at two years old is showing signs of developing argumentative skills that could lead to a managerial post someday.

Caitlin Horrocks lives in Michigan. Her work has appeared or is forthcoming in *Tin House, Epoch, Colorado Review, The Cincinnati Review*, and elsewhere. She misses Finnish baseball but not Finnish winters.

Matthew McGough is the author of *Bat Boy: Coming of Age with the New York Yankees* (Doubleday, 2005). From 2006 to 2010, he was a writer for NBC's *Law & Order*. His next book, about the Stephanie Lazarus cold case and the Los Angeles Police Department, is forthcoming from Henry Holt. His author website is www.matthewmcgough.com.

Susan Perabo is writer-in-residence and an associate professor of English at Dickinson College. She is the author of *Who I Was Supposed to Be*, a collection of short stories, and *The Broken Places*, a novel.

George Plimpton (1927–2003) was the long-time editor of *The Paris Review* and the author of several books about competing in professional sports, among them *Paper Lion,* about training as a backup quarterback for the Detroit Lions, and *Out of My League*, about pitching against National League All-Stars in 1960.

Katherine A. Powers is a book critic, a columnist for Barnes and Noble Review, and the editor of *Suitable Accommodations: An Autobiographical Story of Family Life: The Letters of J. F. Powers, 1942 – 1963* (Farrar, Straus & Giroux). She received the 2013 Nona Balakian Citation for Excellence in Reviewing from the National Book Critics Circle. She lives in Cambridge, Mass.

J. D. Scrimgeour's book *Themes for English B: A Professor's Education In and Out of Class* won the AWP Award for Creative Nonfiction in 2005 and was published by the University of Georgia Press in 2006. He is also the author of another book of nonfiction, *Spin Moves*, and a collection of poetry, *The Last Miles*. His essays have appeared in several venues, including the *Boston Globe Magazine* and *The Chronicle of Higher Education*. He is coordinator of creative writing at Salem State College in Salem, Massachusetts, and the assistant coach on his sons' baseball team.

Michael Shapiro is the author of five nonfiction books, most recently *The Last Good Season*. His work has appeared in such publications as *The New Yorker*,

Esquire, *The New York Times Magazine*, and *Sports Illustrated*. He teaches journalism at Columbia University and is founder of The Big Roundtable, a narrative nonfiction digital publisher.

Gay Talese, author of twelve books, began his professional career as a feature writer in *The New York Times'* sports department, in 1966. During his sixty years of writing, he has continued with his interest in sports, including a collection of the best of his sports writing, *The Silent Season of a Hero*.

John Thorn is the Official Historian of Major League Baseball. Apart from his creation, with Pete Palmer, of Total Baseball, he is often visible on ESPN, MLBTV, and other media outlets. He was a major on-screen presence in and chief consultant to Ken Burns's PBS film, *Baseball*. His many baseball books over the past three decades include *The Hidden Game of Baseball*, *The Armchair Books of Baseball*, *Treasures of the Baseball Hall of Fame*, *The Game for All America*, and *Our Game*, a history of the game which supplies the title for his blog. In 2011 Simon & Schuster published his major work, *Baseball in the Garden of Eden: A Secret History of the Early Game*.

George Vecsey is still recovering from four years on the road with Casey Stengel from 1962 through 1965, when he was a young reporter and Stengel was the self-styled Slickest Manager in Baseball. Vecsey is a Contributing Sports Columnist for the *New York Times* after writing a column regularly from 1982 through the end of 2011. He has written over a dozen books, including five best sellers, the most recent being *Stan Musial: An American Life*, published by Ballantine/ESPN Books. For 2014, he has been preparing a personal memory, *Eight World Cups: My Journey Through the Beauty and Dark Side of Soccer*, for Henry Holt/Times Books, in time for the World Cup in Brazil in 2014. In 2013, he received the Colin Jose Media Award from the National Soccer Hall of Fame. "The Old Man" was originally published in *Coach: 25 Writers Reflect on People Who Made a Difference* (Warner Books, 2005).

Sean Wilentz is the author of several books, including *The Rise of American Democracy: Jefferson to Lincoln*, which won the Bancroft Prize in 2006. He teaches history at Princeton University.

Matt Wood is a graduate of the Master of Arts in Creative Writing program at Northwestern University, where his final thesis, "Through an Unlocked Door," won the 2006–2007 Distinguished Thesis Award. He lives with his family in Chicago.

Jake Young is from Los Angeles, California, and has studied writing at Princeton and Arizona State Universities. He is currently at work on a novel.

About the Editors

LEE GUTKIND is the founding editor of *Creative Nonfiction* and prize-winning author or editor of more than two dozen books, including *The Best Seat in Baseball, But You Have to Stand!: The Game as Umpires See It*. He is Distinguished Writer in Residence in the Consortium for Science, Policy & Outcomes at Arizona State University and a professor, School for the Future of Innovation in Society.

ANDREW BLAUNER is a literary agent and editor of *Coach: 25 Writers Reflect on People Who Made a Difference, Brothers: 26 Stories of Love and Rivalry, Central Park: An Anthology, Our Boston: Writers Celebrate the City They Love,* and *The Good Book: Writers Reflect on Favorite Bible Passages.*